THE FIRST AND SECOND
BOOKS OF SAMUEL

THE IGNATIUS CATHOLIC STUDY BIBLE

REVISED STANDARD VERSION
SECOND CATHOLIC EDITION

THE FIRST AND SECOND BOOKS OF SAMUEL

With Introduction, Commentary, and Notes

by

Scott Hahn and Curtis Mitch

with

Michael Barber

and

with Study Questions by

Dennis Walters

IGNATIUS PRESS SAN FRANCISCO

Published with ecclesiastical approval

Original RSV Bible text:
Revised Standard Version, Catholic Edition
Nihil obstat: Thomas Hanlon, S.T.L., L.S.S., Ph.L.
Imprimatur: + Peter W. Bartholome, D.D.
Bishop of Saint Cloud, Minnesota
May 11, 1966

Introduction, commentaries, and notes:
Nihil obstat: Dr. Ruth Ohm Sutherland, Ph.D., Censor Deputatus
Imprimatur: + The Most Reverend Salvatore Cordileone
Archbishop of San Francisco
February 29, 2016

The *nihil obstat* and *imprimatur* are official declarations that a book or pamphlet is free of doctrinal or moral error. No implication is contained therein that those who have granted the *nihil obstat* and *imprimatur* agree with the contents, opinions, or statements expressed.

Second Catholic Edition approved by the
National Council of the Churches of Christ in the USA

Cover art: *David Slaying Goliath*
Anonymous, 19th century, © 1860.
Ann Ronan Picture Library, London, Great Britian
Photo: HIP / Art Resource, N.Y.

Cover design by Riz Boncan Marsella

Published by Ignatius Press in 2016

CONTENTS

INTRODUCTION TO
THE IGNATIUS CATHOLIC STUDY BIBLE

by Scott Hahn, Ph.D.

You are approaching the "word of God". This is the title Christians most commonly give to the Bible, and the expression is rich in meaning. It is also the title given to the Second Person of the Blessed Trinity, God the Son. For Jesus Christ became flesh for our salvation, and "the name by which he is called is The Word of God" (Rev 19:13; cf. Jn 1:14).

The word of God is Scripture. The Word of God is Jesus. This close association between God's *written* word and his *eternal* Word is intentional and has been the custom of the Church since the first generation. "All Sacred Scripture is but one book, and this one book is Christ, 'because all divine Scripture speaks of Christ, and all divine Scripture is fulfilled in Christ'[1]" (CCC 134). This does not mean that the Scriptures are divine in the same way that Jesus is divine. They are, rather, divinely inspired and, as such, are unique in world literature, just as the Incarnation of the eternal Word is unique in human history.

Yet we can say that the inspired word resembles the incarnate Word in several important ways. Jesus Christ is the Word of God incarnate. In his humanity, he is like us in all things, except for sin. As a work of man, the Bible is like any other book, except without error. Both Christ and Scripture, says the Second Vatican Council, are given "for the sake of our salvation" (*Dei Verbum* 11), and both give us God's definitive revelation of himself. We cannot, therefore, conceive of one without the other: the Bible without Jesus, or Jesus without the Bible. Each is the interpretive key to the other. And because Christ is the subject of all the Scriptures, St. Jerome insists, "Ignorance of the Scriptures is ignorance of Christ"[2] (CCC 133).

When we approach the Bible, then, we approach Jesus, the Word of God; and in order to encounter Jesus, we must approach him in a prayerful study of the inspired word of God, the Sacred Scriptures.

Inspiration and Inerrancy The Catholic Church makes mighty claims for the Bible, and our acceptance of those claims is essential if we are to read the Scriptures and apply them to our lives as the Church intends. So it is not enough merely to nod at words like "inspired", "unique", or "inerrant". We have to understand what the Church means by these terms, and we have to make that understanding our own. After all, what we believe about the Bible will inevitably influence the way we read the Bible. The way we read the Bible, in turn, will determine what we "get out" of its sacred pages.

These principles hold true no matter what we read: a news report, a search warrant, an advertisement, a paycheck, a doctor's prescription, an eviction notice. How (or whether) we read these things depends largely upon our preconceived notions about the reliability and authority of their sources—and the potential they have for affecting our lives. In some cases, to misunderstand a document's authority can lead to dire consequences. In others, it can keep us from enjoying rewards that are rightfully ours. In the case of the Bible, both the rewards and the consequences involved take on an ultimate value.

What does the Church mean, then, when she affirms the words of St. Paul: "All Scripture is inspired by God" (2 Tim 3:16)? Since the term "inspired" in this passage could be translated "God-breathed", it follows that God breathed forth his word in the Scriptures as you and I breathe forth air when we speak. This means that God is the primary author of the Bible. He certainly employed human authors in this task as well, but he did not merely assist them while they wrote or subsequently approve what they had written. God the Holy Spirit is the *principal* author of Scripture, while the human writers are *instrumental* authors. These human authors freely wrote everything, and only those things, that God wanted: the word of God in the very words of God. This miracle of dual authorship extends to the whole of Scripture, and to every one of its parts, so that whatever the human authors affirm, God likewise affirms through their words.

The principle of biblical inerrancy follows logically from this principle of divine authorship. After all, God cannot lie, and he cannot make mistakes. Since the Bible is divinely inspired, it must be without error in everything that its divine and human authors affirm to be true. This means that biblical inerrancy is a mystery even broader in scope than infallibility, which guarantees for us that the Church will always teach the truth concerning faith and morals. Of course the mantle of inerrancy likewise covers faith and morals, but it extends even farther to ensure that all the facts and events of salvation history are accurately presented for us in

---

[1] Hugh of St. Victor, *De arca Noe* 2, 8: PL 176, 642: cf. ibid. 2, 9: PL 176, 642–43.
[2] *DV* 25; cf. Phil 3:8 and St. Jerome, *Commentariorum in Isaiam libri xviii*, prol.: PL 24, 17b.

the Scriptures. Inerrancy is our guarantee that the words and deeds of God found in the Bible are unified and true, declaring with one voice the wonders of his saving love.

The guarantee of inerrancy does not mean, however, that the Bible is an all-purpose encyclopedia of information covering every field of study. The Bible is not, for example, a textbook in the empirical sciences, and it should not be treated as one. When biblical authors relate facts of the natural order, we can be sure they are speaking in a purely descriptive and "phenomenological" way, according to the way things appeared to their senses.

Biblical Authority Implicit in these doctrines is God's desire to make himself known to the world and to enter a loving relationship with every man, woman, and child he has created. God gave us the Scriptures not just to inform or motivate us; more than anything he wants to save us. This higher purpose underlies every page of the Bible, indeed every word of it.

In order to reveal himself, God used what theologians call "accommodation". Sometimes the Lord stoops down to communicate by "condescension"—that is, he speaks as humans speak, as if he had the same passions and weakness that we do (for example, God says he was "sorry" that he made man in Genesis 6:6). Other times he communicates by "elevation"—that is, by endowing human words with divine power (for example, through the Prophets). The numerous examples of divine accommodation in the Bible are an expression of God's wise and fatherly ways. For a sensitive father can speak with his children either by condescension, as in baby talk, or by elevation, by bringing a child's understanding up to a more mature level.

God's word is thus saving, fatherly, and personal. Because it speaks directly to us, we must never be indifferent to its content; after all, the word of God is at once the object, cause, and support of our faith. It is, in fact, a test of our faith, since we see in the Scriptures only what faith disposes us to see. If we believe what the Church believes, we will see in Scripture the saving, inerrant, and divinely authored revelation of the Father. If we believe otherwise, we see another book altogether.

This test applies not only to rank-and-file believers but also to the Church's theologians and hierarchy, and even the Magisterium. Vatican II has stressed in recent times that Scripture must be "the very soul of sacred theology" (*Dei Verbum* 24). As Joseph Cardinal Ratzinger, Pope Benedict XVI echoed this powerful teaching with his own, insisting that "the *normative theologians* are the authors of Holy Scripture" (emphasis added). He reminded us that Scripture and the Church's dogmatic teaching are tied tightly together, to the point of being inseparable: "Dogma is by definition nothing other than an interpretation of Scripture." The defined dogmas of our faith, then, encapsulate the Church's infallible interpretation of Scripture, and theology is a further reflection upon that work.

The Senses of Scripture Because the Bible has both divine and human authors, we are required to master a different sort of reading than we are used to. First, we must read Scripture according to its *literal* sense, as we read any other human literature. At this initial stage, we strive to discover the meaning of the words and expressions used by the biblical writers as they were understood in their original setting and by their original recipients. This means, among other things, that we do not interpret everything we read "literalistically", as though Scripture never speaks in a figurative or symbolic way (it often does!). Rather, we read it according to the rules that govern its different literary forms of writing, depending on whether we are reading a narrative, a poem, a letter, a parable, or an apocalyptic vision. The Church calls us to read the divine books in this way to ensure that we understand what the human authors were laboring to explain to God's people.

The literal sense, however, is not the only sense of Scripture, since we interpret its sacred pages according to the *spiritual* senses as well. In this way, we search out what the Holy Spirit is trying to tell us, beyond even what the human authors have consciously asserted. Whereas the literal sense of Scripture describes a historical reality—a fact, precept, or event—the spiritual senses disclose deeper mysteries revealed through the historical realities. What the soul is to the body, the spiritual senses are to the literal. You can distinguish them; but if you try to separate them, death immediately follows. St. Paul was the first to insist upon this and warn of its consequences: "God ... has qualified us to be ministers of a new covenant, not in a written code but in the Spirit; for the written code kills, but the Spirit gives life" (2 Cor 3:5–6).

Catholic tradition recognizes three spiritual senses that stand upon the foundation of the literal sense of Scripture (see CCC 115). **(1)** The first is the *allegorical* sense, which unveils the spiritual and prophetic meaning of biblical history. Allegorical interpretations thus reveal how persons, events, and institutions of Scripture can point beyond themselves toward greater mysteries yet to come (OT) or display the fruits of mysteries already revealed (NT). Christians have often read the Old Testament in this way to discover how the mystery of Christ in the New Covenant was once hidden in the Old and how the full significance of the Old Covenant was finally made manifest in the New. Allegorical significance is likewise latent in the New Testament, especially in the life and deeds of Jesus recorded in the Gospels. Because Christ is the Head of the Church and the source of her spiritual life, what was accomplished in Christ the Head during his earthly life prefigures what he continually produces in his members through grace. The allegorical sense builds up the virtue of faith. **(2)** The second is the *tropological* or *moral* sense, which reveals how the actions of God's people in the Old Testament and the life of Jesus in the New Testament prompt us to form virtuous habits in our own lives. It therefore draws from Scripture warnings against sin and vice as well as inspirations to pursue holiness and purity. The moral sense is intended to build up the virtue of charity. **(3)** The third is the *anagogical* sense, which points upward to heavenly glory. It shows us how countless events in the Bible prefigure our final union with God in eternity and how things that are "seen" on earth are figures of things "unseen" in heaven. Because the anagogical sense leads us to contemplate our destiny, it is meant to build up the virtue of hope. Together with the literal sense, then, these spiritual senses draw out the fullness of what God wants to give us through his Word and as such comprise what ancient tradition has called the "full sense" of Sacred Scripture.

All of this means that the deeds and events of the Bible are charged with meaning beyond what is immediately apparent to the reader. In essence, that meaning is Jesus Christ and the salvation he died to give us. This is especially true of the books of the New Testament, which proclaim Jesus explicitly; but it is also true of the Old Testament, which speaks of Jesus in more hidden and symbolic ways. The human authors of the Old Testament told us as much as they were able, but they could not clearly discern the shape of all future events standing at such a distance. It is the Bible's divine Author, the Holy Spirit, who could and did foretell the saving work of Christ, from the first page of the Book of Genesis onward.

The New Testament did not, therefore, abolish the Old. Rather, the New fulfilled the Old, and in doing so, it lifted the veil that kept hidden the face of the Lord's bride. Once the veil is removed, we suddenly see the world of the Old Covenant charged with grandeur. Water, fire, clouds, gardens, trees, hills, doves, lambs—all of these things are memorable details in the history and poetry of Israel. But now, seen in the light of Jesus Christ, they are much more. For the Christian with eyes to see, water symbolizes the saving power of Baptism; fire, the Holy Spirit; the spotless lamb, Christ crucified; Jerusalem, the city of heavenly glory.

The spiritual reading of Scripture is nothing new. Indeed, the very first Christians read the Bible this way. St. Paul describes Adam as a "type" that prefigured Jesus Christ (Rom 5:14). A "type" is a real person, place, thing, or event in the Old Testament that foreshadows something greater in the New. From this term we get the word "typology", referring to the study of how the Old Testament prefigures Christ (CCC 128–30). Elsewhere St. Paul draws deeper meanings out of the story of Abraham's sons, declaring, "This is an allegory" (Gal 4:24). He is not suggesting that these events of the distant past never really happened; he is saying that the events both happened *and* signified something more glorious yet to come.

The New Testament later describes the Tabernacle of ancient Israel as "a copy and shadow of the heavenly sanctuary" (Heb 8:5) and the Mosaic Law as a "shadow of the good things to come" (Heb 10:1). St. Peter, in turn, notes that Noah and his family were "saved through water" in a way that "corresponds" to sacramental Baptism, which "now saves you" (1 Pet 3:20–21). It is interesting to note that the expression translated as "corresponds" in this verse is a Greek term that denotes the fulfillment or counterpart of an ancient "type".

We need not look to the apostles, however, to justify a spiritual reading of the Bible. After all, Jesus himself read the Old Testament this way. He referred to Jonah (Mt 12:39), Solomon (Mt 12:42), the Temple (Jn 2:19), and the brazen serpent (Jn 3:14) as "signs" that pointed forward to him. We see in Luke's Gospel, as Christ comforted the disciples on the road to Emmaus, that "beginning with Moses and all the prophets, he interpreted to them in all the Scriptures the things concerning himself" (Lk 24:27). It was precisely this extensive spiritual interpretation of the Old Testament that made such an impact on these once-discouraged travelers, causing their hearts to "burn" within them (Lk 24:32).

Criteria for Biblical Interpretation We, too, must learn to discern the "full sense" of Scripture as it includes both the literal and spiritual senses together. Still, this does not mean we should "read into" the Bible meanings that are not really there. Spiritual exegesis is not an unrestrained flight of the imagination. Rather, it is a sacred science that proceeds according to certain principles and stands accountable to sacred tradition, the Magisterium, and the wider community of biblical interpreters (both living and deceased).

In searching out the full sense of a text, we should always avoid the extreme tendency to "over-spiritualize" in a way that minimizes or denies the Bible's literal truth. St. Thomas Aquinas was well aware of this danger and asserted that "all other senses of Sacred Scripture are based on the literal" (*STh* I, 1, 10, *ad* 1, quoted in CCC 116). On the other hand, we should never confine the meaning of a text to the literal, intended sense of its human author, as if the divine Author did not intend the passage to be read in the light of Christ's coming.

Fortunately the Church has given us guidelines in our study of Scripture. The unique character and divine authorship of the Bible call us to read it "in the Spirit" (*Dei Verbum* 12). Vatican II outlines this teaching in a practical way by directing us to read the Scriptures according to three specific criteria:

1. We must "[b]e especially attentive 'to the content and unity of the whole Scripture'" (CCC 112).

2. We must "[r]ead the Scripture within 'the living Tradition of the whole Church'" (CCC 113).

3. We must "[b]e attentive to the analogy of faith" (CCC 114; cf. Rom 12:6).

These criteria protect us from many of the dangers that ensnare readers of the Bible, from the newest inquirer to the most prestigious scholar. Reading Scripture out of context is one such pitfall, and probably the one most difficult to avoid. A memorable cartoon from the 1950s shows a young man poring over the pages of the Bible. He says to his sister: "Don't bother me now; I'm trying to find a Scripture verse to back up one of my preconceived notions." No doubt a biblical text pried from its context can be twisted to say something very different from what its author actually intended.

The Church's criteria guide us here by defining what constitutes the authentic "context" of a given biblical passage. The first criterion directs us to the literary context of every verse, including not only the words and paragraphs that surround it, but also the entire corpus of the biblical author's writings and, indeed, the span of the entire Bible. The *complete* literary context of any Scripture verse includes every text from Genesis to Revelation—because the Bible is a unified book, not just a library of different books. When the Church canonized the Book of Revelation, for example, she recognized it to be incomprehensible apart from the wider context of the entire Bible.

The second criterion places the Bible firmly within the context of a community that treasures a "living tradition". That community is the People of God down through the ages. Christians lived out their faith for well over a millennium before the printing press was invented. For centuries, few believers owned copies of the Gospels, and few people could read anyway. Yet they absorbed the gospel—through the sermons of their bishops and clergy, through prayer and meditation, through Christian art, through liturgical celebrations, and through oral tradition. These were expressions of the one "living tradition", a culture of living faith that stretches from ancient Israel to the contemporary Church. For the early Christians, the gospel could not be understood apart from that tradition. So it is with us. Reverence for the Church's tradition is what protects us from any sort of chronological or cultural provincialism, such as scholarly fads that arise and carry away a generation of interpreters before being dismissed by the next generation.

The third criterion places scriptural texts within the framework of faith. If we believe that the Scriptures are divinely inspired, we must also believe them to be internally coherent and consistent with all the doctrines that Christians believe. Remember, the Church's dogmas (such as the Real Presence, the papacy, the Immaculate Conception) are not something *added* to Scripture; rather, they are the Church's infallible interpretation *of* Scripture.

Using This Study Guide This volume is designed to lead the reader through Scripture according to the Church's guidelines—faithful to the canon, to the tradition, and to the creeds. The Church's interpretive principles have thus shaped the component parts of this book, and they are designed to make the reader's study as effective and rewarding as possible.

Introductions: We have introduced the biblical book with an essay covering issues such as authorship, date of composition, purpose, and leading themes. This background information will assist readers to approach and understand the text on its own terms.

Annotations: The basic notes at the bottom of every page help the user to read the Scriptures with understanding. They by no means exhaust the meaning of the sacred text but provide background material to help the reader make sense of what he reads. Often these notes make explicit what the sacred writers assumed or held to be implicit. They also provide a great deal of historical, cultural, geographical, and theological information pertinent to the inspired narratives—information that can help the reader bridge the distance between the biblical world and his own.

Cross-References: Between the biblical text at the top of each page and the annotations at the bottom, numerous references are listed to point readers to other scriptural passages related to the one being studied. This follow-up is an essential part of any serious study. It is also an excellent way to discover how the content of Scripture "hangs together" in a providential unity. Along with biblical cross-references, the annotations refer to select paragraphs from the *Catechism of the Catholic Church*. These are not doctrinal "proof texts" but are designed to help the reader interpret the Bible in accordance with the mind of the Church. The *Catechism* references listed either handle the biblical text directly or treat a broader doctrinal theme that sheds significant light on that text.

Topical Essays, Word Studies, Charts: These features bring readers to a deeper understanding of select details. The *topical essays* take up major themes and explain them more thoroughly and theologically than the annotations, often relating them to the doctrines of the Church. Occasionally the annotations are supplemented by *word studies* that put readers in touch with the ancient languages of Scripture. These should help readers to understand better and appreciate the inspired terminology that runs throughout the sacred books. Also included are various *charts* that summarize biblical information "at a glance".

Icon Annotations: Three distinctive icons are interspersed throughout the annotations, each one corresponding to one of the Church's three criteria for biblical interpretation. Bullets indicate the passage or passages to which these icons apply.

Notes marked by the book icon relate to the "content and unity" of Scripture, showing how particular passages of the Old Testament illuminate the mysteries of the New. Much of the information in these notes explains the original context of the citations and indicates how and why this has a direct bearing on Christ or the Church. Through these notes, the reader can develop a sensitivity to the beauty and unity of God's saving plan as it stretches across both Testaments.

Notes marked by the dove icon examine particular passages in light of the Church's "living tradition". Because the Holy Spirit both guides the Magisterium and inspires the spiritual senses of Scripture, these annotations supply information along both of these lines. On the one hand, they refer to the Church's doctrinal teaching as presented by various popes, creeds, and ecumenical councils; on the other, they draw from (and paraphrase) the spiritual interpretations of various Fathers, Doctors, and saints.

Notes marked by the keys icon pertain to the "analogy of faith". Here we spell out how the mysteries of our faith "unlock" and explain one another. This type of comparison between Christian beliefs displays the coherence and unity of defined dogmas, which are the Church's infallible interpretations of Scripture.

Putting It All in Perspective Perhaps the most important context of all we have saved for last: the interior life of the individual reader. What we get out of the Bible will largely depend on how we approach the Bible. Unless we are living a sustained and disciplined life of prayer, we will never have the reverence, the profound humility, or the grace we need to see the Scriptures for what they really are.

You are approaching the "word of God". But for thousands of years, since before he knit you in your mother's womb, the Word of God has been approaching you.

One Final Note. The volume you hold in your hands is only a small part of a much larger work still in production. Study helps similar to those printed in this booklet are being prepared for *all* the books of the Bible and will appear gradually as they are finished. Our ultimate goal is to publish a single, one-volume Study Bible that will include the entire text of Scripture, along with all the annotations, charts, cross-references, maps, and other features found in the following pages. Individual booklets will be published in the meantime, with the hope that God's people can begin to benefit from this labor before its full completion.

We have included a long list of Study Questions in the back to make this format as useful as possible, not only for individual study, but for group settings and discussions as well. The questions are designed to help readers both "understand" the Bible and "apply" it to their lives. We pray that God will make use of our efforts and yours to help renew the face of the earth! «

INTRODUCTION TO THE FIRST BOOK OF SAMUEL

Author and Date The author or authors of 1 Samuel are unnamed and unknown. Jewish tradition maintained that everything before the death of Samuel in chap. 25 was written by the prophet Samuel himself and that everything that follows was written by the prophets Nathan and Gad (Babylonian Talmud, *Baba Bathra* 14b, 15a). There is nothing improbable about such prominent figures recording events that occurred during their lifetime. On the contrary, Samuel reportedly wrote guidelines for Israelite kingship in a book (10:25), while Nathan and Gad are both credited with written accounts of the reign of King David (1 Chron 29:29). Nonetheless, these individuals are more likely to have produced some of the source materials incorporated into 1 Samuel than the final form of the book. A majority of scholars concur that 1 Samuel reads more like a compilation of ancient stories and traditions drawn together into a single work than a composition written from scratch by a single author.

This makes dating 1 Samuel rather difficult. On the one hand, the narrative abounds in vivid and realistic detail, with the humanity of the leading characters given a particularly convincing presentation. Indeed, the Books of Samuel do little to idealize the personalities of Samuel and David but relate their sins and shortcomings with a warts-and-all honesty that inspires confidence in the objectivity and antiquity of their sources. On the other hand, the compiler of 1 Samuel seems to have been working after 930 B.C., which saw the breakup of David and Solomon's empire into the rival kingdoms of "Israel" in the north and "Judah" in the south. Allusions to this political situation appear in 11:8; 17:52; 18:16; 27:6. Besides this, modern scholarship has come to regard 1 and 2 Samuel as part of a larger work known as the Deuteronomistic History. This is the name given to the biblical account of Israel's life in Canaan, beginning with its entrance into the land and ending with its exile from the land. Canonically, it encompasses all the books from Joshua to 2 Kings (minus Ruth). Since these works bear the marks of a common theological outlook based on the Book of Deuteronomy, there is reason to think they were edited together as a collection. And since the storyline of this collection extends to the Babylonian Exile of Judah in 586 B.C., it is not unreasonable to date the finished, canonical books to this time.

Questions of authorship and date are thus bound up with the stages of development that apparently stand behind the final edition of the Books of Samuel.

A degree of educated guesswork is unavoidable, but one could reasonably posit **(1)** the appearance of written stories about Samuel, Saul, David, and perhaps the Ark of the Covenant within a generation of the events recorded, **(2)** an initial effort to join these accounts into a connected narrative in the period of the divided monarchy, and **(3)** a concluding stage of editing at the time of the Babylonian Exile in the sixth century B.C.

Title The Books of Samuel have borne several different titles over the centuries. Originally, they constituted a single continuous work rather than two separate volumes. The Hebrew title was simply *Shemu'el*, "Samuel". In the first or second century B.C., the Greek Septuagint divided the Hebrew text into two books and grouped them together with the Books of Kings under the heading "Kingdoms". First Samuel was thus known as *Basileiōn Alpha*, "First Kingdoms". Saint Jerome altered this in the Latin Vulgate by calling the four volumes, *Libri Regum*, "The Books of Kings". Modern editions of the Bible typically adopt the Hebrew title but follow the Greek and Latin tradition of dividing the text of Samuel into two books.

Place in the Canon First Samuel stands after Judges and Ruth in the arrangement of the Old Testament because it completes the story of that era. In the Hebrew Bible, it is the third of the "Former Prophets", a collection of books running from Joshua to 2 Kings (excluding Ruth) that relates the experiences of Israel in Canaan from the perspective of the prophets, whose main concern was to evaluate the success and failure of the nation in relation to its observance or nonobservance of the Mosaic covenant. Christian tradition regards 1 Samuel as one of the "Historical Books" of the Bible without prejudice to its prophetic outlook.

Structure First Samuel may be divided up in different ways. The simplest is to read it as a threefold story about its three main characters: Samuel, Saul, and David. **(1)** Chapters 1–7 feature the birth and ministry of Samuel, the prophet and judge who provides trustworthy leadership for Israel in a time of spiritual decline. **(2)** Chapters 8–15 see the rise and fall of King Saul, who leads Israel to victory against its enemies but whose shallow commitment to the Lord brings his reign to an early and disappointing end. **(3)** Chapters 16–31 relate the story of God choosing David for kingship over

Israel, helping him to bring down the mighty Goliath, and shielding him from the plots and pursuits of an envious Saul.

Content and Themes First Samuel is a theological history of how Israel, a confederation of twelve tribes, was transformed into a kingdom ruled by kings. The storyline covers roughly a century from the birth of Samuel, the last of the judges (ca. 1115 B.C.), to the death of Saul, the first of Israel's kings (ca. 1010 B.C.). This transition from theocracy to monarchy, from the direct rule of Yahweh exercised through judges and tribal deliverers to a succession of kings anointed for royal office, marks a momentous change in covenant administration that was destined to shape the history of Israel for centuries to come.

Samuel himself plays a significant part in this story. He is a prophet (3:20) and judge (7:15–17) as well as a "kingmaker" who lays the foundation for the Israelite monarchy by anointing the nation's first two kings, Saul (10:1) and David (16:13). Curiously, no one is more opposed to institutionalized kingship than Samuel, who disapproves of the popular demand for a king (8:6) because he realizes that Israel's desire to have a ruler "like all the nations" (8:5) is a backhanded rejection of Yahweh as the divine King of Israel (8:7). The people clamor for a more tangible form of rule because they think it will bring them the security and stability that was sorely lacking in the time of the judges. But this was to misdiagnose the problem as political rather than spiritual. The Lord will grant Israel a human king (8:22), but Samuel warns that Israel's national welfare is in no way guaranteed by this new form of government. Blessings of peace and prosperity can only come from a total adherence to the Lord and his covenant (12:14).

The risks and rewards of a monarchy are dramatized in the lives of Saul and David, the first men in Israel anointed for this high office. **(1)** On the one hand, Saul *falters* as king of Israel because he refuses to submit to the word of God. Although he has many natural gifts for leadership (9:1–2), his heart is uncommitted to the Lord. Within a week of his anointing, Saul transgresses the prophet Samuel's instruction to "wait" for his coming at Gilgal (10:8). For this act of impatient disobedience, the Lord denies Saul a family dynasty (13:8–15). Later the prophetic word comes again to Saul as a command to make war on the Amalekites (15:1–3), and again Saul refuses to carry out what is asked of him (15:4–21). As a consequence, God strips Saul of his own right to rule (15:23–28), and the Spirit of the Lord that anointed him for kingship withdraws from him (16:14). Things go from bad to worse in the latter chapters of the book, where Saul, consumed with envy and paranoia, displays fits of rage (18:10–11; 19:9–10; 20:33; 22:17–19) and spends much of his time chasing David from

hideout to hideout, plotting his demise (19:1, 11; 23:14–29; 26:1–5). Saul's tragic life unravels to its tragic end when, in a battle with the Philistines, he makes the fateful decision to throw courage and valor aside and run himself through with a sword (31:1–4). **(2)** David, on the other hand, *flourishes* as the king-elect of Israel since he is a man after God's heart (13:14). One could say that 1 Samuel casts David as an ideal candidate for Israelite kingship, as one who embodies the practical and spiritual qualities most necessary for a royal representative of Yahweh. For instance, David does not rely on his own strength to do the Lord's work but calls upon God in time of need. This is clearest when he fells Goliath with nothing but a small stone flung in the name of the Lord (17:41–51). Nor does David rely on his own wisdom, since several times we see him consulting the Lord before taking action, and he is quick to observe every command of the Lord when action is called for (22:5; 23:9–13; 30:7–10). David likewise displays God's mercy, for twice Saul comes into his grasp, and both times he refuses to avenge himself by laying violent hands on the Lord's anointed (24:1–7; 26:6–12). These and other incidents show David to be a man of unusual faith and fidelity. Because David allows God to direct his way, the Spirit of the Lord remains with him (16:13) and prospers all his endeavors (18:14).

Besides these historical and theological dimensions of the Books of Samuel, one also notices an apologetic concern underlying the story, especially in 1 Samuel 16—2 Samuel 5. These chapters implicitly but repeatedly vindicate David as the legitimate successor to King Saul, presumably because of suspicions surrounding the stormy transfer of kingship from the house of Saul (tribe of Benjamin) to the house of David (tribe of Judah). In view of the protracted war between these two royal houses (2 Sam 3:1), the author portrays David as innocent of any treachery or selfish ambition that would indicate he was a usurper of Saul's throne. Several considerations lend support to this interpretation. **(1)** It is true that David was advantageously wedded to Saul's daughter, the princess Michal; however, the marriage was proposed by Saul himself and had nothing to do with political opportunism on David's part (1 Sam 18:17–22). **(2)** It is true that David withdrew from his service in Saul's court and attracted supporters of his own; however, his flight from Saul was necessitated by the king's attempts on his life (1 Sam 18:10–11; 19:9–10). It was not a calculated attempt by David to build a rival government. **(3)** It is true that David, while running from Saul, found refuge among the Philistines; however, David was no defector to the enemy (1 Sam 27:1–12). Instead, he deceived the Philistines about his intentions and used his circumstances to bring benefit to Israel (1 Sam 28:8–11; 30:1–31). **(4)** It is true that Saul harbored a jealous hatred for David; however, the animosity was not mutual. Twice David found himself in a position to eliminate Saul, and both times he reverently declined (1 Sam 24:1–7; 26:1–12). **(5)** It is true that Saul, his sons, and his military officer all suffered violent deaths in the unsettled times leading up to David's rule; however, no bloodguilt can be imputed to David himself. Before Saul and three of his sons were slain in a clash with the Philistines (1 Sam 31:1–7), David and his men had been ordered to return home before the battle even began (1 Sam 29:1–5). Likewise, neither the murder of Abner, Saul's army commander, nor the assassination of Ish-bosheth, Saul's surviving son, formed part of a plot to eradicate the last remnants of the house of Saul (2 Sam 3:22–30; 4:5–12). To the contrary, David disapproved of these actions and was quick to punish the perpetrators. **(6)** It is true that David seemed unstoppable in his rise to kingship and that Saul's every attempt at retaining power failed; however, this cannot be explained solely in terms of tactical maneuvering. Ultimately it was the outworking of the Lord's plan. It was Yahweh who withdrew his favor from Saul (1 Sam 16:14) and who cleared the path for David to reign over all Israel (1 Sam 16:18; 18:12, 14, 28; 2 Sam 5:10). Taken together, these observations create a strong impression that 1 and 2 Samuel were written in part to set the record straight on David's legitimacy as the royal successor to King Saul.

Christian Perspective Christian tradition sees in 1 Samuel several prophetic glimpses of the gospel. An image of Mary is seen in the pious and prayerful Hannah, who comes to the Temple and dedicates her first-born to the Lord (1:9–27; Lk 2:22–28). Striking parallels in thought and expression indicate that Mary's *Magnificat* in Lk 1:46–55 is practically a Christian version of Hannah's Song in 2:1–10. An image of Jesus Christ is seen in the person of David. Beyond the fact that Jesus has a Davidic genealogy that links him with this ancient king (Mt 1:1–16), it is significant that Jesus was born in David's hometown of Bethlehem (17:12; Mt 2:1), that he was baptized by John the Baptist, a Levitical prophet and Nazirite (Mk 1:9–10; Lk 3:21–22), just as David was anointed by Samuel, a Levitical prophet and Nazirite (16:13), and that he claimed to be the Good Shepherd who, like David, was willing to risk his life for his sheep (17:34–35; Jn 10:11). These connections are not playful inventions of the early Church, for Jesus himself laid the groundwork for Davidic typology when he declared that he and his disciples were comparable to David and his men, who had eaten holy bread on a Sabbath day in 1 Samuel (21:1–6; Mt 12:1–4).

OUTLINE OF THE FIRST BOOK OF SAMUEL

1. The Career of Samuel (chaps. 1–7)
   A. Samuel's Birth and Youth (1:1—3:21)
   B. Philistines Capture the Ark (4:1—7:2)
   C. Samuel the Judge (7:3–17)

2. The Rise and Fall of Saul (chaps. 8–15)
   A. Saul Is Anointed King (8:1—11:15)
   B. Samuel Delivers a Speech (12:1–25)
   C. Saul Leads Israel in War (13:1—15:9)
   D. Saul Is Rejected by God (15:10–35)

3. The Rise of David (chaps. 16–31)
   A. David Is Anointed King (16:1–23)
   B. David and Goliath (17:1–58)
   C. David Flees from Saul (18:1—30:31)
   D. The Death of Saul (31:1–13)

THE FIRST BOOK OF
SAMUEL

Samuel's Birth and Dedication

1 There was a certain man of Ramatha′imzo′phim of the hill country of E′phraim, whose name was Elka′nah the son of Jero′ham, son of Eli′hu, son of To′hu, son of Zuph, an E′phraimite. [2]He had two wives; the name of the one was Hannah, and the name of the other Penin′nah. And Peninnah had children, but Hannah had no children.

3 Now this man used to go up year by year from his city to worship and to sacrifice to the LORD of hosts at Shiloh,* where the two sons of Eli, Hoph′ni and Phin′ehas, were priests of the LORD. [4]On the day when Elka′nah sacrificed, he would give portions to Penin′nah his wife and to all her sons and daughters; [5]and, although[a] he loved Hannah, he would give Hannah only one portion, because the LORD had closed her womb. [6]And her rival used to provoke her sorely, to irritate her, because the LORD had closed her womb. [7]So it went on year by year; as often as she went up to the house of the LORD, she used to provoke her. Therefore Hannah wept and would not eat. [8]And Elka′nah, her husband, said to her, "Hannah, why do you weep? And why do you not eat? And why is your heart sad? Am I not more to you than ten sons?"

9 After they had eaten and drunk in Shiloh, Hannah rose. Now Eli the priest was sitting on the seat beside the doorpost of the temple of the LORD. [10]She was deeply distressed and prayed to the LORD, and wept bitterly. [11]And she vowed a vow and said, "O LORD of hosts, if you will indeed look on the affliction of your maidservant, and remember me, and not forget your maidservant, but will give to your maidservant a son, then I will give him to the LORD all the days of his life, and no razor shall touch his head."

1:1 Ramathaimzophim: Often located at modern Rentis, less than 20 miles west of Shiloh. It is unclear whether this is the same place as the "Ramah" mentioned hereafter in the story as the home of Samuel's family (1:19; 2:11; 7:17; 8:4; 25:1). **Ephraimite:** Geographically, not genealogically. Elkanah lives in the territory of the tribe of Ephraim but descends from the Kohathite clan of the tribe of Levi (1 Chron 6:16–28). The Kohathites were given a handful of towns and pasturelands in Ephraim (Josh 21:20–22; 24:33).

1:2 two wives: Polygamy deviates from the standard of monogamy established at creation (Gen 1:27; 2:24), and yet it was tolerated in early biblical history as a concession to human weakness (Gen 29:15–30; Deut 21:15–17). Most likely, Elkanah married **Hannah** first, but when she proved to be infertile, he took **Peninnah** as a second wife in the hope of fathering an heir. In Hebrew, the name Hannah means "favor" and Peninnah means "fruitful".

1:3 the LORD of hosts: The first time Yahweh is given this title in the Bible. It describes him as the Commander of holy armies, i.e., the angelic hosts of heaven (Josh 5:14) as well as the military forces of Israel (17:45). The epithet appears often in the OT writings, especially in the Psalms and the Prophets. **Shiloh:** A town in Ephraimite territory about 20 miles north of Jerusalem (modern Khirbet Seilun). Shiloh is home to the Mosaic Tabernacle for much of the settlement period (Josh 18:1; 19:51; Judg 18:31).

1:4 portions: Selections of meat from an animal "peace offering" (Lev 7:11–17).

1:5 closed her womb: The Lord is sovereign over human fertility and infertility, meaning that he can grant (1:19; Gen 29:31) or withhold the conception of children according to his will (Gen 16:2; 30:2).

1:7 house of the LORD: Seems to indicate that the Mosaic Tabernacle is stationed within a building or walled enclosure that has solid doors (3:15) and sleeping quarters for priests and Levites (3:3). The Shiloh sanctuary could thus be called a "temple" (1:9).

1:9 Eli the priest: The senior Levitical priest at the Shiloh sanctuary.

1:11 she vowed: I.e., she makes a solemn commitment to the Lord. Vows in the Bible are conditional promises (if … then …) that depend upon God's willingness to answer specific prayers (cf. Gen 28:20–21; Judg 11:30–31; 2 Sam 15:8). Married women in Israel could only be released from a vow if their husbands disapproved of it (Num 30:6–15) (CCC 2102). • *Allegorically*, Hannah is a type of the Church at prayer. She speaks to God, not with noisy requests, but in the silence of her heart, for she knows that the Lord hears the heart rather than the voice. And she receives what she asks for because she asks with faith (St. Cyprian, *On the Lord's Prayer* 5). *Morally*, because Hannah's rival distresses her and causes her pain, her prayer is made the more strenuous, and God is moved to answer it with the birth of Samuel. If we are likewise vigilant, our enemies will bring us great benefit in making us more zealous, provided we utter prayers rather than insults against them (St. John Chrysostom, *Homilies on Hannah* 1). **the affliction of your maidservant:** Rendered "the low estate of your handmaiden" in the Greek LXX, an expression taken up by Mary, the mother of Jesus, in Lk 1:48. See note on 2:1–10. **no razor:** A reference to Num 6:5, implying that Hannah's son will be dedicated to Yahweh as a Nazirite. Persons in this state refrained from cutting their hair, among other things. See note on Num 6:1–21. • Samuel, like Samson before him and John the Baptist after him, is born by a miracle to childless parents and is consecrated from the womb to follow a Nazirite way of life (Judg 13:2–7, 24; Lk 1:7–15).

The First and Second Books of Samuel (the First and Second Books of Kings): Samuel was traditionally supposed to have written these books—hence the title. The Latin Vulgate, following the Greek tradition, links these books with 1 and 2 Kings, calling them 1–4 Kings (Greek, 1–4 Kingdoms). 1 and 2 Samuel cover the early period of the monarchy and are, in fact, composed of two main traditions; this at times makes the sequence of events difficult to follow. The narrative makes plain the difficulty of centralizing the government of the tribes. David's character and achievement are well brought out, and there is special emphasis on the Messianic importance of both. Yet at the end the signs of possible schism are already manifest. The books were probably written during the period of the divided monarchy.

[a] Gk: Heb obscure.

*1:3, *Shiloh:* At this time, the central sanctuary of the tribes and the residence of the ark, the visible assurance of the presence of Yahweh, Lord of the hosts of Israel.

12 As she continued praying before the Lord, Eli observed her mouth. ¹³Hannah was speaking in her heart; only her lips moved, and her voice was not heard; therefore Eli took her to be a drunken woman. ¹⁴And Eli said to her, "How long will you be drunken? Put away your wine from you." ¹⁵But Hannah answered, "No, my lord, I am a woman sorely troubled; I have drunk neither wine nor strong drink, but I have been pouring out my soul before the Lord. ¹⁶Do not regard your maidservant as a base woman, for all along I have been speaking out of my great anxiety and vexation." ¹⁷Then Eli answered, "Go in peace, and the God of Israel grant your petition which you have made to him." ¹⁸And she said, "Let your maidservant find favor in your eyes." Then the woman went her way and ate, and her countenance was no longer sad.

19 They rose early in the morning and worshiped before the Lord; then they went back to their house at Ra′mah. And Elka′nah knew Hannah his wife, and the Lord remembered her; ²⁰and in due time Hannah conceived and bore a son, and she called his name Samuel, for she said, "I have asked him of the Lord."

21 And the man Elka′nah and all his house went up to offer to the Lord the yearly sacrifice, and to pay his vow. ²²But Hannah did not go up, for she said to her husband, "As soon as the child is weaned, I will bring him, that he may appear in the presence of the Lord, and abide there for ever." ²³Elka′nah her husband said to her, "Do what seems best to you, wait until you have weaned him; only, may the Lord establish his word." So the woman remained and nursed her son, until she weaned him. ²⁴And when she had weaned him, she took him up with her, along with a three-year-old bull,ᵇ an ephah of flour, and a skin of wine; and she brought him to the house of the Lord at Shiloh; and the child was young. ²⁵Then they slew the bull, and they brought the child to Eli. ²⁶And she said, "Oh, my lord! As you live, my lord, I am the woman who was standing here in your presence, praying to the Lord. ²⁷For this child I prayed; and the Lord has granted me my petition which I made to him. ²⁸Therefore I have lent him to the Lord; as long as he lives, he is lent to the Lord."

And theyˣ worshiped the Lord there.

Hannah's Prayer

2 Hannah also prayed and said,*
  "My heart exults in the Lord;
    my strength is exalted in the Lord.
My mouth derides my enemies,
    because I rejoice in your salvation.

2:1–10: Lk 1:46–55.

1:13 drunken: This would be a serious offense, especially in the sanctuary (Lev 10:9).

1:18 no longer sad: Hannah leaves reassured and hopeful that God will answer her pleas.

1:19 Ramah: Ramathaim-zophim in the territory of Ephraim (1:1), or possibly the town of Ramah just north of Jerusalem in the territory of Benjamin (modern er-Ram). **the Lord remembered:** Not that God is forgetful of his people in the midst of their trials. On the contrary, Scripture uses the language of "remembering" to signal a turning point when God acts to put the next phase of his covenant plan into effect (Gen 8:1; Ex 6:5).

1:20 Samuel: The Hebrew *shemu′el* either means "the name of God" or is meant to evoke the expression "one who is from God". Samuel is thus understood as God's gift to Hannah for her prayerful request (1:17, 27), just as Hannah's dedication of the boy is her grateful return of the gift back to the Lord (1:28). Indeed, the same Hebrew verb underlies the expressions "petition" and "lent", thus illustrating by means of a word play the proper human response to divine generosity. The divine gift of the boy can be understood as the response of God to the prayerful request Hannah asked of him, e.g., what she asked from God (1:17, 27). Her response is the return of the gift, when Hannah has "lent him to the Lord" (1:28). The word play thus illustrates the covenantal relationship between God's gift and human response that is evident throughout biblical history. • Several parallels between the Samuel story and the Pentateuch suggest that Samuel is a new Moses. **(1)** Samuel and Moses are both parted from their mothers in childhood to be raised by others (2:18-19; Ex 2:1-10); **(2)** both are called by God in the same way, and both respond to God in the same way (3:4; Ex 3:4); **(3)** both serve the Lord in the three offices of prophet (3:20; Deut 34:10), priest (7:9; Lev 8:14-29; Ps 99:6), and judge (7:6; Ex 18:13); **(4)** both are remembered as powerful intercessors on behalf of Israel (7:8-9; Num 14:19-20; Jer 15:1); **(5)** both have two sons (8:2; Ex 18:2-3); **(6)** both write a book with laws for Israel's kings to be kept in the Lord's presence (10:25; Deut 17:14-20; 31:24-26); **(7)** both anoint others for sacred office (10:1; 16:13; Lev 8:10-12); and **(8)** both deliver farewell speeches highlighting the two ways of obedience and disobedience to the covenant (12:1-25; Deut 28-30). Behind these parallels is the expectation of a "prophet like Moses" who would deliver God's word to Israel (Deut 18:15-18). Samuel is viewed as a preliminary fulfillment of this prophecy; however, the expectation is fully met only in Jesus Christ (Acts 3:18-24).

1:22 weaned: At about age three (2 Mac 7:27).

1:24 bull ... flour ... wine: An animal offering, cereal offering, and drink offering brought for the fulfillment of a vow (Num 15:8-10).

2:1-10 Hannah's Song. It is a prayer of praise, celebrating Hannah's deliverance from years of childlessness (1:2) and verbal abuse (1:6-7), as well as a prophetic utterance that foresees the establishment of the monarchy in Israel (2:10). The theme of the song is the "reversal of fortunes"—the belief that Yahweh can turn society upside down, toppling the high and mighty and lifting up the lowly and afflicted. This pattern is worked out in several ways through the book. **(1)** Peninnah, a fertile but insulting woman, bears several children but drops quickly out of the story, whereas Hannah, an infertile and stigmatized woman, is blessed with a child who will alter the course of Israel's history. **(2)** Eli, the head priest and judge at Shiloh, is cast down for allowing wickedness to flourish under his supervision,

---

ᵇGk Syr: Heb *three bulls*.

ˣHeb *he*.

*2:1–10: This song, though certainly touched up at a later period (e.g., the reference to a king in verse 10), is meant to express Hannah's sentiments. It has profoundly influenced the Magnificat.

²"There is none holy like the Lord,
  there is none besides you;
  there is no rock like our God.
³Talk no more so very proudly,
  let not arrogance come from your mouth;
 for the Lord is a God of knowledge,
  and by him actions are weighed.
⁴The bows of the mighty are broken,
  but the feeble gird on strength.
⁵Those who were full have hired themselves out
    for bread,
  but those who were hungry have ceased to
    hunger.
 The barren has borne seven,
  but she who has many children is forlorn.
⁶The Lord kills and brings to life;
  he brings down to Sheol and raises up.
⁷The Lord makes poor and makes rich;
  he brings low, he also exalts.
⁸He raises up the poor from the dust;
  he lifts the needy from the dung heap,
 to make them sit with princes
  and inherit a seat of honor.
 For the pillars of the earth are the Lord's,
  and on them he has set the world.

⁹"He will guard the feet of his faithful ones;
  but the wicked shall be cut off in darkness;
  for not by might shall a man prevail.
¹⁰The adversaries of the Lord shall be broken to
    pieces;
  against them he will thunder in heaven.

 The Lord will judge the ends of the earth;
  he will give strength to his king,
  and exalt the power of his anointed."

Eli's Wicked Sons

11 Then Elka′nah went home to Ra′mah. And the boy ministered to the Lord, in the presence of Eli the priest.

12 Now the sons of Eli were worthless men; they had no regard for the Lord. ¹³The custom of the priests with the people was that when any man offered sacrifice, the priest's servant would come, while the meat was boiling, with a three-pronged fork in his hand, ¹⁴and he would thrust it into the pan, or kettle, or caldron, or pot; all that the fork brought up the priest would take for himself.^c So they did at Shiloh to all the Israelites who came there. ¹⁵Moreover, before the fat was burned, the priest's servant would come and say to the man who was sacrificing, "Give meat for the priest to roast; for he will not accept boiled meat from you, but raw." ¹⁶And if the man said to him, "Let them burn the fat first, and then take as much as you wish," he would say, "No, you must give it now; and if not, I will take it by force." ¹⁷Thus the sin of the young men was very great in the sight of the Lord; for the men treated the offering of the Lord with contempt.

The Boy Samuel

18 Samuel was ministering before the Lord, a boy girded with a linen ephod.* ¹⁹And his mother used to make for him a little robe and take it to him each year, when she went up with her husband to offer the yearly sacrifice. ²⁰Then Eli would bless

---

whereas Samuel, also a priestly figure and judge, is raised up for uncompromising spiritual leadership. (3) Saul, chosen as king for impressive credentials, is stripped of his crown for disobedience to the word of God, whereas David, an insignificant shepherd boy, is elevated to kingship because of his trustful reliance on the Lord. Also, there are notable parallels between Hannah's Song, at the beginning of the Books of Samuel (1 Sam 2:1–10), and David's Song, which appears at the end (2 Sam 22:1–51). The two prayers form a frame around the main narrative, announcing its leading themes. • Hannah's Song has links with other biblical poems, such as the Song of Moses in Deut 32 and Ps 113. Even more, it is the primary inspiration behind Mary's *Magnificat* in Lk 1:46–55. Like her blessed ancestress, Mary pours forth the praise of her heart (2:1; Lk 1:47) to the saving Lord (2:1; Lk 1:47) for confounding the proud and the mighty (2:3–4; Lk 1:51–52), feeding the hungry (2:5; Lk 1:53), and exalting those of low estate (2:7–8; Lk 1:52) (CCC 489).

2:2 holy ... none besides ... rock: Descriptions of Yahweh drawn from the Pentateuch (Lev 11:44; 19:2; Deut 4:35; 32:4, 15, 18).

2:6 kills and brings to life: An allusion to Deut 32:39. **Sheol:** Hebrew name for the realm of the dead. See word study: *Sheol* at Num 16:30.

2:8 the pillars: Several biblical passages imagine the earth supported and stabilized from below by subterranean columns (Job 9:6; Ps 75:3; 104:5). In all these cases, the description is poetic rather than scientific. In fact, it may be linked to the scriptural view of the world as a cosmic temple (Rev 3:12). See essay: *Theology of the Temple* at 2 Chron 5.

2:10 he will thunder: Anticipates the Lord's action in 7:10. **his anointed:** A title initially used for the priests of Israel (Lev 4:3) but here a prophetic reference to the kings of Israel (2 Sam 22:51), who will soon be anointed for office (Saul, 10:1; David, 16:13; Solomon, 1 Kings 1:39, etc.). The term translated "anointed" (Heb., *mashiah*) was used in early Judaism as a title for the royal and priestly "Messiah" to come (CCC 436). See word study: *Christ* at Mk 14:61.

2:11 ministered: The Hebrew *sheret* is elsewhere used of priestly and Levitical service in the sanctuary (Num 8:26; 18:2; Ezek 44:12, 16). This indirectly confirms the genealogy in 1 Chron 6:16–28, which identifies Samuel as a Levite.

2:12–25 A priestly scandal at Shiloh is exposed. Eli's sons engage in promiscuous sexual activity (2:22), intimidation of worshipers (2:16), and abuse of the clerical right to receive food portions of sacrificial animals (2:13–14). The portions of meat designated for priests are strictly defined in Lev 7:28–36 and Deut 18:3.

2:16 the fat: Forbidden to eat and so dedicated to the Lord by fire (Lev 7:22–25).

2:18 linen ephod: A liturgical vestment worn by the sanctuary priests (22:18). This is not the highly decorated ephod worn by the high priest (Ex 28:5–13).

2:20 bless: A priestly gesture (Lev 9:22; Num 6:22–27).

---

^c Gk Syr Vg: Heb *with it.*
*2:18, *ephod:* The ephod was either a distinctive priestly garment as here, or a means of divination used by the priest, possibly a container for the sacred lots; cf. 2:28.

Elka'nah and his wife, and say, "The LORD give you children by this woman for the loan which she lent to[d] the LORD"; so then they would return to their home.

21 And the LORD visited Hannah, and she conceived and bore three sons and two daughters. And the boy Samuel grew in the presence of the LORD.

Eli Tries to Correct His Sons

22 Now Eli was very old, and he heard all that his sons were doing to all Israel, and how they lay with the women who served at the entrance to the tent of meeting. ²³And he said to them, "Why do you do such things? For I hear of your evil dealings from all the people. ²⁴No, my sons; it is no good report that I hear the people of the LORD spreading abroad. ²⁵If a man sins against a man, God will mediate for him; but if a man sins against the LORD, who can intercede for him?" But they would not listen to the voice of their father; for it was the will of the LORD to slay them.

Samuel's Virtues

26 Now the boy Samuel continued to grow both in stature and in favor with the LORD and with men.

A Prophecy against Eli's Household

27 And there came a man of God to Eli, and said to him, "Thus the LORD has said, 'I revealed[e] myself to the house of your father when they were in Egypt subject to the house of Pharaoh. ²⁸And I chose him out of all the tribes of Israel to be my priest, to go up to my altar, to burn incense, to wear an ephod before me; and I gave to the house of your father all my offerings by fire from the sons of Israel. ²⁹Why then look with greedy eye at[f] my sacrifices and my offerings which I commanded, and honor your sons above me by fattening yourselves upon the choicest parts of every offering of my people Israel?' ³⁰Therefore the LORD the God of Israel declares: 'I promised that your house and the house of your father should go in and out before me for ever'; but now the LORD declares: 'Far be it from me; for those who honor me I will honor, and those who despise me shall be lightly esteemed. ³¹Behold, the days are coming, when I will cut off your strength and the strength of your father's house, so that there will not be an old man in your house. ³²Then in distress you will look with envious eye on all the prosperity which shall be bestowed upon Israel; and there shall not be an old man in your house for ever. ³³The man of you whom I shall not cut off from my altar shall be spared to weep out his[g] eyes and grieve his[g] heart; and all the increase of your house shall die by the sword of men.[h] ³⁴And this which shall befall your two sons, Hoph'ni and Phin'ehas, shall be the sign to you: both of them shall die on the same day. ³⁵And I will raise up for myself a faithful priest, who shall do according to what is in my heart and in my mind; and I will build him a sure house, and he shall go in and out before my anointed for ever. ³⁶And every one who is left in your house shall come to implore him for a piece of silver or a loaf of bread, and shall say, "Put me, I

2:26: Lk 2:52.

2:21 sons ... daughters: God responds to generosity with generosity. Because Hannah makes Samuel a gift to the Lord, she receives from the Lord the blessing of five more children.

2:22 women who served: Little is known about the activities and responsibilities of these female ministers at the Israelite sanctuary, though reference is made to them in Ex 38:8 as well. Later sources, describing the personnel of the Second Temple, speak of female virgins who lived as wards of the Temple (*Protoevangelium of James* 7-8; cf. 2 Mac 3:19) and who made the sanctuary veils, baked showbread, prepared incense, etc. (Mishnah *Shekalim* 8, 5-6; *Pesiqta Rabbati* 26, 6; Babylonian Talmud, *Ketubbot* 106a). Here the consecrated women at Shiloh act more like the cult prostitutes of Canaanite religion who are condemned in the Bible (Deut 23:17; 2 Kings 23:7; Hos 4:14).

2:25 would not listen: The sons of Eli remain defiant because the grace of repentance is withheld from them. On this form of divine judgment, see note on Ex 4:21.

2:26 in stature and in favor: This notice of Samuel's development is echoed in the description of Jesus in Lk 2:52.

2:27 man of God: A way of describing a prophet (1 Kings 13:1; 2 Kings 5:8).

2:28 my priest: The tribe of Levi has received a covenant of priesthood to be exercised by the family line of Aaron (Ex 40:12-15; Mal 2:4).

2:31-36 An oracle of doom. It announces the fall of the priestly house of Eli as punishment for the sacrilege of his sons as well as his own failure to administer parental discipline (3:13). The end will come when Solomon banishes Eli's great-great-grandson, the priest Abiathar, from service at the sanctuary (1 Kings 2:26-27). In the context of 1 Samuel, the fall of the *priestly* house of Eli, foretold by a prophet and anticipated by the death of Eli and his sons (4:17-18), mirrors the fall of the *royal* house of Saul, also foretold by a prophet (13:13-14) and anticipated by the death of Saul and three of his sons at the end of the book (31:2-6). • *Allegorically,* the end of the house of Eli prefigures the end of the house of Aaron and the transference of the priesthood to Jesus Christ (St. Augustine, *City of God* 17, 5).

2:33 die by the sword: Anticipates the massacre of the priests at Nob in 22:18.

2:35 faithful priest: Foretells the rise of the high priest Zadok, who will stay faithful to Solomon (1 Kings 1:32-40) and whose descendants will hold the high priesthood in Jerusalem for centuries until Maccabean times (Ezek 44:15-31; 2 Mac 4:23-50). It is the Zadokite line of Aaronic priests that will constitute the **sure house** built by the Lord. See word study: *Sure House* at 25:28. • Christian faith recognizes a provisional fulfillment of the oracle in Zadok but sees its ultimate fulfillment in the Messiah. This is clearest in the Book of Hebrews, where Jesus is called the "faithful high priest" (Heb 2:17).

---

d Or *for the petition which she asked of.*
e Gk Tg: Heb *Did I reveal.*
f Or *treat with scorn.* Gk: Heb *kick at.*
g Gk: Heb *your.*
h Gk: Heb *die as men.*

beg you, in one of the priest's places, that I may eat a morsel of bread."'"

The Lord Calls Samuel

3 *Now the boy Samuel was ministering to the Lord under Eli. And the word of the Lord was rare in those days; there was no frequent vision.

2 At that time Eli, whose eyesight had begun to grow dim, so that he could not see, was lying down in his own place; ³the lamp of God had not yet gone out, and Samuel was lying down within the temple of the Lord, where the ark of God was. ⁴Then the Lord called, "Samuel! Samuel!" ⁱ and he said, "Here I am!" ⁵and ran to Eli, and said, "Here I am, for you called me." But he said, "I did not call; lie down again." So he went and lay down. ⁶And the Lord called again, "Samuel!" And Samuel arose and went to Eli, and said, "Here I am, for you called me." But he said, "I did not call, my son; lie down again." ⁷Now Samuel did not yet know the Lord, and the word of the Lord had not yet been revealed to him. ⁸And the Lord called Samuel again the third time. And he arose and went to Eli, and said, "Here I am, for you called me." Then Eli perceived that the Lord was calling the boy. ⁹Therefore Eli said to Samuel, "Go, lie down; and if he calls you, you shall say, 'Speak, Lord, for your servant hears.'" So Samuel went and lay down in his place.

10 And the Lord came and stood forth, calling as at other times, "Samuel! Samuel!" And Samuel said, "Speak, for your servant hears." ¹¹Then the Lord said to Samuel, "Behold, I am about to do a thing in Israel, at which the two ears of every one that hears it will tingle. ¹²On that day I will fulfil against Eli all that I have spoken concerning his house, from beginning to end. ¹³And I tell him that I am about to punish his house for ever, for the iniquity which he knew, because his sons were blaspheming God, ʲ and he did not restrain them. ¹⁴Therefore I swear to the house of Eli that the iniquity of Eli's house shall not be expiated by sacrifice or offering for ever."

15 Samuel lay until morning; then he opened the doors of the house of the Lord. And Samuel was afraid to tell the vision to Eli. ¹⁶But Eli called Samuel and said, "Samuel, my son." And he said, "Here I am." ¹⁷And Eli said, "What was it that he told you? Do not hide it from me. May God do so to you and more also, if you hide anything from me of all that he told you." ¹⁸So Samuel told him everything and hid nothing from him. And he said, "It is the Lord; let him do what seems good to him."

Samuel's Prophecy and the Capture of the Ark of God

19 And Samuel grew, and the Lord was with him and let none of his words fall to the ground. ²⁰And all Israel from Dan to Be′er-she′ba knew that Samuel was established as a prophet of the Lord. ²¹And the Lord appeared again at Shiloh, for the Lord revealed himself to Samuel at Shiloh by the word of the Lord. **4** ¹And the word of Samuel came to all Israel.

3:1 rare in those days: The absence of prophecy can be a sign that God is disciplining his wayward people (Ps 74:9; Amos 8:11–12). **vision:** A sensory encounter with God when divine revelation is given (Gen 15:1; Dan 8:15).

3:3 the lamp: The golden lampstand, called the *menorah*, that burns through the night in the sanctuary (Ex 27:20–21; 2 Chron 13:11). **temple:** Perhaps a walled enclosure around the Tabernacle. See note on 1:7. **the ark:** Veiled from sight inside the sanctuary's innermost chamber. Yahweh spoke from the top of the ark (Ex 25:22).

3:2–14 The call of Samuel to be a prophet (3:20). In this first encounter with the Lord, he receives, not new revelation, but a divine confirmation of the oracle already spoken against Eli in 2:27–36. A decisive new chapter in salvation history begins with Samuel's acceptance of the prophetic vocation, for he will facilitate Israel's move from being a nation of tribes to being a kingdom under the rule of a monarch.

3:4 Samuel! Samuel!: Reminiscent of the call of Moses to be a prophet (Ex 3:4). For other parallels between the two figures, see note on 1:20. **Here I am!:** The reply of one ready and eager to heed the Lord's instruction (Gen 22:1; Ex 3:4; Is 6:8) (CCC 2578). • *Morally*, the boy Samuel exemplifies the highest kind of obedience, which neither questions commands that are given nor stands in judgment over them, but renounces one's personal judgment (St. Gregory the Great, *On First Kings* 2, 4).

3:13 did not restrain: The failure to discipline wanton rebellion ensures the ruin of Eli's family and its future.

3:14 I swear: Yahweh swears a divine oath to bring judgment on the priestly family of Eli, which revels in blasphemy, impurity, and scandal (2:17, 22–23). For the initial indictment, see 2:27–36.

3:17 God do so to you: An abbreviated oath formula. It invokes a conditional curse upon Samuel should he conceal any information from Eli. The nature of the curse is not specified in the oath but may have been acted out in a symbolic gesture. For similar formulas, see 2 Sam 3:35 and 2 Kings 6:31.

3:19 with him: A sign that Yahweh will prosper Samuel's way and accomplish great things through him. Success and failure in doing the Lord's will depend on his active presence in one's life, as indicated later in the book (see 16:14, 18; 18:12–14). **let none of his words fall:** Samuel is recognized as a true prophet and spokesman for God because none of his words fail to come true (9:6; Deut 18:21–22).

3:20 Dan to Beer-sheba: Cities marking the northern and southern borders of the land of Israel (Judg 20:1; 2 Sam 24:15).

3:21 Shiloh: Location of the Israelite sanctuary. See note on 1:3.

4:1–11 The battle of Aphek. It is a day of triumph for the Philistines but a day of slaughter for the Israelites, who suffer heavy casualties and are forced to scatter from the battlefield in retreat. Even worse, it is a day when the Ark of the Covenant is captured and carried off as a trophy of war. In this catastrophe, Israel is made to experience the painful discipline of the Lord.

4:1 Philistines: Predominantly Aegean immigrants who settled in southwest Canaan in the late second millennium. For background, see note on Judg 3:3. **Ebenezer:** Translates "stone of help" and located at modern Izbet Sartah. It appears to be the same location mentioned in 7:12. **Aphek:** In the lowlands west of the hill country of Ephraim. It stands at the upper end

---

ⁱ Gk See 3:10: Heb *the Lord called Samuel.*

ʲ Another reading is *for themselves.*

*3:1: This account of the prophetic vocation of Samuel (cf. Is 6) is meant to begin a new chapter in the spiritual history of Israel.

*Now Israel went out to battle against the Philis'tines; they encamped at Ebenezer, and the Philistines encamped at A'phek. ²The Philis'tines drew up in line against Israel, and when the battle spread, Israel was defeated by the Philistines, who slew about four thousand men on the field of battle. ³And when the troops came to the camp, the elders of Israel said, "Why has the LORD put us to rout today before the Philis'tines? Let us bring the ark of the covenant of the LORD here from Shiloh, that he may come among us and save us from the power of our enemies." ⁴So the people sent to Shiloh, and brought from there the ark of the covenant of the LORD of hosts, who is enthroned on the cherubim; and the two sons of Eli, Hoph'ni and Phin'ehas, were there with the ark of the covenant of God.

5 When the ark of the covenant of the LORD came into the camp, all Israel gave a mighty shout, so that the earth resounded. ⁶And when the Philis'tines heard the noise of the shouting, they said, "What does this great shouting in the camp of the Hebrews mean?" And when they learned that the ark of the LORD had come to the camp, ⁷the Philis'tines were afraid; for they said, "A god has come into the camp." And they said, "Woe to us! For nothing like this has happened before. ⁸Woe to us! Who can deliver us from the power of these mighty gods? These are the gods who struck the Egyptians with every sort of plague in the wilderness. ⁹Take courage, and acquit yourselves like men, O Philis'tines, lest you become slaves to the Hebrews as they have been to you; acquit yourselves like men and fight."

10 So the Philis'tines fought, and Israel was defeated, and they fled, every man to his home; and there was a very great slaughter, for there fell of Israel thirty thousand foot soldiers. ¹¹And the ark of God was captured; and the two sons of Eli, Hoph'ni and Phin'ehas, were slain.

Death of Eli

12 A man of Benjamin ran from the battle line, and came to Shiloh the same day, with his clothes torn and with earth upon his head. ¹³When he arrived, Eli was sitting upon his seat by the road watching, for his heart trembled for the ark of God. And when the man came into the city and told the news, all the city cried out. ¹⁴When Eli heard the sound of the outcry, he said, "What is this uproar?" Then the man hastened and came and told Eli. ¹⁵Now Eli was ninety-eight years old and his eyes were set, so that he could not see. ¹⁶And the man said to Eli, "I am he who has come from the battle; I fled from the battle today." And he said, "How did it go, my son?" ¹⁷He who brought the tidings answered and said, "Israel has fled before the Philis'tines, and there has also been a great slaughter among the people; your two sons also, Hoph'ni and Phin'ehas, are dead, and the ark of God has been captured." ¹⁸When he mentioned the ark of God, Eli fell over

---

of Philistine territory, suggesting they planned to extend their northern frontier.

4:3 ark of the covenant: A representation of Yahweh's throne (4:4) and battle chariot (1 Chron 28:18). In times past, it proved to be a devastating weapon against Israel's enemies (Num 10:35; Josh 6:1–21). The problem, in this case, is that Israel is acting presumptuously, assuming the Lord will give victory in battle despite the brazen iniquities of the priests and the people (2:12–17; Judg 21:25). **Shiloh:** Location of the Israelite sanctuary (1:9).

4:4 cherubim: Two angelic images perched on the lid of the ark. Their wings stretch out to form the visible throne of Yahweh (Ps 99:1). See notes on Ex 25:10 and 25:18.

4:8 mighty gods: A mistaken assumption that Israel venerates many gods. The Philistines had little reason to think otherwise, as polytheism was universal in the religious culture of the ancient Near East.

4:11 Hophni and Phinehas: Slain in battle on the same day, as foretold in 2:34.

4:12 ran: Roughly 18 miles from Aphek to Shiloh. **clothes ... head:** Tearing one's garments and sprinkling dirt on one's head are expressions of extreme distress (2 Sam 1:2; 13:19).

4:18 heavy: Helps to explain how Eli's fall could be fatal. Beyond this, it harkens back to the comment in 2:29 that the priests of Shiloh fattened themselves on portions of sacrificial meat bullied from the laity. **judged:** Eli the priest is counted among the judges that guided Israel between the death of Joshua and the rise of King Saul. It is possible that the 40-year judgeship of Eli overlapped part of the 20-year judgeship of Samson (Judg 15:20).

---

*4:1: Here begins a new phase in the epic struggle against the Philistines, which the editor has skilfully woven into the story of the ark and of Samuel.

WORD STUDY

Glory (4:22)

Kabod (Heb.): often translated "glory", the term is used in a variety of ways in Scripture. It can refer to wealth and material abundance (Gen 31:1), outward splendor or magnificence (Hag 2:3), or even the honor that one person bestows upon another (Prov 11:16). When the glory of God is meant, it refers to the visible manifestation of his presence (Lev 9:6), usually in the form of a dark or fiery cloud (Ex 16:10), like the one that enveloped the top of Mt. Sinai (Ex 24:15–17). This is the glory of his presence that sanctified the Tent of Meeting when God proclaimed that he will come to meet the people of Israel (Ex 29:43), the glory that filled the Mosaic Tabernacle (Ex 40:34) and later the Solomonic Temple (1 Kings 8:11). Since the Hebrew noun "glory" (*kabod*) is related to the verb "be heavy" (*kabed*), it is likely the Israelites understood the glory of the Lord to be the immeasurable heaviness of his Being (see Paul's comment at 2 Cor 4:17). This would explain why, in 1 Samuel, the glory that departs from Israel (1 Sam 4:22) presses heavy upon the Philistines in the form of crushing judgments (1 Sam 5:6–7, 11) that could only be lightened if "glory" was rendered back to the God of Israel (1 Sam 6:5).

backward from his seat by the side of the gate; and his neck was broken and he died, for he was an old man, and heavy. He had judged Israel forty years.

19 Now his daughter-in-law, the wife of Phin'ehas, was with child, about to give birth. And when she heard the tidings that the ark of God was captured, and that her father-in-law and her husband were dead, she bowed and gave birth; for her pains came upon her. [20]And about the time of her death the women attending her said to her, "Fear not, for you have borne a son." But she did not answer or give heed. [21]And she named the child Ich'abod,* saying, "The glory has departed from Israel!" because the ark of God had been captured and because of her father-in-law and her husband. [22]And she said, "The glory has departed from Israel, for the ark of God has been captured."

The Philistines and the Ark

5 When the Philis'tines captured the ark of God, they carried it from Ebenezer to Ash'dod; [2]then the Philis'tines took the ark of God and brought it into the house of Da'gon and set it up beside Dagon. [3]And when the people of Ash'dod rose early the next day, behold, Da'gon had fallen face downward on the ground before the ark of the LORD. So they took Dagon and put him back in his place. [4]But when they rose early on the next morning, behold, Da'gon had fallen face downward on the ground before the ark of the LORD, and the head of Dagon and both his hands were lying cut off upon the threshold; only the trunk of Dagon was left to him. [5]This is why the priests of Da'gon and all who enter the house of Dagon do not tread on the threshold of Dagon in Ash'dod to this day.

6 The hand of the LORD was heavy upon the people of Ash'dod, and he terrified and afflicted them with tumors, both Ashdod and its territory. [7]And when the men of Ash'dod saw how things were, they said, "The ark of the God of Israel must not remain with us; for his hand is heavy upon us and upon Da'gon our god." [8]So they sent and gathered together all the lords of the Philis'tines, and said, "What shall we do with the ark of the God of Israel?" They answered, "Let the ark of the God of Israel be brought around to Gath." So they brought the ark of the God of Israel there. [9]But after they had brought it around, the hand of the LORD was against the city, causing a very great panic, and he afflicted the men of the city, both young and old, so that tumors broke out upon them. [10]So they sent the ark of God to Ek'ron. But when the ark of God came to Ekron, the people of Ekron cried out, "They have brought around to us the ark of the God of Israel to slay us and our people." [11]They sent therefore and gathered together all the lords of the Philis'tines, and said, "Send away the ark of the God of Israel, and let it return to its own place, that it may not slay us and our people." For there was a deathly panic throughout the whole city. The hand of God was very heavy there; [12]the men who did not die were stricken with tumors, and the cry of the city went up to heaven.

The Ark Returned to Israel

6 The ark of the LORD was in the country of the Philis'tines seven months. [2]And the Philis'tines called for the priests and the diviners and said, "What shall we do with the ark of the LORD? Tell us with what we shall send it to its place." [3]They said, "If you send away the ark of the God of Israel, do not send it empty, but by all means return him a guilt offering. Then you will be healed, and it will be known to you why his hand

---

4:21 Ichabod: Translates "no glory" or "Where is the glory?" The name memorializes how Yahweh's glorious presence, symbolized by the ark, was taken away from Israel. It was through Ichabod's brother Ahitub (14:3) that the priestly line of Eli continued for two more generations in the brothers Ahijah (14:3) and Ahimelech (22:9) and then in Abiathar, son of Ahimelech (22:20; 1 Kings 2:27).

5:1–12 The ark is taken to three Philistine cites in succession, leading to an outbreak of tumors (5:6), possibly bubonic plague, and an infestation of mice (6:4). In all likelihood, the rodents carried and spread the disease. • The plagues that ravaged Philistia, forcing the lords of the cities to release the captive ark, recall the plagues that terrorized Egypt, forcing the Pharaoh to release captive Israel. In both cases, the judgments of God came upon the people, their land, and their "gods" (6:5; Ex 12:12). The Exodus event is explicitly recalled in 4:8 and 6:6.

5:1 Ashdod: A coastal city more than 30 miles west of Jerusalem. It was part of a league of five Philistine cities in southwest Canaan, the others being Gaza, Ashkelon, Gath, and Ekron (6:17). Ashdod was also home to the temple of Dagon, an ancient Semitic grain god and the head of the Phi-

listine pantheon (5:2). The city was known as "Azotus" in later times (1 Mac 10:83–84; Acts 8:40). See note on Judg 16:23.

5:3 face downward: The image of Dagon slams down in front of the ark. Although capture of the ark seemed to imply that Dagon was stronger than Yahweh, the truth of the matter is now revealed, as the idol lies toppled and prostrate like a subject before his superior.

5:4 lying cut off: The statue is decapitated and dismembered like an enemy taken in battle (31:9; Judg 1:6; 2 Sam 4:12). **upon the threshold:** The incident gave rise to a Philistine superstition against stepping on the temple threshold (5:5).

5:6 The hand: Note the contrast between Dagon, whose hands are broken off, and Yahweh, whose hand presses hard upon the Philistines with his judgment (5:7, 11).

5:8 the lords: The rulers of the five Philistine cities (6:17). **Gath:** Location uncertain. Many identify it with a site 12 miles east of Ashdod.

5:10 Ekron: More than ten miles northeast of Ashdod.

6:1 seven months: The time frame covered by the events in chap. 5.

6:2 diviners: Practitioners of occult spiritual discernment. They are here consulted on the most effective way to propitiate an offended deity. Pagan divination was strictly prohibited in Israel (Deut 18:9–12).

6:3 guilt offering: A reparation offering for inadvertent sins committed against holy things (Lev 5:15). The compensation offered in this case is gold (6:4).

---

*4:21, *Ichabod:* The name means "The Glory is not"; i.e., the glory of the Lord enthroned over the ark has departed. Then followed the years during which the sanctuary of Shiloh was desolate and of which Jeremiah long afterward was acutely conscious; cf. Jer 7:12, 14; 26:6.

does not turn away from you." ⁴And they said, "What is the guilt offering that we shall return to him?" They answered, "Five golden tumors and five golden mice, according to the number of the lords of the Philis′tines; for the same plague was upon all of you and upon your lords. ⁵So you must make images of your tumors and images of your mice that ravage the land, and give glory to the God of Israel; perhaps he will lighten his hand from off you and your gods and your land. ⁶Why should you harden your hearts as the Egyptians and Pharaoh hardened their hearts? After he had made sport of them, did not they let the people go, and they departed? ⁷Now then, take and prepare a new cart and two milch cows upon which there has never come a yoke, and yoke the cows to the cart, but take their calves home, away from them. ⁸And take the ark of the Lᴏʀᴅ and place it on the cart, and put in a box at its side the figures of gold, which you are returning to him as a guilt offering. Then send it off, and let it go its way. ⁹And watch; if it goes up on the way to its own land, to Beth-she′mesh, then it is he who has done us this great harm; but if

not, then we shall know that it is not his hand that struck us, it happened to us by chance."

10 The men did so, and took two milch cows and yoked them to the cart, and shut up their calves at home. ¹¹And they put the ark of the Lᴏʀᴅ on the cart, and the box with the golden mice and the images of their tumors. ¹²And the cows went straight in the direction of Beth-she′mesh along one highway, lowing as they went; they turned neither to the right nor to the left, and the lords of the Philis′tines went after them as far as the border of Beth-shemesh. ¹³Now the people of Beth-she′mesh were reaping their wheat harvest in the valley; and when they lifted up their eyes and saw the ark, they rejoiced to see it. ¹⁴The cart came into the field of Joshua of Beth-she′mesh, and stopped there. A great stone was there; and they split up the wood of the cart and offered the cows as a burnt offering to the Lᴏʀᴅ. ¹⁵And the Levites took down the ark of the Lᴏʀᴅ and the box that was beside it, in which were the golden figures, and set them upon the great stone; and the men of Beth-she′mesh offered burnt offerings and sacrificed sacrifices on that day to the Lᴏʀᴅ.

6:5 give glory: See word study: *Glory* at 4:22.

6:7 never come a yoke: Calls for two cows that never pulled a wagon or ploughed a field. The idea is that profane work makes animals unfit for sacred purposes (Num 19:2; Deut 21:3). **take their calves:** A test to see if the Lord would direct the wagon (6:9). Cows that have just delivered would naturally want to suckle their young. Perhaps their "lowing" is viewed as a protest to leaving their newborn calves behind (6:12).

6:9 Beth-shemesh: Translates "house of the sun". Several locations in ancient Canaan bear this name. Here the reference is to a border town of Israel a few miles east of Ekron. It was home to Levitical descendants of Aaron (Josh 21:16).

6:14 great stone: Qualifies as an altar (Judg 13:19), provided it was untouched by an iron tool (Ex 20:25).

6:15 the Levites: The only persons among the Israelites authorized to transport the Ark of the Covenant (Num 3:31; Deut 10:8).

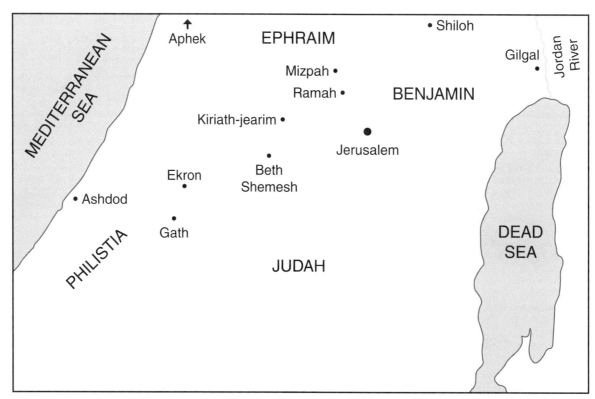

The Ministry of Samuel the Prophet

¹⁶And when the five lords of the Philis′tines saw it, they returned that day to Ek′ron.

17 These are the golden tumors, which the Philis′tines returned as a guilt offering to the LORD: one for Ash′dod, one for Gaza, one for Ash′kelon, one for Gath, one for Ek′ron; ¹⁸also the golden mice, according to the number of all the cities of the Philis′tines belonging to the five lords, both fortified cities and unwalled villages. The great stone, beside which they set down the ark of the LORD, is a witness to this day in the field of Joshua of Beth-she′mesh.

The Ark at Kiriath-jearim

19 And he slew some of the men of Beth-she′mesh, because they looked into the ark of the LORD; he slew seventy men of them,ᵏ and the people mourned because the LORD had made a great slaughter among the people. ²⁰Then the men of Beth-she′mesh said, "Who is able to stand before the LORD, this holy God? And to whom shall he go up away from us?" ²¹So they sent messengers to the inhabitants of Kir′iath-je′arim, saying, "The Philis′tines have returned the ark of the LORD. Come down and take it up to you." ¹And the men of Kir′iath-je′arim came and took up the ark of the LORD, and brought it to the house of Abin′adab on the hill; and they consecrated his son, Elea′zar, to have charge of the ark of the LORD. ²From the day that the ark was lodged at Kir′iath-je′arim, a long time passed, some twenty years, and all the house of Israel lamented after the LORD.*

Samuel as Judge of Israel

3 Then Samuel said to all the house of Israel, "If you are returning to the LORD with all your heart, then put away the foreign gods and the Ash′taroth from among you, and direct your heart to the LORD, and serve him only, and he will deliver you out of the hand of the Philis′tines." ⁴So Israel put away the Ba′als and the Ash′taroth, and they served the LORD only.

5 Then Samuel said, "Gather all Israel at Mizpah, and I will pray to the LORD for you." ⁶So they gathered at Mizpah, and drew water and poured it out before the LORD, and fasted on that day, and said there, "We have sinned against the LORD." And Samuel judged the sons of Israel at Mizpah. ⁷Now when the Philis′tines heard that the sons of Israel had gathered at Mizpah, the lords of the Philistines went up against Israel. And when the sons of Israel heard of it they were afraid of the Philistines. ⁸And the sons of Israel said to Samuel, "Do not cease to cry to the LORD our God for us, that he may save us from the hand of the Philis′tines." ⁹So Samuel took a suckling lamb and offered it as a whole burnt offering to the LORD; and Samuel cried to the LORD for Israel, and the LORD answered him. ¹⁰As Samuel was offering up the burnt offering, the Philis′tines drew near to attack Israel; but the LORD thundered with a mighty voice that day against the Philistines and threw them into confusion; and they were routed before Israel. ¹¹And the men of Israel went out of Mizpah and pursued the Philis′tines, and struck them, as far as below Beth-car.

12 Then Samuel took a stone and set it up between Mizpah and Jesha′nah,¹ and called its name Ebenezer;ᵐ for he said, "Hitherto the LORD has helped us." ¹³So the Philis′tines were subdued and

---

6:19 looked into the ark: The men, unauthorized to handle the ark, must have lifted off its golden lid to look inside. To touch the ark with unconsecrated hands was a fatal mistake, as also indicated in 2 Sam 6:7.

6:21 Kiriath-jearim: Translates "town of forests". Roughly nine miles northeast of Beth-shemesh, it belonged to the tribe of Judah and lay near its border with Benjamin's territory (Josh 18:14). The Ark of the Covenant stayed in Kiriath-jearim for about 20 years (7:2) until David moved it to its permanent home in Jerusalem (2 Sam 6:1–19).

7:1 house of Abinadab: Not mentioned again until David comes to retrieve the ark (2 Sam 6:3). Abinadab and his son may have been Levites, since the name **Eleazar** appears often in Levitical genealogies (Ex 6:23; 1 Chron 23:21; Ezra 8:33; Neh 12:42).

7:3–4 Samuel preaches repentance to Israel. The people, wearied by Philistine aggression and domination, respond to the prophet's call by renouncing their idols (7:4), confessing their sins (7:6), and begging Samuel to intercede with the Lord on their behalf (7:8). God's swift answer to his prayer (7:9) helps to establish Samuel as one of the great intercessors in Israel (Ps 99:6; Jer 15:1; CCC 2578).

7:3 with all your heart: The strength and depth of commitment to the Lord required by the Deuteronomic covenant (Deut 6:4–6). **Ashtaroth:** Idol figurines of the Semitic fertility goddess, Ashtoreth. See note on Judg 2:13. **serve him only:** Exclusive allegiance to Yahweh is stipulated in the Deuteronomic covenant (Deut 6:13). Jesus may have had the wording of this passage in mind when he quoted Deuteronomy against the temptation of the devil (Mt 4:10; Lk 4:8).

7:4 Baals: Baal is the storm and fertility god of Canaanite religion. See note on Judg 2:11.

7:5 Mizpah: Seven miles north of Jerusalem in the tribal territory of Benjamin.

7:6 poured it out: Symbolic of pouring out one's soul before the Lord in prayer (1:15; Ps 62:8). **judged:** Samuel provides leadership and administers justice to the Israelites (7:15–17), perhaps by adjudicating disputes, just as Moses did (Ex 18:13–27). Samuel and his sons are the last of the judges in biblical history (8:1–2). For parallels between Samuel and Moses, see note on 1:20.

7:10 the LORD thundered: Anticipated by the final verse of Hannah's Song (2:10).

7:11 Beth-car: Location unknown, but presumably west of Mizpah.

7:12 Ebenezer: Translates "stone of help". The boulder is propped upright as a memorial to Yahweh, who delivers his people when at last they turn to him with repentant hearts. The location marks a reversal in the story: this appears to be the place where sinful Israel encamped earlier before a crushing defeat by the Philistines (4:1; 5:1); but now that Israel has renounced its former ways, the Lord grants victory over the Philistines (7:10).

7:13 the Philistines were subdued: Temporarily, not decisively. Conflict will resume in the days of Saul (13:3; 14:52; 31:1).

ᵏ Cn: Heb *of the people seventy men, fifty thousand men.*
¹ Gk Syr: Heb *Shen.*
ᵐ That is *Stone of help.*
*7:2: The story of the ark, which comes from a special source, is continued in 2 Sam 6.

Samuel is the Judge + High Priest

did not again enter the territory of Israel. And the hand of the LORD was against the Philistines all the days of Samuel. [14]The cities which the Philis'tines had taken from Israel were restored to Israel, from Ek'ron to Gath; and Israel rescued their territory from the hand of the Philistines. There was peace also between Israel and the Am'orites.

15 Samuel judged Israel all the days of his life. [16]And he went on a circuit year by year to Bethel, Gilgal, and Mizpah; and he judged Israel in all these places. [17]Then he would come back to Ra'mah, for his home was there, and there also he administered justice to Israel. And he built there an altar to the LORD.

Israel Asks for a King

8 When Samuel became old, he made his sons judges over Israel. [2]The name of his first-born son was Joel, and the name of his second, Abi'jah; they were judges in Be'er-she'ba. [3]Yet his sons did not walk in his ways, but turned aside after gain; they took bribes and perverted justice.

4 Then all the elders of Israel gathered together and came to Samuel at Ra'mah, [5]and said to him, "Behold, you are old and your sons do not walk in your ways; now appoint for us a king to govern us like all the nations." [6]But the thing displeased Samuel when they said, "Give us a king to govern us." And Samuel prayed to the LORD. [7]And the LORD said to Samuel, "Listen to the voice of the people in all that they say to you; for they have not rejected you, but they have rejected me from being king over them. [8]According to all the deeds which they have done to me,[n] from the day I brought them up out of Egypt even to this day, forsaking me and serving other gods, so they are also doing to you. [9]Now then, listen to their voice; only, you shall solemnly warn them, and show them the ways of the king who shall reign over them."

10 So Samuel told all the words of the LORD to the people who were asking a king from him.* [11]He said, "These will be the ways of the king who will reign over you: he will take your sons and appoint them to his chariots and to be his horsemen, and to run before his chariots; [12]and he will appoint for himself commanders of thousands and commanders of fifties, and some to plow his ground and to reap his harvest, and to make his implements of war and the equipment of his chariots. [13]He will take your daughters to be perfumers and cooks and bakers. [14]He will take the best of your fields and vineyards and olive orchards and give them to his servants. [15]He will take the tenth of your grain and of your vineyards and give it to his officers and to his servants. [16]He will take your menservants and maidservants, and the best of your cattle° and your donkeys, and put them to his work. [17]He will take the tenth of your flocks, and you shall be his slaves. [18]And in that day you will cry out because of your king, whom you have chosen for yourselves; but the LORD will not answer you in that day."

7:14 Amorites: Inhabitants of Canaan who survived the Israelite conquest of the land and retained control of certain areas (Judg 1:34–36).

7:16 Bethel: Roughly ten miles north of Jerusalem in the central highlands. **Gilgal:** Directly northeast of Jericho in the western Jordan valley.

7:17 Ramah: Hometown of Samuel. See notes on 1:1 and 1:19.

8:1–22 Israel clamors for a king, and a new phase of biblical history begins. The transition from judges to kings is occasioned by a crisis of corrupt leadership (2:12–17; 8:3) and a growing secular desire to be "like all the nations" (8:5). Demand for a model of government adopted by Gentiles (monarchy) amounts to a rejection of Israel's special vocation to live as a people set apart under the direct rule of Yahweh as King (theocracy). Scholars often view these verses as antimonarchical in outlook and thus deriving from a source that opposed kingship in Israel. The hypothesis is open to question, however, since it is unclear whether Samuel's resistance relates to the establishment of a royal government per se; instead, he appears displeased that Israel wishes to adopt the ways of other nations, and, beyond that, he seems offended that Israel is rejecting him as their leader (8:7).

8:1 Samuel became old: Many years have passed since the events of chap. 7.

8:2 Beer-sheba: One of the southernmost cities of Israel.

8:5 a king to govern: Kingship is not wrong in itself, since kings were long envisioned to come from Abraham through the line of Judah (Gen 17:6; 35:11; 49:10). Moses likewise made provision for an Israelite monarchy in the Torah (Deut 17:14–20). The problem here is that Israel is seeking national security and prosperity apart from the Lord, thus rejecting the primacy of *his* kingship over their lives (8:7; 10:19). This is not the first time the desire for a king has come to the surface in the turbulent age of the judges (see Judg 8:22–23).

8:9 the ways of the king: I.e., the drawbacks of having a king. Eventually the burdens of a monarchy will outweigh its blessings, and God's people will groan with regret for having demanded it. Among the royal policies to come, Israel can expect **(1)** state conscription of young men to be soldiers, officers, farmers, and craftsmen (8:11–12), **(2)** recruitment of young women to pamper the royal family and prepare its extravagant banquets (8:13), **(3)** requisition of property for royal estates and landholdings (8:14), and **(4)** heavy taxes on produce and livestock (8:15–17). Theologically, the divine concession to grant Israel a king includes a measure of divine discipline: God will allow his people to experience the painful bitterness that comes with rejecting his plan in favor of their own.

8:10 asking: Sets up a wordplay for the story that follows. The Hebrew verb "ask" (*sha'al*) is related to the name of Israel's first king, Saul (*sha'ul*), meaning, "the one asked for". The verb is repeated for emphasis in 12:13, 17, 19.

8:18 the LORD will not answer: Once granted, no amount of prayerful remorse will deliver Israel from its decision for kingship.

---

[n]Gk: Heb lacks *to me*.

°Gk: Heb *young men*.

*8:10ff: Choosing a king. Two accounts are discernible—a monarchist and an antimonarchist. In the absence of a central sanctuary and in an atmosphere of defeat, one section of the people demanded a king to reestablish their fortunes; the others preferred to leave it to God to raise up leaders when necessary, as in the days of the judges.

Israel's Demand Granted

19 But the people refused to listen to the voice of Samuel; and they said, "No! but we will have a king over us, [20]that we also may be like all the nations, and that our king may govern us and go out before us and fight our battles." [21]And when Samuel had heard all the words of the people, he repeated them in the ears of the LORD. [22]And the LORD said to Samuel, "Listen to their voice, and make them a king." Samuel then said to the men of Israel, "Go every man to his city."

Saul Chosen to Be King

9 There was a man of Benjamin whose name was Kish, the son of Abi'el, son of Ze'ror, son of Beco'rath, son of Aphi'ah, a Benjaminite, a man of wealth; [2]and he had a son whose name was Saul, <u>a handsome young man</u>. There was not a man among the sons of Israel more handsome than he; from his shoulders upward he was taller than any of the people.

3 Now the donkeys of Kish, Saul's father, were lost. So Kish said to Saul his son, "Take one of the servants with you, and arise, go and look for the donkeys." [4]And they[p] passed through the hill country of E'phraim and passed through the land of Shal'ishah, but they did not find them. And they passed through the land of Sha'alim, but they were not there. Then they passed through the land of Benjamin, but did not find them.

5 When they came to the land of Zuph, Saul said to his servant who was with him, "Come, let us go back, lest my father cease to care about the donkeys and become anxious about us." [6]But he said to him, "Behold, there is a man of God in this city, and he is a man that is held in honor; all that he says comes true. Let us go there; perhaps he can tell us

about the journey on which we have set out." [7]Then Saul said to his servant, "But if we go, what can we bring the man? For the bread in our sacks is gone, and there is no present to bring to the man of God. What have we?" [8]The servant answered Saul again, "Here, I have with me the fourth part of a shekel of silver, and I will give it to the man of God, to tell us our way." [9](Formerly in Israel, when a man went to inquire of God, he said, "Come, let us go to the seer"; for he who is now called a prophet was formerly called a seer.) [10]And Saul said to his servant, "Well said; come, let us go." So they went to the city where the man of God was.

11 As they went up the hill to the city, they met young maidens coming out to draw water, and said to them, "Is the seer here?" [12]They answered, "He is; behold, he is just ahead of you. Make haste; he has come just now to the city, because the people have a sacrifice today on the high place. [13]As soon as you enter the city, you will find him, before he goes up to the high place* to eat; for the people will not eat till he comes, since he must bless the sacrifice; afterward those eat who are invited. Now go up, for you will meet him immediately." [14]So they went up to the city. As they were entering the city, they saw Samuel coming out toward them on his way up to the high place.

15 Now the day before Saul came, the LORD had revealed to Samuel: [16]"Tomorrow about this time I will send to you a man from the land of Benjamin, and you shall anoint him to be prince over my people Israel. He shall save my people from the hand of the Philis'tines; for I have seen the affliction of[q] my people, because their cry has come to me." [17]When Samuel saw Saul, the LORD told him, "Here is the man of whom I spoke to you! He it is who

---

9:1–2 Introduction of Saul and his résumé. From a human standpoint, Saul has impressive credentials for leadership: he hails from a wealthy family, stands out for being young and attractive, and towers over his kinsmen in physical stature. Even so, none of these natural qualifications carries weight with the Lord, who sees past outward appearances into the hiddenness of the heart (16:7). Notice that the lineage of Saul, who is God's answer to the request of the people, is traced back five generations (Kish, Abiel, Zeror, Becorath, Aphiah), just as the lineage of Samuel, who is God's answer to the prayer of Hannah, was also traced back five generations in 1:1 (Elkanah, Jeroham, Elihu, Tohu, Zuph).

9:4 passed through: The search proceeds northward, presumably from the town of Gibeah (home of Saul, 10:26) to the town of Ramah (home of Samuel, 7:17).

9:5 land of Zuph: Apparently named after Samuel's ancestor Zuph (1:1).

9:6 man of God: The prophet Samuel (9:14).

9:8 fourth part: Roughly one-tenth of an ounce of silver. It was customary in ancient Israel to offer a gift in return for the services of a prophet (1 Kings 14:3; 2 Kings 8:7–9).

9:9 seer: Basically a prophet, i.e., someone with a privileged knowledge of the Lord's plan for his people. Folks inquired about the divine will through the mediation of a seer (10:22) or priest (22:10). The parenthetical explanation is offered in view of the following story, which preserves the archaic title "seer" in the dialogues (9:11, 18–19).

9:12 high place: A cultic sanctuary in Ramah, perhaps a Canaanite shrine converted into an Israelite house of worship. Local sanctuaries such as this will be outlawed once Solomon builds the Jerusalem Temple and the law of the central sanctuary (Deut 12:1–14) goes into effect (2 Kings 18:4; 23:8).

📖 **9:16 you shall anoint him:** Fulfilled in 10:1. **prince:** The Hebrew term *nagid* means "leader, chief, sovereign". It is later used to describe Solomon as the crown prince destined to succeed David as king (1 Kings 1:35; rendered "ruler" in the RSV). Here, too, it means one designated to assume the reins of royal government (i.e., "king-elect"). **save my people:** National defense is set as the top priority for Saul's reign. **I have seen the affliction ... their cry:** Yahweh spoke similar words to Moses when he revealed his plan to rescue Israel from the hand of the Egyptians (Ex 3:7-8), only now he foretells deliverance for his people from **the hand of the Philistines.**

---

[p] Gk Vg: Heb *he.*

[q] Heb lacks *the affliction of.*

*9:13, *high place*: It was customary in early Israel to worship God on raised platforms or hilltops, as the Canaanites did their gods. Later such practices were forbidden as leading to idolatry, and worship was allowed only in Jerusalem; cf. Deut 12:2ff.

shall rule over my people." [18]Then Saul approached Samuel in the gate, and said, "Tell me where is the house of the seer?" [19]Samuel answered Saul, "I am the seer; go up before me to the high place, for today you shall eat with me, and in the morning I will let you go and will tell you all that is on your mind. [20]As for your donkeys that were lost three days ago, do not set your mind on them, for they have been found. And for whom is all that is desirable in Israel? Is it not for you and for all your father's house?" [21]Saul answered, "Am I not a Benjaminite, from the least of the tribes of Israel? And is not my family the humblest of all the families of the tribe of Benjamin? Why then have you spoken to me in this way?"

22 Then Samuel took Saul and his servant and brought them into the hall and gave them a place at the head of those who had been invited, who were about thirty persons. [23]And Samuel said to the cook, "Bring the portion I gave you, of which I said to you, 'Put it aside.'" [24]So the cook took up the leg and the upper portion [r] and set them before Saul; and Samuel said, "See, what was kept is set before you. Eat; because it was kept for you until the hour appointed, that you might eat with the guests." [s]

So Saul ate with Samuel that day. [25]And when they came down from the high place into the city, a bed was spread for Saul [t] upon the roof, and he lay down to sleep. [26]Then at the break of dawn [u] Samuel called to Saul upon the roof, "Up, that I may send you on your way." So Saul arose, and both he and Samuel went out into the street.

God is the leader - in control of everything

Samuel Anoints Saul

27 As they were going down to the outskirts of the city, Samuel said to Saul, "Tell the servant to pass on before us, and when he has passed on stop here yourself for a while, that I may make known to you the word of God."

10 Then Samuel took a vial of oil and poured it on his head, and kissed him and said, "Has not the LORD anointed you to be prince over his people Israel? And you shall reign over the people of the LORD and you will save them from the hand of their enemies round about. And this shall be the sign to you that the LORD has anointed you to be prince [w] over his heritage. [2]When you depart from me today you will meet two men by Rachel's tomb in the territory of Benjamin at Zelzah, and they will say to you, 'The donkeys which you went to seek are found, and now your father has ceased to care about the donkeys and is anxious about you, saying, "What shall I do about my son?"' [3]Then you shall go on from there further and come to the oak of Ta'bor; three men going up to God at Bethel will meet you there, one carrying three kids, another carrying three loaves of bread, and another carrying a skin of wine. [4]And they will greet you and give you two loaves of bread, which you shall accept from their hand. [5]After that you shall come to Gib'eath-elo'him, [x] where there is a garrison of the Philis'tines; and there, as you come to the city, you will meet a band of prophets [*] coming down from the high place with harp, tambourine, flute, and lyre before them, prophesying. [6]Then the spirit of the

---

9:20 for whom ...?: The question is slightly obscure. One possibility in view of the context is the meaning: "Why fuss over donkeys when you have been chosen as king and everything in Israel is at your disposal?" So understood, **all that is desirable** is a reference to the royal privileges enumerated in 8:11–17. Another possibility is that Saul himself is meant, insofar as Israel's desires for a king have all converged on him.

9:21 the least of the tribes: Benjamin was the youngest of Jacob's twelve sons (Gen 35:16–18; 43:29). **the humblest of all the families:** Saul belongs to the clan of Matrites (10:21).

9:24 the leg: Perhaps the portion of meat from a peace offering that was usually reserved for the officiating priest (Lev 7:32).

10:1–27 Chapter 10 recounts the *private* anointing of Saul by Samuel (10:1–8) as well as his *public* acceptance as king before an assembly of Israelites (10:17–27). Reassurance that Yahweh has chosen Saul for kingship (10:24) is given to Saul himself by three providential encounters (10:2–6) and is given to the people by a threefold casting of lots (10:20–21).

10:1 vial of oil: An earthen flask of olive oil. In the rite of anointing, used for priests (Lev 8:12), prophets (1 Kings 19:16), and kings (1 Kings 1:39), the flask is emptied onto the head of the recipient so that the oil runs over him (Ps 133:2). Anointing is a sign of the Spirit and his grace pouring down upon the officeholder (16:13; Is 61:1) (CCC 695).

10:2 Rachel's tomb: Burial place of the patriarch Jacob's favored wife (Gen 29:18). Here it is located north of Jerusalem near the Benjaminite town of Ramah (Jer 31:15). The Book of Genesis preserves another tradition, which locates the tomb south of Jerusalem near the Judahite town of Bethlehem (Gen 35:19–20). **Zelzah:** Meaning obscure.

10:3 oak of Tabor: A landmark of unknown location. **going up to God at Bethel:** Indicates there was a place of worship in the highland town of Bethel. See note on Judg 1:23.

10:5 Gibeath-elohim: Translates "hill of God" and probably refers to a cultic site in or near Saul's hometown of Gibeah. See note on 10:26. **garrison:** An outpost of Philistine soldiers in Benjaminite territory (13:3; 14:1). **a band of prophets:** Prophets in Israel could minister as individuals or unite to form prophetic guilds comprised of a teacher ("father", 2 Kings 2:12) and a ring of disciples ("sons", 2 Kings 2:5). The prophet Samuel is the head of such a company (19:20). Seized by the Spirit of God, these figures deliver inspired utterances, perform on musical instruments, and sometimes engage in bizarre forms of behavior that could be mistaken for madness (19:24; 2 Kings 9:11).

10:6 the spirit of the LORD: Brings the grace and power of God to leaders and deliverers in Israel (16:13; Judg 14:6; 15:14). See note on Judg 3:10. **another man:** Suggests the onset of an altered state of consciousness. Scholars often imagine Saul thrown into an ecstatic state.

---

[r] Heb obscure.

[s] Cn: Heb *saying, I have invited the people.*

[t] Gk: Heb *and he spoke with Saul.*

[u] Gk: Heb *and they arose early and at break of dawn.*

[w] Gk: Heb lacks *over his people Israel? And you shall ... to be prince.*

[x] Or *the hill of God.*

[*] 10:5, *prophets:* An inferior kind of prophet who flourished for a time in Israel. They were quite different from the writing prophets, in that they cultivated states of ecstasy and even used musical instruments for the purpose.

LORD will come mightily upon you, and you shall prophesy with them and be turned into another man. ⁷Now when these signs meet you, do whatever your hand finds to do, for God is with you. ⁸And you shall go down before me to Gilgal; and behold, I am coming to you to offer burnt offerings and to sacrifice peace offerings. Seven days you shall wait, until I come to you and show you what you shall do."

Saul Prophesies

9 When he turned his back to leave Samuel, God gave him another heart; and all these signs came to pass that day. ¹⁰When they came to Gib′e-ah,ᶻ behold, a band of prophets met him; and the spirit of God came mightily upon him, and he prophesied among them. ¹¹And when all who knew him before saw how he prophesied with the prophets, the people said to one another, "What has come over the son of Kish? Is Saul also among the prophets?" ¹²And a man of the place answered, "And who is their father?" Therefore it became a proverb, "Is Saul also among the prophets?" ¹³When he had finished prophesying, he came to the high place.

14 Saul's uncle said to him and to his servant, "Where did you go?" And he said, "To seek the donkeys; and when we saw they were not to be found, we went to Samuel." ¹⁵And Saul's uncle said, "Please, tell me what Samuel said to you." ¹⁶And Saul said to his uncle, "He told us plainly that the donkeys had been found." But about the matter of the kingdom, of which Samuel had spoken, he did not tell him anything.

Saul Proclaimed King

17 Now Samuel called the people together to the LORD at Mizpah; ¹⁸and he said to the sons of Israel, "Thus says the LORD, the God of Israel, 'I brought up Israel out of Egypt, and I delivered you from the hand of the Egyptians and from the hand of all the kingdoms that were oppressing you.' ¹⁹But you have this day rejected your God, who saves you from all your calamities and your distresses; and you have said, 'No! but set a king over us.' Now therefore present yourselves before the LORD by your tribes and by your thousands."

20 Then Samuel brought all the tribes of Israel near, and the tribe of Benjamin was taken by lot. ²¹He brought the tribe of Benjamin near by its families, and the family of the Ma′trites was taken by lot; finally he brought the family of the Matrites near man by man,ᵃ and Saul the son of Kish was taken by lot. But when they sought him, he could not be found. ²²So they inquired again of the LORD, "Did the man come here?"ᵇ and the LORD said, "Behold, he has hidden himself among the baggage." ²³Then they ran and fetched him from there; and when he stood among the people, he was taller than any of the people from his shoulders upward. ²⁴And Samuel said to all the people, "Do you see him whom the LORD has chosen? There is none like him among all the people." And all the people shouted, "Long live the king!"

25 Then Samuel told the people the rights and duties of the kingship; and he wrote them in a book and laid it up before the LORD. Then Samuel sent all the people away, each one to his home. ²⁶Saul also went to his home at Gib′e-ah, and with him went men of valor whose hearts God had touched. ²⁷But some worthless fellows said, "How can this man save us?" And they despised him, and brought him no present. But he held his peace.

Saul Defeats the Ammonites

11 Then Na′hash the Am′monite went up and besieged Ja′besh-gil′ead; and all the men of Ja′besh said to Nahash, "Make a treaty with us, and

---

10:11–12: 19:23, 24.

10:7 whatever your hand finds: May insinuate that Saul, now strengthened by the Spirit, is invited to lead an attack on the Philistine garrison of 10:5, just as his son Jonathan will do in 13:3 and 14:1–23. **God is with you:** So long as Saul remains faithful to the Lord and his calling. Unfortunately, the time will come when the Spirit withdraws from Saul because of his stubborn disobedience (16:14; 18:12).
  10:8 Gilgal: Directly northeast of Jericho in the western Jordan valley. **Seven days:** A test of obedience that will prove to be Saul's undoing (see 13:8–15).
  10:14 Saul's uncle: Probably his uncle Ner (14:50–51).
  10:17 Mizpah: Seven miles north of Jerusalem in the tribal territory of Benjamin (7:5).
  10:20–21 For another instance of singling out an individual by lot, see Josh 7:16–18.
  10:22 hidden himself: Saul appears reluctant to accept the crown. His silence regarding the kingdom in 10:16 points in the same direction.

10:25 duties of the kingship: Samuel, like Moses, provides the kings of Israel with a written set of guidelines for the governance of Yahweh's people (see Deut 17:14–20). Note that Samuel's scroll, like the Book of Deuteronomy, is kept in sacred storage **before the LORD,** i.e., beside or near the Ark of the Covenant (see Deut 31:24–26).
  10:26 Gibe-ah: Translates "hill" and refers to a town of Benjamin (13:2) less than five miles northwest of Jerusalem (modern Jaba'). Besides being the hometown of Saul, it also serves as a functional capital from which he rules over Israel. It thus becomes known as "Gibeah of Saul" (11:4; 15:34; Is 10:29).
  10:27 no present: No tribute or goodwill offering in recognition of Saul's rule (2 Sam 8:2).
  11:1 Nahash: A king according to 12:12. His name means "serpent". **Ammonite:** Ammon was an eastern neighbor of Israel whose ancestry is traced back to Abraham's nephew Lot (Gen 19:30–38). This is not the first time the Ammonites have taken hostile action against Israelites living east of the Jordan (Judg 3:13; 11:4). **Jabesh-gilead:** Eight miles east of the upper Jordan, in the region of Gilead. Saul may have had family connections with the town, since the Benjaminites intermarried with the women of Jabesh according to Judg 21:8–15. His rush to defend the city would thus be readily explained. **treaty:**

ᶻ Or *the hill.*
ᵃ Gk: Heb lacks *finally ... man by man.*
ᵇ Gk: Heb *Is there yet a man to come here?*

we will serve you." ²But Na'hash the Am'monite said to them, "On this condition I will make a treaty with you, that I gouge out all your right eyes, and thus put disgrace upon all Israel." ³The elders of Ja'besh said to him, "Give us seven days respite that we may send messengers through all the territory of Israel. Then, if there is no one to save us, we will give ourselves up to you." ⁴When the messengers came to Gib'e-ah of Saul, they reported the matter in the hearing of the people; and all the people wept aloud.

5 Now Saul was coming from the field behind the oxen; and Saul said, "What ails the people, that they are weeping?" So they told him the tidings of the men of Ja'besh. ⁶And the spirit of God came mightily upon Saul when he heard these words, and his anger was greatly kindled. ⁷He took a yoke of oxen, and cut them in pieces and sent them throughout all the territory of Israel by the hand of messengers, saying, "Whoever does not come out after Saul and Samuel, so shall it be done to his oxen!" Then the dread of the Lᴏʀᴅ fell upon the people, and they came out as one man. ⁸When he mustered them at Be'zek, the men of Israel were three hundred thousand, and the men of Judah thirty thousand.* ⁹And they said to the messengers who had come, "Thus shall you say to the men of Ja'besh-gil'ead: 'Tomorrow, by the time the sun is hot, you shall have deliverance.'" When the messengers came and told the men of Ja'besh, they were glad. ¹⁰Therefore the men of Ja'besh said, "Tomorrow we will give ourselves up to you, and you may do to us whatever seems good to you." ¹¹And the next day Saul put the people in three companies; and they came into the midst of the camp in the morning watch, and cut down the Am'monites until the heat of the day; and those who survived were scattered, so that no two of them were left together.

12 Then the people said to Samuel, "Who is it that said, 'Shall Saul reign over us?' Bring the men, that we may put them to death." ¹³But Saul said, "Not a man shall be put to death this day, for today the Lᴏʀᴅ has wrought deliverance in Israel." ¹⁴Then Samuel said to the people, "Come, let us go to Gilgal and there renew the kingdom." ¹⁵So all the people went to Gilgal, and there they made Saul king before the Lᴏʀᴅ in Gilgal. There they sacrificed peace offerings before the Lᴏʀᴅ, and there Saul and all the men of Israel rejoiced greatly.

Samuel's Farewell Address

12 And Samuel said to all Israel, "Behold, I have listened to your voice in all that you have said to me, and have made a king over you. ²And now, behold, the king walks before you; and I am old and gray, and behold, my sons are with you; and I have walked before you from my youth until this day. ³Here I am; testify against me before the Lᴏʀᴅ and before his anointed. Whose ox have I taken? Or whose donkey have I taken? Or whom have I defrauded? Whom have I oppressed? Or from whose hand have I taken a bribe to blind my eyes with it? Testify against me ᶜ and I will restore it to you." ⁴They said, "You have not defrauded us or oppressed us or taken anything from any man's hand." ⁵And he said to them, "The Lᴏʀᴅ is witness against you, and his anointed is witness this day, that you have not found anything in my hand." And they said, "He is witness."

6 And Samuel said to the people, "The Lᴏʀᴅ is witness, ᵈ who appointed Moses and Aaron and brought your fathers up out of the land of Egypt. ⁷Now therefore stand still, that I may plead with

---

Preferring servitude to slaughter, the townsmen propose a covenant to make Jabesh-gilead a vassal city under the rule of Ammonite overlords.

11:2 gouge out ... eyes: Bodily impairment was a humiliation, but also a way of crippling a vassal's ability to rise up in rebellion.

11:4 Gibe-ah of Saul: See note on 10:26.

11:6 the spirit of God: Anoints Saul with the courage and determination to rescue Jabesh from the Ammonite threat. See note on 10:6. **came mightily upon:** Recalls the exploits of Samson, who was kindled by the Spirit to vent his righteous anger on the enemies of Israel (Judg 14:19; 15:14–15).

11:7 cut them in pieces: A mustering of fighters for war and a conditional curse invoked upon those who fail to heed the summons (cf. Judg 19:29).

11:8 Bezek: Located at modern Khirbet Ibziq, about ten miles east of the Jordan, opposite Jabesh-gilead. **Israel ... Judah:** Here, collective names for the northern and southern tribes of Israel, respectively.

11:11 three companies: A traditional military tactic in early Israel (Judg 7:16; 9:43; 2 Sam 18:2). **morning watch:** The final hours of darkness before 6 A.M.

11:12 Bring the men: Presumably the "worthless fellows" of 10:27 are meant.

11:14 Gilgal: Directly northeast of Jericho in the western Jordan valley. **there renew the kingdom:** Probably means accepting "the rights and duties of the kingship" drawn up by Samuel (10:25) and renewing the Deuteronomic covenant mediated through Moses, which incorporates the royal office into the structure of Israel's relationship with Yahweh (Deut 17:14–20).

11:15 they made Saul king: The public acceptance of Saul's kingship in 10:24 is formally ratified after his successful demonstration of national leadership against the Ammonites in 11:11. Military prowess is precisely what the Israelites want in a king (see 8:19–20). In the Greek LXX, Samuel performs the rite of coronation rather than the assembly (the text reads: "and there Samuel anointed Saul to be king"). At this point, the period of the judges is officially over.

12:1–25 Samuel's farewell speech. He vigorously affirms his innocence in dealing with the people (12:1–5), while accusing Israel of wrongdoing against the Lord (12:17). His career as a judge is ending now that the kingship of Saul is established. Nevertheless, it is not strictly a retirement speech, since Samuel will continue to instruct and intercede for the people as a prophet (12:23–25).

12:2 my sons: Joel and Abijah (8:2).

12:3 his anointed: Saul, anointed king in 10:1. See note on 2:10.

ᶜ Gk: Heb lacks *Testify against me.*
ᵈ Gk: Heb lacks *is witness.*
*11:8: These figures are probably a later insertion.

you before the Lord concerning all the saving deeds of the Lord which he performed for you and for your fathers. [8]When Jacob went into Egypt and the Egyptians oppressed them,[e] then your fathers cried to the Lord and the Lord sent Moses and Aaron, who brought forth your fathers out of Egypt, and made them dwell in this place. [9]But they forgot the Lord their God; and he sold them into the hand of Sis′era, commander of the army of Ja′bin king of[f] Ha′zor, and into the hand of the Philis′tines, and into the hand of the king of Moab; and they fought against them. [10]And they cried to the Lord, and said, 'We have sinned, because we have forsaken the Lord, and have served the Ba′als and the Ash′taroth; but now deliver us out of the hand of our enemies, and we will serve you.' [11]And the Lord sent Jerubba′al* and Barak,[g] and Jephthah, and Samuel, and delivered you out of the hand of your enemies on every side; and you dwelt in safety. [12]And when you saw that Na′hash the king of the Am′monites came against you, you said to me, 'No, but a king shall reign over us,' when the Lord your God was your king. [13]And now behold the king whom you have chosen, for whom you have asked; behold, the Lord has set a king over you. [14]If you will fear the Lord and serve him and listen to his voice and not rebel against the commandment of the Lord, and if both you and the king who reigns over you will follow the Lord your God, it will be well; [15]but if you will not listen to the voice of the Lord, but rebel against the commandment of the Lord, then the hand of the Lord will be against you and your king.[h] [16]Now therefore stand still and see this great thing, which the Lord will do before your eyes. [17]Is it not wheat harvest today? I will call upon the Lord, that he may send thunder and rain; and you shall know and see that your wickedness is great, which you have done in the sight of the Lord, in asking for yourselves a king." [18]So Samuel called upon the Lord, and the Lord sent thunder and rain that day; and all the people greatly feared the Lord and Samuel.

19 And all the people said to Samuel, "Pray for your servants to the Lord your God, that we may not die; for we have added to all our sins this evil, to ask for ourselves a king." [20]And Samuel said to the people, "Fear not; you have done all this evil, yet do not turn aside from following the Lord, but serve the Lord with all your heart; [21]and do not turn aside after[i] vain things which cannot profit or save, for they are vain. [22]For the Lord will not cast away his people, for his great name's sake, because it has pleased the Lord to make you a people for himself. [23]Moreover as for me, far be it from me that I should sin against the Lord by ceasing to pray for you; and I will instruct you in the good and the right way. [24]Only fear the Lord, and serve him faithfully with all your heart; for consider what great things he has done for you. [25]But if you still do wickedly, you shall be swept away, both you and your king."†

Saul's Unlawful Sacrifice

13 Saul was...[j] years old when he began to reign; and he reigned...and two[k]‡ years over Israel.

12:8 Egypt ... this place: Summarizes the biblical story from Gen 46, where Jacob moves his family to Egypt, to Josh 3–4, where Israel crosses the Jordan into the Promised Land.

12:9 Sisera: Commander of Canaanite forces who was killed in secret by the woman Jael (Judg 4:1–24). **Philistines:** A menace to Israel since the time of the judges (Judg 3:31; 10:7; 13:1). **king of Moab:** Eglon, assassinated by the judge Ehud (Judg 3:12–30).

12:10 Baals ... Ashtaroth: Idols worshiped by the Canaanites. See notes on Judg 2:11 and 2:13.

12:11 Jerubbaal: The judge Gideon (Judg 6–8). **Barak:** Commander of Israel's forces at the Battle of Megiddo (Judg 4:4–16). **Jephthah:** Recruited to lead Israel to victory over the Ammonites (Judg 11:1–33). **Samuel:** Samuel ranks himself among the judges, and rightly so, for he preaches repentance (7:3–4), administers justice (7:15–17), and prays Israel to victory over the Philistines (7:7–14).

12:12 No, but a king: The vote for a human king is really a vote of "no confidence" in the Lord, and this despite centuries of Yahweh saving and protecting his people from enemies and oppressors (summarized in 12:7–11). See note on 8:1–22.

12:13 asked: A wordplay on the name Saul. See note on 8:10.

12:14 fear the Lord: Required by the Deuteronomic covenant (Deut 6:24; 10:12; 31:12). **it will be well:** Hope is kept alive for Israel's future despite its failings in the past. The choice between blessings and curses is a choice between loyalty and disloyalty to Yahweh and the stipulations of his covenant (Deut 11:26–28; 30:15–20).

12:17 wheat harvest: In late spring, during the dry season in Israel. It is a miracle that a thunderstorm should roll through at this time. For Samuel as a powerful intercessor, see note on 7:3–4.

12:20 with all your heart: See note on 7:3.

12:21 vain things: Idols (Is 44:9–10).

12:22 a people for himself: Reaffirms the Lord's lasting commitment to Israel, his beloved people (Ps 94:14; Rom 11:1).

13:1 Saul was ... years: Two words seem to have been lost from the Hebrew text, one that specified Saul's *age* at his coronation and another that indicated the *length* of his reign. The Greek LXX offers little help in filling in the blanks: some manuscripts state that Saul was 30 years old when he began his reign, without reference to the length of his kingship, and one major manuscript tradition omits 13:1 entirely. The historian Josephus contends that Saul ruled over Israel for 20 years (*Antiquities of the Jews* 10, 143). Paul, perhaps relying on an uncorrupted text, specifies the length of his reign as 40 years (Acts 13:21). On the apostle's reckoning, Saul would have been king from ca. 1050 to 1010 B.C.

---

[e] Gk: Heb lacks *and the Egyptians oppressed them.*
[f] Gk: Heb lacks *Jabin king of.*
[g] Gk Syr: Heb *Bedan.*
[h] Gk: Heb *fathers.*
[i] Gk Syr Tg Vg: Heb *because after.*
[j] The number is lacking in Heb.
[k] *Two* is not the entire number. Something has dropped out.
*12:11, *Jerubbaal:* i.e., Gideon.
†12:20–25: Samuel here summarizes the antimonarchist attitude; cf. Josh 24.
‡13:1: Acts 13:21 says Saul reigned forty years; but so did David (2 Sam 5:5). These must be round numbers, to indicate a fairly long rule.

2 Saul chose three thousand men of Israel; two thousand were with Saul in Mich'mash and the hill country of Bethel, and a thousand were with Jonathan in Gib'e-ah of Benjamin; the rest of the people he sent home, every man to his tent. ³Jonathan defeated the garrison of the Philis'tines which was at Ge'ba; and the Philistines heard of it. And Saul blew the trumpet throughout all the land, saying, "Let the Hebrews hear." ⁴And all Israel heard it said that Saul had defeated the garrison of the Philis'tines, and also that Israel had become odious to the Philistines. And the people were called out to join Saul at Gilgal.

5 And the Philis'tines mustered to fight with Israel, thirty thousand chariots, and six thousand horsemen, and troops like the sand on the seashore in multitude; they came up and encamped in Mich'-mash, to the east of Beth-a'ven. ⁶When the men of Israel saw that they were in straits (for the people were hard pressed), the people hid themselves in caves and in holes and in rocks and in tombs and in cisterns, ⁷or crossed the fords of the Jordan¹ to the land of Gad and Gilead. Saul was still at Gilgal, and all the people followed him trembling.

8 He waited seven days, the time appointed by Samuel; but Samuel did not come to Gilgal, and the people were scattering from him. ⁹So Saul said, "Bring the burnt offering here to me, and the peace offerings." And he offered the burnt offering. ¹⁰As soon as he had finished offering the burnt offering, behold, Samuel came; and Saul went out to meet him and salute him. ¹¹Samuel said, "What have you done?" And Saul said, "When I saw that the people were scattering from me, and that you did not come within the days appointed, and that the Philis'tines had mustered at Mich'mash, ¹²I said, 'Now the Philis'tines will come down upon me at Gilgal and I have not entreated the favor of the Lord'; so I forced myself, and offered the burnt offering." ¹³And Samuel said to Saul, "You have done foolishly; you have not kept the commandment of the Lord your God, which he commanded you; for now the Lord would have established your kingdom over Israel for ever. ¹⁴But now your kingdom shall not continue; the Lord has sought out a man after his own heart; and the Lord has appointed him to be prince over his people, because you have not kept what the Lord commanded you." ¹⁵And Samuel arose, and went up from Gilgal to Gib'e-ah of Benjamin.

And Saul numbered the people who were present with him, about six hundred men. ¹⁶And Saul, and Jonathan his son, and the people who were present with them, stayed in Ge'ba of Benjamin; but the Philis'tines encamped in Mich'mash. ¹⁷And raiders came out of the camp of the Philis'tines in three companies; one company turned toward Oph'rah, to the land of Shual, ¹⁸another company turned toward Beth-ho'ron, and another company turned toward the border that looks down upon the valley of Zebo'im toward the wilderness.

Preparations for Battle

19 Now there was no smith to be found throughout all the land of Israel; for the Philis'tines said, "Lest the Hebrews make themselves swords or spears"; ²⁰but every one of the Israelites went down to the Philis'tines to sharpen his plowshare, his mattock,

---

13:14: Acts 13:22.

13:2 Saul chose: A selection of 3000 fighting men from the army of 330,000 mustered for his campaign against the Ammonites (11:8). **Michmash:** Over four miles northeast of Saul's home at Gibeah. Both towns are within the territory of Benjamin. **Jonathan:** Saul's oldest son (14:49). **Gibe-ah:** See note on 10:26.

13:3 garrison: An outpost of Philistine soldiers in Israelite territory. **Geba:** Close to Gibeah (Judg 20:33–34). **trumpet:** Blown to assemble Israel for war. See word study: *Trumpet* at Judg 6:34.

13:4 Gilgal: Directly northeast of Jericho in the western Jordan valley. Samuel has promised to rendezvous with Saul at this location seven days after his anointing (10:8).

13:5 thirty thousand: Possibly a textual corruption. The number 3000 appears in certain LXX and Syriac manuscripts. Solomon, at the height of his glory, had only 1400 chariots at his command (1 Kings 10:26). **Beth-aven:** Exact location uncertain, but west of Michmash in the territory of Benjamin (Josh 18:12).

13:8–15 Saul panics and forfeits the privilege of founding a Saulide dynasty of kings.

13:9 he offered: A double act of disobedience. Saul refuses to wait for Samuel as instructed in 10:8; and, as a layman, he is forbidden to officiate at a liturgy of sacrifice. According to the Torah, the king of Israel must submit himself to the word of the Lord (Deut 17:18–20), and only the Levitical priests are authorized to sacrifice to the Lord (Num 18:1–7). That Samuel was a minister from the tribe of Levi, see note on 2:11.

13:14 your kingdom shall not continue: Saul is denied a dynasty. The Lord offered to make his family a royal family "for ever" (13:13), but Saul's disobedience ensures that he will be the first and last king of his line. Notice that, for the time being, Saul is allowed to retain his kingship; later, when he defies the Lord a second time, he will be stripped of his own right to rule (15:23, 28). **man after his own heart:** An advance reference to David (16:6–13). The significance of this statement is that God—not Saul—will choose the next king of Israel. • *Allegorically*, the change from Saul to David foreshadows the change in covenants from the Old to the New and the transformation of priesthood and kingship in the eternal priest-king, Jesus Christ (St. Augustine, *City of God* 17, 4).

13:17 raiders: Philistine marauders sent out to terrorize central Israel and prevent troop reinforcements from the northern tribes reaching Saul's camp at Geba. They fan out in three groups, one going north, another west, and another east.

13:19–23 Saul's army is disadvantaged by a lack of metal weaponry. The Philistines held a monopoly on the secrets of ironworking in the late second millennium b.c.; as a result, their armaments were far superior to those of their Israelite neighbors.

---

¹ Cn: Heb *Hebrews crossed the Jordan.*

his axe, or his sickle;[m] [21]and the charge was a pim for the plowshares and for the mattocks, and a third of a shekel for sharpening the axes and for setting the goads.[n] [22]So on the day of the battle there was neither sword nor spear found in the hand of any of the people with Saul and Jonathan; but Saul and Jonathan his son had them. [23]And the garrison of the Philis'tines went out to the pass of Mich'mash.

Jonathan Surprises the Philistines

14 One day Jonathan the son of Saul said to the young man who bore his armor, "Come, let us go over to the Philis'tine garrison on yonder side." But he did not tell his father. [2]Saul was staying in the outskirts of Gib'e-ah under the pomegranate tree which is at Migron; the people who were with him were about six hundred men, [3]and Ahi'jah

---

13:21 a pim: Two-thirds of a shekel (= about 8 grams of silver). The prices set for servicing Israelite farm equipment are quite exorbitant, meaning the Philistines are taking full advantage of their specialized knowledge of metallurgy.

14:2 Migron: Possibly a threshing floor (cf. 1 Kings 22: 10).

---

[m] Gk: Heb *plowshare.*
[n] The Heb of this verse is obscure.

14:3 Ahijah: Great-grandson of Eli, formerly the senior Levitical priest at Shiloh (1:9). Saul takes him into his service as a royal chaplain and advisor (14:18–19). Ahijah's brother, Ahimelech, ministers as priest at the Tabernacle, stationed in Nob (21:1). **Ichabod:** Born on the day that his parents, his uncle, and his grandfather died (4:11, 18, 20–21). **ephod:** A linen vestment worn by priests (22:18). Ahijah dons the special ephod of the high priest, which was worn beneath a breastpiece containing the sacred lots of discernment, Urim and Thummim (see 14:41).

Old Testament Chronology

The dates below are based on the internal chronology of the Bible. Scholars often prefer a different time line, which shortens the chronology of early Israel before the founding of the monarchy. Based mainly on interpretations of the archaeological record, this reconstructed time line affects the date of the Exodus from Egypt and the Conquest of Canaan, which are moved into the 1200s B.C. (instead of the 1400s, as in 1 Kings 6:1), as well as the length of Israel's sojourn in Egypt, which is shortened to four or five generations (instead of 430 years, as in Ex 12:40). Minor differences of opinion also exist for dates in the period of the Israelite monarchy, but these have little bearing on the overall chronology of the OT.

Event	Date	Verses
Early History to the Exodus from Egypt		
Primeval History	Undateable	Gen 1–11
Call of Abraham	2090 B.C.	Gen 12:1–3
Jacob Moves to Egypt	1876 B.C.	Gen 46:8–27 (Ex 12:40)
Exodus from Egypt	1446 B.C.	Ex 12–13 (1 Kings 6:1)
Conquest and Settlement of Canaan		
40 Years of Wilderness Wandering	1446–1406 B.C.	Num 14:34–35; Deut 2:7
Conquest of Canaan Begins	1406 B.C.	Josh 1–11
Period of the Judges	1350–1050 B.C.	Judg 1—1 Sam 9 (Judg 11:26)
The United Monarchy		
Reign of King Saul	1050–1010 B.C.	Acts 13:21
Reign of King David	1010–970 B.C.	2 Sam 5:3–5
Reign of King Solomon	970–930 B.C.	1 Kings 11:42
Construction begins on Jerusalem Temple	966 B.C.	1 Kings 6:1
The Divided Monarchy		
Israel Divides into Two Kingdoms	930 B.C.	1 Kings 12
Assyrian Exile of Northern Tribes	722 B.C.	2 Kings 17
Babylonian Exile of Southern Tribes	586 B.C.	2 Kings 24–25
Period of Restoration		
End of the Babylonian Exile	538 B.C.	Ezra 1
Returnees Rebuild Jerusalem Temple	520–515 B.C.	Ezra 6:14–15
Nehemiah Rebuilds Walls of Jerusalem	445 B.C.	Neh 1–6
Period of Maccabean Rule		
Persecution by Antiochus Epiphanes IV	167–164 B.C.	1 Mac 1:20–64
Judas Maccabeus Cleanses the Temple	164 B.C.	1 Mac 4:36–61
Jonathan Becomes King and High Priest	152 B.C.	1 Mac 10:18–21
Palestine Becomes Roman Territory	63 B.C.	-----

the son of Ahi'tub, Ich'abod's brother, son of Phin'-
ehas, son of Eli, the priest of the LORD in Shiloh,
wearing an ephod. And the people did not know that
Jonathan had gone. [4]In the pass,[o] by which Jonathan
sought to go over to the Philis'tine garrison, there
was a rocky crag on the one side and a rocky crag
on the other side; the name of the one was Bozez,
and the name of the other Se'neh. [5]The one crag rose
on the north in front of Mich'mash, and the other on
the south in front of Ge'ba.
6 And Jonathan said to the young man who bore
his armor, "Come, let us go over to the garrison of
these uncircumcised; it may be that the LORD will
work for us; for nothing can hinder the LORD from
saving by many or by few." [7]And his armor-bearer
said to him, "Do all that your mind inclines to;[p]
behold, I am with you, as is your mind so is mine."[q]
[8]Then said Jonathan, "Behold, we will cross over
to the men, and we will show ourselves to them. [9]If
they say to us, 'Wait until we come to you,' then we
will stand still in our place, and we will not go up to
them. [10]But if they say, 'Come up to us,' then we will
go up; for the LORD has given them into our hand.
And this shall be the sign to us." [11]So both of them
showed themselves to the garrison of the Philis'tines;
and the Philistines said, "Look, Hebrews are coming
out of the holes where they have hid themselves."
[12]And the men of the garrison hailed Jonathan and
his armor-bearer, and said, "Come up to us, and we
will show you a thing." And Jonathan said to his
armor-bearer, "Come up after me; for the LORD has
given them into the hand of Israel." [13]Then Jonathan
climbed up on his hands and feet, and his armor-
bearer after him. And they fell before Jonathan,
and his armor-bearer killed them after him; [14]and
that first slaughter, which Jonathan and his armor-
bearer made, was of about twenty men within as
it were half a furrow's length in an acre[r] of land.
[15]And there was a panic in the camp, in the field,
and among all the people; the garrison and even the
raiders trembled; the earth quaked; and it became a
very great panic.
16 And the watchmen of Saul in Gib'e-ah of
Benjamin looked; and behold, the multitude was
surging here and there.[s] [17]Then Saul said to the
people who were with him, "Number and see who has
gone from us." And when they had numbered, behold,
Jonathan and his armor-bearer were not there. [18]And
Saul said to Ahi'jah, "Bring the ark of God here." For
the ark of God went at that time with the sons of
Israel. [19]And while Saul was talking to the priest, the
tumult in the camp of the Philis'tines increased more
and more; and Saul said to the priest, "Withdraw
your hand." [20]Then Saul and all the people who were
with him rallied and went into the battle; and behold,
every man's sword was against his fellow, and there
was very great confusion. [21]Now the Hebrews who
had been with the Philis'tines before that time and
who had gone up with them into the camp, even they
also turned to be with[t] the Israelites who were with
Saul and Jonathan. [22]Likewise, when all the men of
Israel who had hid themselves in the hill country
of E'phraim heard that the Philis'tines were fleeing,
they too followed hard after them in the battle. [23]So
the LORD delivered Israel that day; and the battle
passed beyond Beth-a'ven.

Saul's Rash Oath

24 And the men of Israel were distressed that
day; for Saul laid an oath on the people, saying,
"Cursed be the man who eats food until it is evening
and I am avenged on my enemies." So none of the
people tasted food. [25]And all the people[u] came into
the forest; and there was honey on the ground.
[26]And when the people entered the forest, behold,

14:4 the pass: A deep ravine between Michmash and Geba (modern Wadi Suweinit).

14:6 these uncircumcised: A derogatory epithet for the Philistines (Judg 14:3). **nothing can hinder the LORD:** The statement brims with confidence and faith, much like David's confession before Goliath (17:45–47). In both cases, heroic trust in God paves the way for a triumph over powerful enemies (14:13–15).

14:11 out of the holes: The hiding places mentioned in 13:6.

14:14 about twenty men: Slain by a mere two men. This confirms Jonathan's faith that the Lord can achieve victory "by few" (14:6).

14:18 the ark: As stated in the Hebrew text. Important manuscripts of the Greek LXX read "ephod" rather than "ark" at this point. This alternative Greek wording may be original, since **(1)** the ephod was just mentioned in 14:3, **(2)** the context suggests Saul is looking for guidance from the Lord rather than for help on the battlefield, and **(3)** the ark is by and large neglected in the days of Saul (1 Chron 13:3).

14:19 Withdraw your hand: The priest is just about to cast the sacred lots, Urim and Thummim, when the king makes him stop. Saul is making a rash decision to charge into battle without first seeking God's will. Contrast this with Jonathan's careful discernment in 14:8–10.

14:21 Hebrews: This verse distinguishes between Hebrews and Israelites, whereas 13:3–4 and 14:11 seem to equate them. One possibility is that these Hebrews are Semites living in Canaan without a firm political commitment either to Philistia or to Israel. Their presence in the land is unexplained, but perhaps they are descended from the "mixed multitude" that came up with Israel out of Egypt (Ex 12:38). According to Scripture, all Israelites are Hebrews (descendants of Eber, Gen 11:16) but most Hebrews are not Israelites (descendants of the Jacob, Ex 1:1–4).

14:22 hill country of Ephraim: Directly north of Benjaminite territory.

14:23 beyond Beth-aven: Exact location uncertain, but evidently west of Michmash in the territory of Benjamin (Josh 18:12).

14:24 laid an oath: A curse is invoked on the soldier who eats before sundown. Jonathan sees this as a foolish move because fasting saps Israel of the energy it needs to rout the enemy more decisively (14:29–30).

[o] Heb *between the passes.*
[p] Gk: Heb *Do all that is in your mind. Turn.*
[q] Gk: Heb lacks *so is mine.*
[r] Heb *yoke.*
[s] Gk: Heb *they went and there.*
[t] Gk Syr Vg Tg: Heb *round about, they also, to be with.*
[u] Heb *land.*

the honey was dropping, but no man put his hand to his mouth; for the people feared the oath. ²⁷But Jonathan had not heard his father charge the people with the oath; so he put forth the tip of the staff that was in his hand, and dipped it in the honeycomb, and put his hand to his mouth; and his eyes became bright. ²⁸Then one of the people said, "Your father strictly charged the people with an oath, saying, 'Cursed be the man who eats food this day.'" And the people were faint. ²⁹Then Jonathan said, "My father has troubled the land; see how my eyes have become bright, because I tasted a little of this honey. ³⁰How much better if the people had eaten freely today of the spoil of their enemies which they found; for now the slaughter among the Philis'tines has not been great."

31 They struck down the Philis'tines that day from Mich'mash to Ai'jalon. And the people were very faint; ³²the people flew upon the spoil, and took sheep and oxen and calves, and slew them on the ground; and the people ate them with the blood. ³³Then they told Saul, "Behold, the people are sinning against the LORD, by eating with the blood." And he said, "You have dealt treacherously; roll a great stone to me here." ᵛ ³⁴And Saul said, "Disperse yourselves among the people, and say to them, 'Let every man bring his ox or his sheep, and slay them here, and eat; and do not sin against the LORD by eating with the blood.'" So every one of the people brought his ox with him that night, and slew them there. ³⁵And Saul built an altar to the LORD; it was the first altar that he built to the LORD.

The People Ransom Jonathan

36 Then Saul said, "Let us go down after the Philis'tines by night and despoil them until the morning light; let us not leave a man of them." And they said, "Do whatever seems good to you." But the priest said, "Let us draw near here to God." ³⁷And Saul inquired of God, "Shall I go down after the Philis'tines? Will you give them into the hand of Israel?" But he did not answer him that day. ³⁸And

Saul said, "Come here, all you leaders of the people; and know and see how this sin has arisen today. ³⁹For as the LORD lives who saves Israel, though it be in Jonathan my son, he shall surely die." But there was not a man among all the people that answered him. ⁴⁰Then he said to all Israel, "You shall be on one side, and I and Jonathan my son will be on the other side." And the people said to Saul, "Do what seems good to you." ⁴¹Therefore Saul said, "O LORD God of Israel, why have you not answered your servant this day? If this guilt is in me or in Jonathan my son, O LORD, God of Israel, give U'rim; but if this guilt is in your people Israel,ʷ give Thummim." And Jonathan and Saul were taken, but the people escaped. ⁴²Then Saul said, "Cast the lot between me and my son Jonathan." And Jonathan was taken.*

43 Then Saul said to Jonathan, "Tell me what you have done." And Jonathan told him, "I tasted a little honey with the tip of the staff that was in my hand; here I am, I will die." ⁴⁴And Saul said, "God do so to me and more also; you shall surely die, Jonathan." ⁴⁵Then the people said to Saul, "Shall Jonathan die, who has wrought this great victory in Israel? Far from it! As the LORD lives, there shall not one hair of his head fall to the ground; for he has wrought with God this day." So the people ransomed Jonathan, that he did not die. ⁴⁶Then Saul went up from pursuing the Philis'tines; and the Philistines went to their own place.

Saul's Continuing Wars

47 When Saul had taken the kingship over Israel, he fought against all his enemies on every side, against Moab, against the Am'monites, against E'dom, against the kings of Zobah, and against the Philis'tines; wherever he turned he put them to the worse. ⁴⁸And he did valiantly, and struck the Amal'ekites, and delivered Israel out of the hands of those who plundered them.

49 Now the sons of Saul were Jonathan, Ishvi, and Mal"chishu'a; and the names of his two daughters were these: the name of the first-born was Merab,

---

14:49: 31:2; 1 Chron 10:2.

14:27 eyes became bright: The honey revives Jonathan's strength after an exhausting day of combat (Ezra 9:8).

14:31 Michmash: Over four miles northeast of Saul's home at Gibeah. **Aijalon:** About 15 miles west of Michmash in the direction of Philistine territory.

14:32 blood: Forbidden for human consumption by the Torah (Lev 17:10; 19:26).

14:33 great stone: Serves as a natural, unhewn altar (Ex 20:25).

14:36 the priest: Ahijah (14:3).

14:39 as the LORD lives: An oath formula.

14:41 Urim ... Thummim: Sacred lots that are cast to determine the Lord's will in specific situations. These items,

whether marked sticks or stones, are kept in the custody of the high priest (Num 27:21; Deut 33:8).

14:44 God do so to me: A conditional self-curse. See note on Ruth 1:17.

14:45 ransomed: Fellow soldiers intervene to save Jonathan's life when his own father condemns him to death. In this case, "ransom" means "rescue from punishment".

14:46 their own place: The Philistines control the coastal region in southwest Canaan.

14:47–48 An inventory of Saul's triumphs as a military leader. He has achieved victories on all sides, in the east (**Moab, Ammonites**), in the south (**Edom, Amalekites**), in the southwest (**Philistines**), and in the far north (**Zobah**). The stage is thus set for David, who eventually makes these nations into vassal states of the kingdom of Israel (2 Sam 8:1–14).

14:49 Ishvi: Also known as "Ish-bosheth" (2 Sam 2:8) or "Eshbaal" (1 Chron 8:33). Saul has a fourth son as well, not listed here, named "Abinadab" (31:2). **Michal:** Later given to David in marriage (18:27).

ᵛ Gk: Heb *this day.*
ʷ Vg Compare Gk: Heb *Saul said to the* LORD, *the God of Israel.*
* 14:38–42: This passage shows how the sacred lots were cast to find out God's will.

and the name of the younger Michal; ⁵⁰and the name of Saul's wife was Ahin'o-am the daughter of Ahim'a-az. And the name of the commander of his army was Abner the son of Ner, Saul's uncle; ⁵¹Kish was the father of Saul, and Ner the father of Abner was the son of Abi'el.

52 There was hard fighting against the Philis'tines all the days of Saul; and when Saul saw any strong man, or any valiant man, he attached him to himself.

Saul Defeats the Amalekites but Disobeys

15 And Samuel said to Saul, "The LORD sent me to anoint you king over his people Israel; now therefore listen to the words of the LORD. ²Thus says the LORD of hosts, 'I will punish what Am'alek did to Israel in opposing them on the way, when they came up out of Egypt. ³Now go and strike Am'alek, and utterly destroy all that they have; do not spare them, but kill both man and woman, infant and suckling, ox and sheep, camel and donkey.'"

4 So Saul summoned the people, and numbered them in Tela'im, two hundred thousand men on foot, and ten thousand men of Judah. ⁵And Saul came to the city of Am'alek, and lay in wait in the valley. ⁶And Saul said to the Kenites, "Go, depart, go down from among the Amal'ekites, lest I destroy you with them; for you showed kindness to all the people of Israel when they came up out of Egypt." So the Kenites departed from among the Amalekites. ⁷And Saul defeated the Amal'ekites, from Hav'ilah as far as Shur, which is east of Egypt. ⁸And he took A'gag the king of the Amal'ekites alive, and utterly destroyed all the people with the edge of the sword. ⁹But Saul and the people spared A'gag, and the best of the sheep and of the oxen and of the fatlings, and the lambs, and all that was good, and would not utterly destroy them; all that was despised and worthless they utterly destroyed.

The Lord Rejects Saul for His Disobedience

10 The word of the LORD came to Samuel: ¹¹"I repent that I have made Saul king; for he has turned back from following me, and has not performed my commandments." And Samuel was angry; and he cried to the LORD all night. ¹²And Samuel rose early to meet Saul in the morning; and it was told Samuel, "Saul came to Carmel, and behold, he set up a monument for himself and turned, and passed on, and went down to Gilgal." ¹³And Samuel came to Saul, and Saul said to him, "Blessed be you to the LORD; I have performed the commandment of the LORD." ¹⁴And Samuel said, "What then is this bleating of the sheep in my ears, and the lowing of the oxen which I hear?" ¹⁵Saul said, "They have brought them from the Amal'ekites; for the people spared the best of the sheep and of the oxen, to sacrifice to the LORD your God; and the rest we have utterly destroyed." ¹⁶Then Samuel said to Saul, "Stop! I will tell you what the LORD said to me this night." And he said to him, "Say on."

17 And Samuel said, "Though you are little in your own eyes, are you not the head of the tribes of Israel? The LORD anointed you king over Israel. ¹⁸And the LORD sent you on a mission, and said, 'Go, utterly destroy the sinners, the Amal'ekites, and fight against them until they are consumed.' ¹⁹Why then did you not obey the voice of the LORD? Why did you swoop on the spoil, and do what was evil in the sight of the LORD?" ²⁰And Saul said to Samuel, "I have obeyed the voice of the LORD, I have gone on the mission on which the LORD sent me, I have brought A'gag the king of Am'alek, and I have utterly destroyed the Amal'ekites. ²¹But the people took of the spoil, sheep and oxen, the best of the things devoted to destruction, to sacrifice to the LORD your God in Gilgal." ²²And Samuel said,

---

15:22: Mk 12:33.

14:52 attached him: I.e., recruited him as a soldier in the royal army.

15:2 Amalek: The Amalekites are a nomadic people of the Sinai Peninsula descended from Esau (Gen 36:12). They became enemies of Israel when they ambushed the exodus pilgrims streaming out of Egypt (Ex 17:8–16). Hostilities continued into later times (Judg 6:3).

15:3 utterly destroy: Means "place under a ban of total destruction". This wartime policy, stipulated in Deuteronomy, requires Israel to destroy enemy peoples in Canaan as an act of dedication to Yahweh (Deut 20:16–18). Strict application of the law means that confiscation of booty is forbidden. See word study: *Devoted* at Josh 6:17.

15:4 Telaim: A city in the territory of Judah also called "Telem" (Josh 15:24). **two hundred thousand:** A flood of new recruits that greatly enlarges Saul's army (compare with 13:2).

15:6 Kenites: Semites who are related to the Midianites and friends of the Israelites. Some settled among the tribe of Judah in southern Palestine (Judg 1:16). **kindness:** Apparently the Kenites acted as guides for Israel journeying through the wilderness (Num 10:29–32).

15:7 Havilah as far as Shur: The location of Havilah is uncertain, but the passage seems to indicate a westward

sweep from Arabia to the top corner of the Sinai Peninsula, bordering northern Egypt.

15:9 spared Agag: A violation of Deuteronomy's ban on taking enemy captives and seizing their possessions as spoils. See note on 15:3.

15:11 I repent: Or "I regret". See note on 15:29. **not performed my commandments:** Use of the plural ("commandments") in the Lord's rebuke stands in contrast to Saul's use of the singular ("commandment") in 15:13. The detail hints that Saul is rejected as king, not for a single trespass against God's word, but for a pattern of disobedience to his decrees.

15:12 Carmel: Seven miles south of Hebron in southern Canaan.

15:15 they ... we: Saul points the finger of blame at his soldiers ("they") while portraying himself as one who obeys the Lord ("we"). He attempts the same in 15:20–21. Samuel, however, is quick to see through the king's evasive ploy. Only after the word of judgment is pronounced (15:22–23) does Saul own up to his wrongdoing (15:24).

15:22 to obey is better: Not that the Lord has no regard for sacrifice, but that obedience is a more perfect form of divine service than animal offerings. Separating the moral life from liturgical life is a contradiction of biblical religion that

"Has the LORD as great delight in burnt offerings
  and sacrifices,
  as in obeying the voice of the LORD?
Behold, to obey is better than sacrifice,
  and to listen than the fat of rams.
²³For rebellion is as the sin of divination,
  and stubbornness is as iniquity and idolatry.
Because you have rejected the word of the LORD,
  he has also rejected you from being king." *

24 And Saul said to Samuel, "I have sinned; for I have transgressed the commandment of the LORD and your words, because I feared the people and obeyed their voice. ²⁵Now therefore, I beg, pardon my sin, and return with me, that I may worship the LORD." ²⁶And Samuel said to Saul, "I will not return with you; for you have rejected the word of the LORD, and the LORD has rejected you from being king over Israel." ²⁷As Samuel turned to go away, Saul laid hold upon the skirt of his robe, and it tore. ²⁸And Samuel said to him, "The LORD has torn the kingdom of Israel from you this day, and has given it to a neighbor of yours, who is better than you. ²⁹And also the Glory of Israel will not lie or repent; for he is not a man, that he should repent." ³⁰Then he said, "I have sinned; yet honor me now before the elders of my people and before Israel, and return with me, that I may worship the LORD your God." ³¹So Samuel turned back after Saul; and Saul worshiped the LORD.

32 Then Samuel said, "Bring here to me A'gag the king of the Amal'ekites." And Agag came to him cheerfully. Agag said, "Surely the bitterness of death is past." ³³And Samuel said, "As your sword has made women childless, so shall your mother be childless among women." And Samuel hewed A'gag in pieces before the LORD in Gilgal.

34 Then Samuel went to Ra'mah; and Saul went up to his house in Gib'e-ah of Saul. ³⁵And Samuel did not see Saul again until the day of his death, but Samuel grieved over Saul. And the LORD repented that he had made Saul king over Israel.

David Anointed as King

16 The LORD said to Samuel, "How long will you grieve over Saul, seeing I have rejected him from being king over Israel? Fill your horn with oil, and go; I will send you to Jesse the Bethlehemite, for I have provided for myself a king among his sons." ²And Samuel said, "How can I go? If Saul hears it, he will kill me." And the LORD said, "Take a heifer with you, and say, 'I have come to sacrifice to the LORD.' ³And invite Jesse to the sacrifice, and I will show you what you shall do; and you shall anoint for me him whom I name to you." ⁴Samuel did what the LORD commanded, and came to Bethlehem. The elders of the city came to meet him trembling, and said, "Do you come peaceably?" ⁵And he said, "Peaceably; I have come to sacrifice to the LORD; consecrate yourselves, and come with me to the sacrifice." And he consecrated Jesse and his sons, and invited them to the sacrifice.

6 When they came, he looked on Eli'ab and thought, "Surely the LORD's anointed is before him."

God finds deeply offensive—so much so that brazen disobedience is on a par with idolatry. In several places, Scripture declares worship an empty and vain gesture without a corresponding submission to the Lord's will (Jud 16:16; Is 1:12–17; Hos 6:6).

15:23 rejected you: Saul is stripped of his kingship. Earlier Saul was denied a dynasty of royal successors; now he is denied the right to continue as king. See note on 13:14.

15:24 I feared: A weakness of character that makes Saul unfit for leadership. Rather than holding his soldiers to the law of God, or steering them back when they depart from it, he succumbs to their wishes to plunder the enemies' choice livestock (15:9).

15:28 torn the kingdom: A similar event occurs in 1 Kings 11:29–32.

15:29 not a man: A clarification offered in view of statements that Yahweh "repents" certain decisions (15:11, 35). Scripture often speaks of God acting in a human way or experiencing human emotions. Nevertheless, other passages, such as this one, insist that God transcends man's propensity to be untruthful, to change his mind, or to retract his words (Num 23:19). Thus, Scripture affirms the impassibility of God (divine immunity to change), even as it sometimes describes God in anthropomorphic terms (as if he possessed human imperfections). Theologians designate the latter a form of "divine accommodation", an instance of God lowering himself, like a parent talking to a child, to communicate with us in ways that correspond to the limitations of our thinking and experience. Samuel's point in this context is that God's word is irrevocable, so it is futile to hope that he will reverse his decision to take the kingship from Saul (15:23). • Holy Scripture uses expressions for God that are quite like our own. It portrays him as getting angry and repenting, and besides this it mentions him sitting and standing and moving, and the like. These things do not actually pertain to God but are not without use as an accommodation for teaching others. To those who grow insolent through prosperity, God's repentance over Saul warns that good fortune is not a certain possession, even if it seems to come from him (St. Gregory of Nyssa, *Answer to the Second Book of Eunomius* 4, 259–60).

15:33 hewed: The utter destruction called for in 15:3.

15:35 repented: See note on 15:29.

16:1—31:13 The latter chapters of 1 Samuel document the rise of David and the decline of Saul. Their stories intersect at many levels, as Saul's affection for David in the beginning (16:21) turns quickly into a murderous hatred for the man destined to replace him as king (18:29; 19:10; 20:33; etc.).

16:1 I have rejected him: The same Hebrew is used to describe how the people "rejected" the Lord from being king over them (8:7). **horn:** A hollow animal horn used as an oil flask (1 Kings 1:39). See note on 10:1. **Jesse:** The father of David and his seven brothers (17:12). He is the grandson of Ruth and Boaz (Ruth 4:21–22) and a member of the tribe of Judah (1 Chron 2:3–12).

16:4 Bethlehem: Five miles south of Jerusalem. • Bethlehem, in addition to being the hometown of David, is also the anticipated birthplace of the Davidic Messiah (Mic 5:2). The evangelist Matthew draws attention to this when he lays out the Davidic ancestry of Jesus (Mt 1:1–16) and locates his nativity in Bethlehem (Mt 2:1–6).

16:5 I have come to sacrifice: True in itself, though not the only reason for the visit. It provides cover so that Samuel can anoint a new king without raising suspicions with Saul.

---

*15:22–23: Samuel does not condemn sacrifices but says obedience is better.

7But the LORD said to Samuel, "Do not look on his appearance or on the height of his stature, because I have rejected him; for the LORD sees not as man sees; man looks on the outward appearance, but the LORD looks on the heart." 8Then Jesse called Abin′adab, and made him pass before Samuel. And he said, "Neither has the LORD chosen this one." 9Then Jesse made Shammah pass by. And he said, "Neither has the LORD chosen this one." 10And Jesse made seven of his sons pass before Samuel. And Samuel said to Jesse, "The LORD has not chosen these." 11And Samuel said to Jesse, "Are all your sons here?" And he said, "There remains yet the youngest, but behold, he is keeping the sheep." And Samuel said to Jesse, "Send and fetch him; for we will not sit down till he comes here." 12And he sent, and brought him in. Now he was ruddy, and had beautiful eyes, and was handsome. And the LORD said, "Arise, anoint him; for this is he." 13Then Samuel took the horn of oil, and anointed him in the midst of his brothers; and the Spirit of the LORD came mightily upon David from that day forward. And Samuel rose up, and went to Ra′mah.

David Plays the Lyre for Saul

14 Now the Spirit of the LORD departed from Saul, and an evil spirit from the LORD tormented him. 15And Saul's servants said to him, "Behold now, an evil spirit from God is tormenting you. 16Let our lord now command your servants, who are before you, to seek out a man who is skilful in playing the lyre; and when the evil spirit from God is upon you, he will play it, and you will be well." 17So Saul said to his servants, "Provide for me a man who can play

well, and bring him to me." 18One of the young men answered, "Behold, I have seen a son of Jesse the Bethlehemite, who is skilful in playing, a man of valor, a man of war, prudent in speech, and a man of good presence; and the LORD is with him." 19Therefore Saul sent messengers to Jesse, and said, "Send me David your son, who is with the sheep." 20And Jesse took a donkey laden with bread, and a skin of wine and a kid, and sent them by David his son to Saul. 21And David came to Saul, and entered his service. And Saul loved him greatly, and he became his armor-bearer. 22And Saul sent to Jesse, saying, "Let David remain in my service, for he has found favor in my sight." 23And whenever the evil spirit from God was upon Saul, David took the lyre and played it with his hand; so Saul was refreshed, and was well, and the evil spirit departed from him.

David and Goliath

17 Now the Philis′tines gathered their armies for battle; and they were gathered at Socoh, which belongs to Judah, and encamped between Socoh and Aze′kah, in E′phes-dam′mim. 2And Saul and the men of Israel were gathered, and encamped in the valley of E′lah, and drew up in line of battle against the Philis′tines. 3And the Philis′tines stood on the mountain on the one side, and Israel stood on the mountain on the other side, with a valley between them. 4And there came out from the camp of the Philis′tines a champion named Goliath, of Gath, whose height was six cubits and a span. 5He had a helmet of bronze on his head, and he was armed with a coat of mail, and the weight of the coat was five thousand shekels of bronze. 6And he had greaves of

---

16:7 height: Not a crucial qualification for leadership. Remember that Saul was a towering figure (9:2), and yet the Lord ousted him from office (15:23). **the outward appearance:** Literally "the eyes". **the heart:** The hidden center of the person where thoughts, actions, and intentions originate. See word study: *Heart* at Deut 30:6.

16:11 youngest: The Lord often bypasses the wiser and stronger of the world, who appear more qualified to accomplish great things, in order to raise up the smaller and weaker for the accomplishment of his purposes (1 Cor 1:25). In part, this is to show that the hand of God is behind their success. See essay: *Blessings and Birthrights* at Gen 48.

16:12 ruddy: David's complexion or hair must have been reddish in color. **handsome:** An added bonus, but not the reason for his divine election. David is chosen because his heart is right with the Lord (13:14; 16:7).

16:13 Spirit of the LORD: The grace and strength of heaven rushes upon David and raises him up as king. The anointing of the Spirit is symbolized by pouring oil upon his head (Is 61:1) (CCC 695). **from that day:** David enjoys an ongoing presence of the Spirit, unlike earlier figures whose possession of the Spirit was intermittent and temporary (e.g., Saul, 10:6; 16:14; and Samson, Judg 14:6, 19; 15:14; 16:20).
• The Spirit descending and abiding with David anticipates the Spirit coming down and remaining on Jesus from the day of his Baptism at the Jordan (Jn 1:32–33).

16:14 evil spirit: A harassing demon (or a disturbed psychological state). David's ability to drive away the spirit and to ease Saul's torments gains him a position as court musician and exorcist. **from the LORD:** Not that Yahweh does evil in the world as well as good, but that he permits even fallen spirits

to work their mischief in view of a greater divine plan. In any case, allowing evil is not the same as approving it or accomplishing it. The expression also underlines the biblical doctrine that God is the Origin of all creatures seen and unseen, in contrast to the polytheism of the Near East, which viewed the gods and spirits of the world as independent beings beholden to the will of no ultimate deity.

16:18 man of war: Sounds overstated at this point, but David's military prowess will be amply attested in his later career (2 Sam 8:1–12; 1 Chron 22:8). **the LORD is with him:** Means that God will anoint David's efforts and bring him success in his many undertakings (18:14).

16:21 entered his service: As a court musician and armor bearer.

16:23 lyre: A stringed instrument with an acoustic sound box.

17:1 Socoh: Roughly 15 miles west of Bethlehem near the border of Philistine territory. **Azekah:** A fortress directly northwest of Socoh.

17:4 Gath: One of the five leading cities of the Philistines (6:17). **six cubits and a span:** Almost ten feet tall. Many scholars think Goliath was actually six and a half feet tall, since the Greek LXX, the Dead Sea scrolls (4QSam), and the historian Josephus (*Antiquities* 6, 171) all list the number as "four" cubits rather than "six" cubits. Either way, Goliath stands at a colossal height, for men of the ancient world were much shorter than most men today.

17:5–7 Goliath is completely covered with body armor, and even a shieldman stands guard in front of him. The only thing exposed is his face (17:49).

17:6 a javelin: Or "a curved sword".

bronze upon his legs, and a javelin of bronze slung between his shoulders. ⁷And the shaft of his spear was like a weaver's beam, and his spear's head weighed six hundred shekels of iron; and his shield-bearer went before him. ⁸He stood and shouted to the ranks of Israel, "Why have you come out to draw up for battle? Am I not a Philis'tine, and are you not servants of Saul? Choose a man for yourselves, and let him come down to me. ⁹If he is able to fight with me and kill me, then we will be your servants; but if I prevail against him and kill him, then you shall be our servants and serve us." ¹⁰And the Philis'tine said, "I defy the ranks of Israel this day; give me a man, that we may fight together." ¹¹When Saul and all Israel heard these words of the Philis'tine, they were dismayed and greatly afraid.

12 Now David was the son of an Eph'rathite of Bethlehem in Judah, named Jesse, who had eight sons. In the days of Saul the man was already old and advanced in years.* ¹³The three eldest sons of Jesse had followed Saul to the battle; and the names of his three sons who went to the battle were Eli'ab the first-born, and next to him Abin'adab, and the third Shammah. ¹⁴David was the youngest; the three eldest followed Saul, ¹⁵but David went back and forth from Saul to feed his father's sheep at Bethlehem. ¹⁶For forty days the Philis'tine came forward and took his stand, morning and evening.

17 And Jesse said to David his son, "Take for your brothers an ephah of this parched grain, and these ten loaves, and carry them quickly to the camp to your brothers; ¹⁸also take these ten cheeses to the commander of their thousand. See how your brothers fare, and bring some token from them."

19 Now Saul, and they, and all the men of Israel, were in the valley of E'lah, fighting with the Philis'tines. ²⁰And David rose early in the morning, and left the sheep with a keeper, and took the provisions, and went, as Jesse had commanded him; and he came to the encampment as the host was going forth to the battle line, shouting the war cry. ²¹And Israel and the Philis'tines drew up for battle, army against army. ²²And David left the

things in charge of the keeper of the baggage, and ran to the ranks, and went and greeted his brothers. ²³As he talked with them, behold, the champion, the Philis'tine of Gath, Goliath by name, came up out of the ranks of the Philistines, and spoke the same words as before. And David heard him.

24 All the men of Israel, when they saw the man, fled from him, and were much afraid. ²⁵And the men of Israel said, "Have you seen this man who has come up? Surely he has come up to defy Israel; and the man who kills him, the king will enrich with great riches, and will give him his daughter, and make his father's house free in Israel." ²⁶And David said to the men who stood by him, "What shall be done for the man who kills this Philis'tine, and takes away the reproach from Israel? For who is this uncircumcised Philistine, that he should defy the armies of the living God?" ²⁷And the people answered him in the same way, "So shall it be done to the man who kills him."

28 Now Eli'ab his eldest brother heard when he spoke to the men; and Eliab's anger was kindled against David, and he said, "Why have you come down? And with whom have you left those few sheep in the wilderness? I know your presumption, and the evil of your heart; for you have come down to see the battle." ²⁹And David said, "What have I done now? Was it not but a word?" ³⁰And he turned away from him toward another, and spoke in the same way; and the people answered him again as before.

31 When the words which David spoke were heard, they repeated them before Saul; and he sent for him. ³²And David said to Saul, "Let no man's heart fail because of him; your servant will go and fight with this Philis'tine." ³³And Saul said to David, "You are not able to go against this Philis'tine to fight with him; for you are but a youth, and he has been a man of war from his youth." ³⁴But David said to Saul, "Your servant used to keep sheep for his father; and when there came a lion, or a bear, and took a lamb from the flock, ³⁵I went after him and struck him and delivered it out of his

---

17:7 six hundred shekels: The spearhead alone weighs more than 15 pounds. Recall that the Philistines possessed iron technology unknown in Israel at this time (13:19–21).

17:11 greatly afraid: Perhaps Saul is implicated by this more than the others; after all, he is the tallest man in Israel and so the most promising contender against the Philistine giant (9:2).

17:12 Ephrathite: Ephrathah is a clan of the tribe of Judah (Ruth 1:2; Mic 5:2).

17:14 the youngest: I.e., the eighth son of Jesse (17:12). See note on 16:11.

17:15 back and forth: Presupposes the background story in 16:6–23.

17:16 forty days: A traditional time of testing. See note on Lk 4:2.

17:25 his daughter: Saul later gives Michal to David in marriage (18:27).

17:28 Eliab's anger: Sparked, it would seem, by resentment that his little brother has the courage that he and his fellow soldiers lack in the face of Goliath (17:24). **evil of your heart:** The very opposite of God's assessment of David, i.e., that his heart is upright (13:14).

17:33 youth: Does not necessarily imply that David is only a boy. It indicates that he is a young man of marriageable age still living with his father (17:58; 18:2, 27).

17:35 delivered it: David is a good shepherd who risks his own life to save his flock from predators. • In this respect, he prefigures Jesus, the Good Shepherd, who lays down his life for his sheep (Jn 10:11–14). • Allegorically, David, who smote the lion and the bear, is a type of Christ, who descended to the dead to rescue the Church from the jaws of death and to free her from the clutches of the devil (St. Caesarius of Arles, *Sermons* 121).

---

*Gk Syr: Heb *among men.*

mouth; and if he arose against me, I caught him by his beard, and struck him and killed him. ³⁶Your servant has killed both lions and bears; and this uncircumcised Philis'tine shall be like one of them, seeing he has defied the armies of the living God." ³⁷And David said, "The Lord who delivered me from the paw of the lion and from the paw of the bear, will deliver me from the hand of this Philis'tine." And Saul said to David, "Go, and the Lord be with you!" ³⁸Then Saul clothed David with his armor; he put a helmet of bronze on his head, and clothed him with a coat of mail. ³⁹And David belted on his sword over his armor, and he tried in vain to go, for he was not used to them. Then David said to Saul, "I cannot go with these; for I am not used to them." And David put them off. ⁴⁰Then he took his staff in his hand, and chose five smooth stones from the brook, and put them in his shepherd's bag or wallet; his sling was in his hand, and he drew near to the Philis'tine.

41 And the Philis'tine came on and drew near to David, with his shield-bearer in front of him. ⁴²And when the Philis'tine looked, and saw David, he disdained him; for he was but a youth, ruddy and comely in appearance. ⁴³And the Philis'tine said to David, "Am I a dog, that you come to me with sticks?" And the Philistine cursed David by his gods. ⁴⁴The Philis'tine said to David, "Come to me, and I will give your flesh to the birds of the air and to the beasts of the field." ⁴⁵Then David said to the Philis'tine, "You come to me with a sword and with a spear and with a javelin; but I come to you in the name of the Lord of hosts, the God of the armies of Israel, whom you have defied. ⁴⁶This day the Lord will deliver you into my hand, and I will strike you down, and cut off your head; and I will give the dead bodies of the host of the Philis'- tines this day to the birds of the air and to the wild beasts of the earth; that all the earth may know that there is a God in Israel, ⁴⁷and that all this assembly may know that the Lord saves not with sword and spear; for the battle is the Lord's and he will give you into our hand."

48 When the Philis'tine arose and came and drew near to meet David, David ran quickly toward the battle line to meet the Philistine. ⁴⁹And David put his hand in his bag and took out a stone, and slung it, and struck the Philis'tine on his forehead; the stone sank into his forehead, and he fell on his face to the ground.

50 So David prevailed over the Philis'tine with a sling and with a stone, and struck the Philistine, and killed him; there was no sword in the hand of David. ⁵¹Then David ran and stood over the Philis'tine, and took his sword and drew it out of its sheath, and killed him, and cut off his head with it. When the Philistines saw that their champion was dead, they fled. ⁵²And the men of Israel and Judah rose with a shout and pursued the Philis'tines as far as Gath ʸ and the gates of Ek'ron, so that the wounded Philistines fell on the way from Sha- ara'im as far as Gath and Ekron. ⁵³And the Israelites came back from chasing the Philis'tines, and they plundered their camp. ⁵⁴And David took the head of the Philis'tine and brought it to Jerusalem; but he put his armor in his tent.

55 When Saul saw David go forth against the Philis'tine, he said to Abner, the commander of the army, "Abner, whose son is this youth?" And Abner said, "As your soul lives, O king, I cannot tell." ⁵⁶And the king said, "Inquire whose son the stripling is." ⁵⁷And as David returned from the slaughter of the Philis'tine, Abner took him, and brought him before Saul with the head of the Philistine in his hand. ⁵⁸And Saul said to him, "Whose son are you, young man?" And David answered, "I am the son of your servant Jesse the Bethlehemite."

Jonathan's Covenant with David

18 When he had finished speaking to Saul, the soul of Jonathan was knit to the soul of David, and Jonathan loved him as his own soul.

17:41–54 The showdown between David and Goliath. From a human standpoint, the duel is a mismatch at every level. Goliath is a fearsome warrior, gigantic and pow- erful, fully armed and armored (17:4-7). David, however, is young and inexperienced, a shepherd and musician with simple weapons and virtually no combat armor (17:38-40). Yet the mighty Philistine is felled because David confronts his foe with faith and relies upon the Lord to fight the battle for him. The lesson for Israel is that Yahweh can accomplish the humanly impossible if only his people will trust him in times of peril and need. • *Morally*, the scene depicts two kinds of life squaring off against each other, the old life and the new. The five stones are the five books of Moses, and their laws are lifted from the stream of human weakness to the bag of divine grace. David relies on this grace, but Goliath relies on himself and his own strength. And because pride carries itself on the brow, he is brought down by a stone hurled at his forehead (St. Augustine, *Sermons* 32).

17:49 forehead: Practically the only part of Goliath's body exposed to attack (17:5-7). **on his face:** Recalls how the statue of Dagon toppled facedown in 5:3. The parallel: just as the Phi- listine god fell prostrate before the Lord's ark, so now the Philis- tine giant falls prostrate before the Lord's Anointed.

17:50 killed him: Not "ended his life", as in 17:51, but "wounded him mortally".

17:54 Jerusalem: Controlled by Jebusites at this time, so perhaps David takes his trophy to a part of the city already occupied by Israel (Josh 15:63; Judg 1:8).

17:55 whose son ...?: An inquiry, not about David's personal identity (already known from 16:14-23), but about David's family background. Saul apparently intends to make good on the promises he made in 17:25.

18:1–30 David soars in popularity with the people but plummets in popularity with Saul. He is "loved" by Saul's son, Jonathan (18:1-3); by Saul's daughter, Michal (18:20); by Saul's servants (18:22); and by the tribes of Israel (18:16, 28). Saul, too, looks upon David with admiration at first (18:5), but his thoughts soon turn to suspicion (18:9), fear (18:12), and murder (18:17, 21, 25). • *Allegorically*, if

---

ʸGk: Heb *Gai*.

Conenents - Adamic

Israel ✓
He woke Struggles with God

Noahide covenant - I wee
never do
then again

Judge = High Priest = religion
Settles disputes In charge
Interpret God word

²And Saul took him that day, and would not let him return to his father's house. ³Then Jonathan made a covenant with David, because he loved him as his own soul. ⁴And Jonathan stripped himself of the robe that was upon him, and gave it to David, and his armor, and even his sword and his bow and his belt. ⁵And David went out and was successful wherever Saul sent him; so that Saul set him over the men of war. And this was good in the sight of all the people and also in the sight of Saul's servants.

6 As they were coming home, when David returned from slaying the Philis'tine, the women came out of all the cities of Israel, singing and dancing, to meet King Saul, with timbrels, with songs of joy, and with instruments ᶻ of music. ⁷And the women sang to one another as they made merry,

"Saul has slain his thousands,
and David his ten thousands."

⁸And Saul was very angry, and this saying displeased him; he said, "They have ascribed to David ten thousands, and to me they have ascribed thousands; and what more can he have but the kingdom?" ⁹And Saul eyed David from that day on.

Saul Tries to Kill David

10 And the next day an evil spirit from God rushed upon Saul, and he raved within his house, while David was playing the lyre, as he did day by day. Saul had his spear in his hand; ¹¹and Saul cast the spear, for he thought, "I will pin David to the wall." But David evaded him twice.

12 Saul was afraid of David, because the Lord was with him but had departed from Saul. ¹³So Saul removed him from his presence, and made him a commander of a thousand; and he went out and came in before the people. ¹⁴And David had success in all his undertakings; for the Lord was with him.

¹⁵And when Saul saw that he had great success, he stood in awe of him. ¹⁶But all Israel and Judah loved David; for he went out and came in before them.

David Marries Michal

17 Then Saul said to David, "Here is my elder daughter Merab; I will give her to you for a wife; only be valiant for me and fight the Lord's battles." For Saul thought, "Let not my hand be upon him, but let the hand of the Philis'tines be upon him." ¹⁸And David said to Saul, "Who am I, and who are my kinsfolk, my father's family in Israel, that I should be son-in-law to the king?" ¹⁹But at the time when Merab, Saul's daughter, should have been given to David, she was given to A'dri-el the Meho'lathite for a wife.

20 Now Saul's daughter Michal loved David; and they told Saul, and the thing pleased him. ²¹Saul thought, "Let me give her to him, that she may be a snare for him, and that the hand of the Philis'tines may be against him." Therefore Saul said to David a second time, ᵃ "You shall now be my son-in-law." ²²And Saul commanded his servants, "Speak to David in private and say, 'Behold, the king has delight in you, and all his servants love you; now then become the king's son-in-law.'" ²³And Saul's servants spoke those words in the ears of David. And David said, "Does it seem to you a little thing to become the king's son-in-law, seeing that I am a poor man and of no repute?" ²⁴And the servants of Saul told him, "Thus and so did David speak." ²⁵Then Saul said, "Thus shall you say to David, 'The king desires no marriage present * except a hundred foreskins of the Philis'tines, that he may be avenged of the king's enemies.'" Now Saul thought to make David fall by the hand of the Philistines. ²⁶And when his servants told David these words, it pleased David well to be the king's son-in-law. Before the

---

18:7: 21:11; 29:5.

---

you want to see the mystery of the Lord prefigured, look upon Abel, who was murdered; Isaac, who was bound; Joseph, who was sold into slavery; Moses, who was exposed; and David, who was persecuted (St. Melito of Sardis, *Homily on Passover* 59).

18:2 not let him return: David has been dividing his time between Saul's royal residence and his father's pastures in Bethlehem (17:15). The passage is a confirmation of Samuel's warning that a king will "take" the sons of Israel for himself (8:11).

18:3 covenant: A mutual commitment of loyalty and goodwill ratified by oath. In Israel, as in the ancient Near East, covenants created legal bonds of kinship, so that the covenant parties accepted obligations normally incumbent upon members of the same family. David thus considers Jonathan a "brother" (2 Sam 1:26).

18:4 stripped ... the robe: Symbolic of Jonathan, the crown prince, relinquishing political ambitions and handing over to David his hereditary claim to be Saul's successor.

Somehow Jonathan has learned that David—not himself—is next in line for the throne (23:17).

18:6 women came out: To lead a victory celebration (Ex 15:20–21; Judg 11:34).

18:8 the kingdom?: Saul begins to suspect that David might be the "neighbor" destined to supplant him as king (15:28).

18:10 evil spirit: See note on 16:14.

18:11 cast the spear: The first of many times that Saul will make an attempt on David's life (19:10).

18:16 Israel and Judah: Refers to the northern and southern tribes of Israel.

18:17–27 Saul pretends to desire David as his son-in-law. His affection is more apparent than real, however, for he marries off his first daughter to another man (18:19) and then promises his younger daughter to David with plans of putting him in harm's way (18:20–25). Ultimately, Saul's attempt to rid himself of David backfires: instead of eliminating him, David's military clashes with the Philistines only enhance his reputation with the people (18:30).

18:25 marriage present: Paid to the father of the prospective bride.

ᶻ Or *triangles*, or *three-stringed instruments.*
ᵃ Heb *by two.*
* 18:25, *marriage present:* The usual payment for a bride.

time had expired, ²⁷David arose and went, along with his men, and killed two hundred of the Philis'tines; and David brought their foreskins, which were given in full number to the king, that he might become the king's son-in-law. And Saul gave him his daughter Michal for a wife. ²⁸But when Saul saw and knew that the LORD was with David, and that all Israel*ᵇ* loved him, ²⁹Saul was still more afraid of David. So Saul was David's enemy continually.

30 Then the princes of the Philis'tines came out to battle, and as often as they came out David had more success than all the servants of Saul; so that his name was highly esteemed.

Jonathan Intercedes for David

19 And Saul spoke to Jonathan his son and to all his servants, that they should kill David. But Jonathan, Saul's son, delighted much in David. ²And Jonathan told David, "Saul my father seeks to kill you; therefore take heed to yourself in the morning, stay in a secret place and hide yourself; ³and I will go out and stand beside my father in the field where you are, and I will speak to my father about you; and if I learn anything I will tell you." ⁴And Jonathan spoke well of David to Saul his father, and said to him, "Let not the king sin against his servant David; because he has not sinned against you, and because his deeds have been of good service to you; ⁵for he took his life in his hand and he slew the Philis'tine, and the LORD wrought a great victory for all Israel. You saw it, and rejoiced; why then will you sin against innocent blood by killing David without cause?" ⁶And Saul listened to the voice of Jonathan; Saul swore, "As the LORD lives, he shall not be put to death." ⁷And Jonathan called David, and Jonathan showed him all these things. And Jonathan brought David to Saul, and he was in his presence as before.

Michal Helps David Escape from Saul

8 And there was war again; and David went out and fought with the Philis'tines, and made a great slaughter among them, so that they fled before him. ⁹Then an evil spirit from the LORD came upon Saul, as he sat in his house with his spear in his hand; and David was playing the lyre. ¹⁰And Saul sought to pin David to the wall with the spear; but he eluded Saul, so that he struck the spear into the wall. And David fled, and escaped.

11 That night Saul*ˣ* sent messengers to David's house to watch him, that he might kill him in the morning. But Michal, David's wife, told him, "If you do not save your life tonight, tomorrow you will be killed." ¹²So Michal let David down through the window; and he fled away and escaped. ¹³Michal took an image*ᶜ* and laid it on the bed and put a pillow*ᵈ* of goats' hair at its head, and covered it with the clothes. ¹⁴And when Saul sent messengers to take David, she said, "He is sick." ¹⁵Then Saul sent the messengers to see David, saying, "Bring him up to me in the bed, that I may kill him." ¹⁶And when the messengers came in, behold, the image*ᶜ* was in the bed, with the pillow*ᵈ* of goats' hair at its head. ¹⁷Saul said to Michal, "Why have you deceived me thus, and let my enemy go, so that he has escaped?" And Michal answered Saul, "He said to me, 'Let me go; why should I kill you?'"

David Joins Samuel in Ramah

18 Now David fled and escaped, and he came to Samuel at Ra'mah, and told him all that Saul had done to him. And he and Samuel went and dwelt at Naioth. ¹⁹And it was told Saul, "Behold, David is at Naioth in Ra'mah." ²⁰Then Saul sent messengers to take David; and when they saw the company of the prophets prophesying, and Samuel standing as head over them, the Spirit of God came upon the messengers of Saul, and they also prophesied. ²¹When it was told Saul, he sent other messengers, and they also prophesied. And Saul sent messengers again the third time, and they also prophesied. ²²Then he himself went to Ra'mah, and came to the great well that is in Secu; and he asked, "Where are

---

18:27 foreskins: Proof that the 200 warriors slain in battle were Philistines (17:26). Most other peoples in the biblical world practiced male circumcision (Jer 9:25–26).

19:1–24 Interventions by Jonathan (19:1–7), Michal (19:11–17), and the Spirit of God (19:18–24) shield David from the sinister plots of Saul.

19:1 delighted: The affection between David and Jonathan is mutual (2 Sam 1:26).

19:4 good service: David has shown nothing but unwavering loyalty to the king.

19:6 swore: The demented Saul will soon renege on this oath (19:11, 15), as he had done earlier in allowing Jonathan to live after swearing to execute violators of his decreed fast (14:24, 39–45).

19:9 evil spirit: See note on 16:14. **lyre:** Similar to a harp. See note on 16:23.

19:10 with the spear: A third attempt to murder David by impaling him (see 18:10–11).

19:12 through the window: Similar nighttime escapes were made by the Jericho spies (Josh 2:15) and the apostle Paul (Acts 9:25). Eluding the ambush ordered by Saul is the backdrop to David's prayers in Ps 59. **he fled away:** David is a fugitive from this point forward. Never again does he return to the service of King Saul as a court musician, armor bearer, or military commander (16:21–23; 18:5).

19:13 an image: The term can refer to "household idols". This one is given hair and clothes to make it look like David is lying sick in bed.

19:17 should I kill you?: Michal lies to her father, probably because she fears his fanatical hatred for David will be unleashed upon her.

19:18 Ramah: The hometown of Samuel in the hill country of Ephraim (1:1; 7:17). **Naioth:** Refers to "encampments" in Ramah, where a band of Israelite prophets live in community under the direction of Samuel (19:20).

19:22 the great well: The Greek LXX reads: "the well of the threshing floor".

ᵇ Gk: Heb *Michal, Saul's daughter.*
ˣ Gk Old Latin: Heb *escaped that night.* ¹¹*And Saul.*
ᶜ Heb *teraphim.*
ᵈ The meaning of the Hebrew word is uncertain.

Samuel and David?" And one said, "Behold, they are at Naioth in Ra′mah." [23]And he went from[f] there to Naioth in Ra′mah; and the Spirit of God came upon him also, and as he went he prophesied, until he came to Naioth in Ramah. [24]And he too stripped off his clothes, and he too prophesied before Samuel, and lay naked all that day and all that night. Hence it is said, "Is Saul also among the prophets?"[*]

The Friendship of David and Jonathan

20 Then David fled from Naioth in Ra′mah, and came and said before Jonathan, "What have I done? What is my guilt? And what is my sin before your father, that he seeks my life?" [2]And he said to him, "Far from it! You shall not die. Behold, my father does nothing either great or small without disclosing it to me; and why should my father hide this from me? It is not so." [3]But David replied,[g] "Your father knows well that I have found favor in your eyes; and he thinks, 'Let not Jonathan know this, lest he be grieved.' But truly, as the LORD lives and as your soul lives, there is but a step between me and death." [4]Then said Jonathan to David, "Whatever you say, I will do for you." [5]David said to Jonathan, "Behold, tomorrow is the new moon, and I should not fail to sit at table with the king; but let me go, that I may hide myself in the field till the third day at evening. [6]If your father misses me at all, then say, 'David earnestly asked leave of me to run to Bethlehem his city; for there is a yearly sacrifice there for all the family.' [7]If he says, 'Good!' it will be well with your servant; but if he is angry, then know that evil is determined by him. [8]Therefore deal kindly with your servant, for you have brought your servant into a sacred covenant[h] with you. But if there is guilt in me, slay me yourself; for why should you bring me to your father?" [9]And Jonathan said, "Far be it from you!

If I knew that it was determined by my father that evil should come upon you, would I not tell you?" [10]Then said David to Jonathan, "Who will tell me if your father answers you roughly?" [11]And Jonathan said to David, "Come, let us go out into the field." So they both went out into the field.

12 And Jonathan said to David, "The LORD, the God of Israel, be witness![i] When I have sounded my father, about this time tomorrow, or the third day, behold, if he is well disposed toward David, shall I not then send and disclose it to you? [13]But should it please my father to do you harm, the LORD do so to Jonathan, and more also, if I do not disclose it to you, and send you away, that you may go in safety. May the LORD be with you, as he has been with my father. [14]If I am still alive, show me the loyal love of the LORD, that I may not die;[j] [15]and do not cut off your loyalty from my house for ever. When the LORD cuts off every one of the enemies of David from the face of the earth, [16]let not the name of Jonathan be cut off from the house of David.[k] And may the LORD take vengeance on David's enemies." [17]And Jonathan made David swear again by his love for him; for he loved him as he loved his own soul.

18 Then Jonathan said to him, "Tomorrow is the new moon; and you will be missed, because your seat will be empty. [19]And on the third day you will be greatly missed;[l] then go to the place where you hid yourself when the matter was in hand, and remain beside yonder stone heap.[m] [20]And I will shoot three arrows to the side of it, as though I shot at a mark. [21]And behold, I will send the lad, saying, 'Go, find the arrows.' If I say to the lad, 'Look, the arrows are on this side of you, take them,' then you are to come, for, as the LORD lives, it is safe for you and there is no danger. [22]But if I say to the youth, 'Look, the arrows are beyond you,' then go; for the LORD

19:23, 24: 10, 11, 12.

19:24 lay naked: Bizarre behavior associated with ecstatic prophecy. Popular perception held that a prophet seized by the Spirit acts so differently than usual that he becomes like "another man" (10:6). **among the prophets?:** Further justifies the saying in 10:11–12.

20:1 and came: Most likely to Gibeah, the hometown of Saul (10:26).

20:5 the new moon: The first day of the new month. This was a holy day in ancient Israel celebrated with trumpets (Num 10:10) and sacrifices to the Lord (Num 28:11–15).

20:6 then say: The excuse is patently untrue and repeated by Jonathan in 20:28–29. The author simply recounts the words and events without offering a moral

judgment. • In Scripture the sins of men are narrated, not praised. It is fitting that God's judgment should be revealed in some cases and concealed in others, so that, when revealed, our ignorance may receive light, and, when concealed, our mind may be exercised to remember what we already know. It is God's writing, but not his doing. He does not propose such things for imitation but holds them out as warnings (St. Augustine, *Against Faustus* 22, 45).

20:8 deal kindly: I.e., in accord with the covenant of brotherhood sealed between David and Jonathan in 18:3. The same term (Heb., *ḥesed*) is translated "loyal love" in 20:14 and "loyalty" in 20:15. For its meaning, see word study: *Merciful Love* at Ex 34:7.

20:13 the LORD do so: A conditional self-curse. See note on Ruth 1:17.

20:14 If I am still alive: Jonathan knows that the founders of new dynasties often slay the potential successors of an old dynasty (1 Kings 15:29; 16:11; 2 Kings 11:1).

20:17 swear again: A renewal of the covenant ratified in 18:3. **he loved him:** The depth of the friendship between David and Jonathan is also noted in 18:1 and 2 Sam 1:26.

20:19 stone heap: Apparently a well-known landmark on the outskirts of Gibeah.

---

[f] Gk: Heb lacks *from.*
[g] Gk: Heb *swore again.*
[h] Heb *a covenant of the* LORD.
[i] Heb lacks *be witness.*
[j] Heb uncertain.
[k] Gk: Heb *earth, and Jonathan made a covenant with the house of David.*
[l] Gk: Heb *go down quickly.*
[m] Gk: Heb *the stone Ezel.*
[*] 19:20–24: cf. 10:5.

has sent you away. 23 And as for the matter of
which you and I have spoken, behold, the LORD is
between you and me for ever."
24 So David hid himself in the field; and when
the new moon came, the king sat down to eat food.
25 The king sat upon his seat, as at other times, upon
the seat by the wall; Jonathan sat opposite,[n] and
Abner sat by Saul's side, but David's place was
empty.
26 Yet Saul did not say anything that day; for
he thought, "Something has befallen him; he is not
clean, surely he is not clean." 27 But on the second
day, the next day after the new moon, David's place
was empty. And Saul said to Jonathan his son, "Why
has not the son of Jesse come to the meal, either
yesterday or today?" 28 Jonathan answered Saul,
"David earnestly asked leave of me to go to Bethlehem;
29 he said, 'Let me go; for our family holds a sacrifice
in the city, and my brother has commanded me to be
there. So now, if I have found favor in your eyes, let
me get away, and see my brothers.' For this reason
he has not come to the king's table."
30 Then Saul's anger was kindled against Jonathan, and he said to him, "You son of a perverse,
rebellious woman, do I not know that you have
chosen the son of Jesse to your own shame, and to
the shame of your mother's nakedness? 31 For as long
as the son of Jesse lives upon the earth, neither you
nor your kingdom shall be established. Therefore
send and fetch him to me, for he shall surely die."
32 Then Jonathan answered Saul his father, "Why
should he be put to death? What has he done?" 33 But
Saul cast his spear at him to strike him; so Jonathan
knew that his father was determined to put David to
death. 34 And Jonathan rose from the table in fierce
anger and ate no food the second day of the month,
for he was grieved for David, because his father had
disgraced him.
35 In the morning Jonathan went out into the
field to the appointment with David, and with him
a little lad. 36 And he said to his lad, "Run and find
the arrows which I shoot." As the lad ran, he shot
an arrow beyond him. 37 And when the lad came
to the place of the arrow which Jonathan had shot,
Jonathan called after the lad and said, "Is not the
arrow beyond you?" 38 And Jonathan called after
the lad, "Hurry, make haste, stay not." So Jonathan's lad gathered up the arrows, and came to his
master. 39 But the lad knew nothing; only Jonathan
and David knew the matter. 40 And Jonathan gave
his weapons to his lad, and said to him, "Go and
carry them to the city." 41 And as soon as the lad
had gone, David rose from beside the stone heap[o]
and fell on his face to the ground, and bowed three
times; and they kissed one another, and wept with
one another, until David recovered himself.[p] 42 Then
Jonathan said to David, "Go in peace, forasmuch as
we have sworn both of us in the name of the LORD,
saying, 'The LORD shall be between me and you, and
between my descendants and your descendants,
for ever.'" And he rose and departed; and Jonathan
went into the city.[q]

David and the Holy Bread

21 [r] Then came David to Nob to Ahim'elech the
priest; and Ahimelech came to meet David
trembling, and said to him, "Why are you alone, and
no one with you?" 2 And David said to Ahim'elech
the priest, "The king has charged me with a matter,
and said to me, 'Let no one know anything of the
matter about which I send you, and with which I
have charged you.' I have made an appointment
with the young men for such and such a place.
3 Now then, what have you at hand? Give me five
loaves of bread, or whatever is here." 4 And the
priest answered David, "I have no common bread at
hand, but there is holy bread; if only the young men

20:25 Abner: Saul's cousin and military commander (14:50).

20:31 nor your kingdom: Saul is still clutching to the dream of a royal dynasty despite the Lord's word of judgment in 13:14.

20:33 cast his spear: Saul again vents his rage in a fit of violence (18:11; 19:10).

20:42 we have sworn: The mutual covenant of 18:3 is meant. **name of the LORD:** Yahweh is invoked by name as a witness and enforcer of the oaths sworn by David and Jonathan. **my descendants:** Years later David will honor his pledge by showing extravagant kindness to Jonathan's son, Mephibosheth (2 Sam 9:1–13).

21:1–9 David flees to Nob in search of food (21:3) and weapons (21:8). He receives both and then leads a small band of fighters into Philistine territory (21:10).

21:1 Nob: Northeast of Jerusalem on the eastern slope of Mt. Scopus. Nob is called the "city of priests" (22:19) because the Shiloh clergy found refuge there after the Philistines captured the ark (4:10–11) and demolished the Shiloh sanctuary (Jer 7:12). The Mosaic Tabernacle is currently stationed in Nob (21:6), although the ark is kept at a separate location west of Jerusalem (7:2). **Ahimelech:** High priest. He is the brother of Ahijah (14:3), the father of Abiathar (22:20), the son of Ahitub (22:9), and the great-grandson of Eli (1:9).

21:2 the young men: David's loyal followers.

21:4 holy bread: The twelve loaves on display in the Tabernacle (Lev 24:5–6). They are known as "the bread of the Presence" (21:6). Only priests were permitted to eat this sanctified bread (Lev 24:9), but Ahimelech makes an exception for David and his men and gives them a special dispensation to eat (21:6). See note on Ex 25:30. • Jesus appeals to this precedent when he and the disciples are accused of unlawful eating on the Sabbath day (Mt 12:1–8; Mk 2:23–28; Lk 6:1–5). **from women:** Sexual relations cause ritual impurity (Lev 15:18), and holy food cannot be eaten in a state of uncleanness (Lev 22:3–6).

---

[n] Cn See Gk: Heb *stood up*.
[o] Gk: Heb *from beside the south*.
[p] Or *exceeded*.
[q] This sentence is 21:1 in Heb.
[r] Ch 21:2 in Heb.

Agape ↓ Saerbeuny smonten giving out of need
—Moral entention   for the good of my people
1 Samuel 21

have kept themselves from women." [5]And David answered the priest, "Of a truth women have been kept from us always when I go on an expedition; the vessels of the young men are holy, even when it is a common journey; how much more today will their vessels be holy?" [6]So the priest gave him the holy bread; for there was no bread there but the bread of the Presence, which is removed from before the Lord, to be replaced by hot bread on the day it is taken away.

[7] Now a certain man of the servants of Saul was there that day, detained before the Lord; his name was Do'eg the E'domite, the chief of Saul's herdsmen.

[8] And David said to Ahim'elech, "And have you not here a spear or a sword at hand? For I have brought neither my sword nor my weapons with me, because the king's business required haste." [9]And the priest said, "The sword of Goliath the Philis'tine, whom you killed in the valley of E'lah, behold, it is here wrapped in a cloth behind the ephod; if you will take that, take it, for there is none but that here." And David said, "There is none like that; give it to me."

David Flees to Gath

[10] And David rose and fled that day from Saul, and went to A'chish the king of Gath. [11]And the servants of A'chish said to him, "Is not this David the king of the land? Did they not sing to one another of him in dances,

'Saul has slain his thousands,
   and David his ten thousands'?"

[12]And David took these words to heart, and was much afraid of A'chish the king of Gath. [13]So he changed his behavior before them, and feigned himself mad in their hands, and made marks on the doors of the gate, and let his spittle run down his beard. [14]Then said A'chish to his servants, "Behold, you see the man is mad; why then have you brought him to me? [15]Do I lack madmen, that

---

21:11: 18:7; 29:5.

21:5 an expedition: Sexual abstinence is required of active-duty soldiers as a spiritual preparation for holy war (Deut 23:9–14).

21:6 removed ... replaced: The weekly exchange of old and new loaves is made on the Sabbath (Lev 24:8–9).

21:7 Doeg: Turns out to be an informant for Saul (22:9–10), just as David suspects (22:22). The treachery of Doeg is the backstory to Ps 52. **Edomite:** Not an Israelite, but a descendant of Jacob's brother, Esau (also called Edom, Gen 36:1).

21:9 sword of Goliath: The very weapon David used to decapitate the Philistine giant (17:51). **ephod:** A liturgical vestment (22:18).

21:10 Gath: One of the five leading cities of the Philistines (6:17).

21:13 feigned himself mad: Faking insanity makes David seem harmless and pitiable. It is a clever way to escape Philistine retribution; after all, David has slain hundreds of their warriors in recent times and is no doubt a wanted man (17:50–51; 18:27, 30).

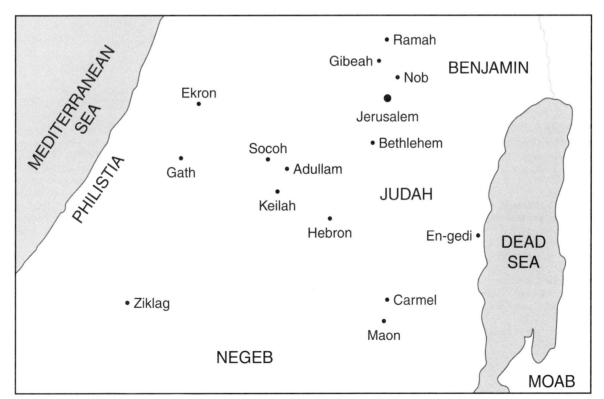

David, The Early Days

you have brought this fellow to play the madman in my presence? Shall this fellow come into my house?"

David and His Followers at Adullam

22 David departed from there and escaped to the cave of Adul′lam; and when his brothers and all his father's house heard it, they went down there to him. ²And every one who was in distress, and every one who was in debt, and every one who was discontented, gathered to him; and he became captain over them. And there were with him about four hundred men.

3 And David went from there to Mizpeh of Moab; and he said to the king of Moab, "Please let my father and my mother stay ˢ with you, till I know what God will do for me." ⁴And he left them with the king of Moab, and they stayed with him all the time that David was in the stronghold. ⁵Then the prophet Gad said to David, "Do not remain in the stronghold; depart, and go into the land of Judah." So David departed, and went into the forest of He′reth.

Saul Slaughters the Priests at Nob

6 Now Saul heard that David was discovered, and the men who were with him. Saul was sitting at Gib′e-ah, under the tamarisk tree on the height, with his spear in his hand, and all his servants were standing about him. ⁷And Saul said to his servants who stood about him, "Hear now, you Benjaminites; will the son of Jesse give every one of you fields and vineyards, will he make you all commanders of thousands and commanders of hundreds, ⁸that all of you have conspired against me? No one discloses to me when my son makes a league with the son of Jesse, none of you is sorry for me or discloses to me that my son has stirred up my servant against me, to lie in wait, as at this day." ⁹Then answered Do′eg the E′domite, who stood by the servants of Saul, "I saw the son of Jesse coming to Nob, to Ahim′elech the son of Ahi′tub, ¹⁰and he inquired of

the LORD for him, and gave him provisions, and gave him the sword of Goliath the Philis′tine."

11 Then the king sent to summon Ahim′elech the priest, the son of Ahi′tub, and all his father's house, the priests who were at Nob; and all of them came to the king. ¹²And Saul said, "Hear now, son of Ahi′tub." And he answered, "Here I am, my lord." ¹³And Saul said to him, "Why have you conspired against me, you and the son of Jesse, in that you have given him bread and a sword, and have inquired of God for him, so that he has risen against me, to lie in wait, as at this day?" ¹⁴Then Ahim′elech answered the king, "And who among all your servants is so faithful as David, who is the king's son-in-law, and captain over ᵗ your bodyguard, and honored in your house? ¹⁵Is today the first time that I have inquired of God for him? No! Let not the king impute anything to his servant or to all the house of my father; for your servant has known nothing of all this, much or little." ¹⁶And the king said, "You shall surely die, Ahim′elech, you and all your father's house." ¹⁷And the king said to the guard who stood about him, "Turn and kill the priests of the LORD; because their hand also is with David, and they knew that he fled, and did not disclose it to me." But the servants of the king would not put forth their hand to fall upon the priests of the LORD. ¹⁸Then the king said to Do′eg, "You turn and fall upon the priests." And Doeg the E′domite turned and fell upon the priests, and he killed on that day eighty-five persons who wore the linen ephod. ¹⁹And Nob, the city of the priests, he put to the sword; both men and women, children and sucklings, oxen, donkeys and sheep, he put to the sword.

20 But one of the sons of Ahim′elech the son of Ahi′tub, named Abi′athar, escaped and fled after David. ²¹And Abi′athar told David that Saul had killed the priests of the LORD. ²²And David said to

---

22:1 cave of Adullam: Over 15 miles southwest of Jerusalem in the territory of Judah. It is here that David, a fugitive and outlaw, begins to gather strength as hundreds of disaffected Israelites (22:2), along with a prophet (22:5) and a priest (22:20), flock to him. David's time in this hideout is the backdrop of Ps 57 and 142.

22:3 Mizpeh: Location unknown. **Moab:** Directly east of the Dead Sea. David travels here with the hope of placing his parents beyond the reach of Saul. Perhaps David has family connections in Moab that suggest this move, e.g., recall that his great-grandmother Ruth was a Moabitess (Ruth 4:13–22).

22:5 prophet Gad: Remains loyal to David and later becomes his royal seer (2 Sam 24:11; 2 Chron 29:25). **forest of Hereth:** Location uncertain.

22:6 his spear: Brings to mind Saul's violent temperament (18:10–11; 20:33).

22:8 a league: Literally "a covenant", as in 18:3 and 20:8.

22:9 Doeg: An informant from Nob. See note on 21:7.

22:11 Ahimelech: High priest. See note on 21:1. **came to the king:** At his hometown of Gibeah (22:6).

22:13 Why have you conspired: A baseless accusation. Ahimelech is not siding with Saul's rival when he furnishes David with a few loaves and a single sword (21:6, 9). David, after all, has tricked him into thinking he is on a secret mission from the king (21:2). **inquired of God:** I.e., seeks the Lord's will by using the sacred lots, Urim and Thummim, which are kept in the custody of the high priest (14:41).

22:17 kill the priests: Reveals the depth of Saul's dementia and paranoia. His own officials refuse to act on this senseless order; only Doeg, the mischievous Edomite, steps forward to comply (22:18–19).

22:18 eighty-five persons: The massacre at Nob fulfills the oracle of doom in 2:33 that foretold the violent death of Eli's priestly house.

22:20 Abiathar: The lone survivor of the priestly line of Eli. David offers him protection (22:23) and later installs him as one of his chief priests (2 Sam 20:25), although Solomon will later expel Abiathar from the priesthood on charges of disloyalty to the rightful Davidic successor (1 Kings 2:26–27).

22:22 I have occasioned: David comes to realize that his trickery (21:2) has resulted in tragedy (22:18–19; cf. 2 Sam 24:17).

ˢ Syr Vg: Heb *come out.*
ᵗ Gk Tg: Heb *and has turned aside to.*

Abi'athar, "I knew on that day, when Do'eg the E'domite was there, that he would surely tell Saul. I have occasioned the death of all the persons of your father's house. ²³Stay with me, fear not; for he that seeks my life seeks your life; with me you shall be in safekeeping."

David Saves the City of Keilah

23 Now they told David, "Behold, the Philis'-tines are fighting against Kei'lah, and are robbing the threshing floors." ²Therefore David inquired of the LORD, "Shall I go and attack these Philis'tines?" And the LORD said to David, "Go and attack the Philistines and save Kei'lah." ³But David's men said to him, "Behold, we are afraid here in Judah; how much more then if we go to Kei'lah against the armies of the Philis'tines?" ⁴Then David inquired of the LORD again. And the LORD answered him, "Arise, go down to Kei'lah; for I will give the Philis'tines into your hand." ⁵And David and his men went to Kei'lah, and fought with the Philis'tines, and brought away their cattle, and made a great slaughter among them. So David delivered the inhabitants of Keilah.

6 When Abi'athar the son of Ahim'elech fled to David to Kei'lah, he came down with an ephod in his hand. ⁷Now it was told Saul that David had come to Kei'lah. And Saul said, "God has given him into my hand; for he has shut himself in by entering a town that has gates and bars." ⁸And Saul summoned all the people to war, to go down to Kei'lah, to besiege David and his men. ⁹David knew that Saul was plotting evil against him; and he said to Abi'athar the priest, "Bring the ephod here." ¹⁰Then said David, "O LORD, the God of Israel, your servant has surely heard that Saul seeks to come to Kei'lah, to destroy the city on my account. ¹¹Will the men of Kei'lah surrender me into his hand? Will Saul come down, as your servant has heard? O LORD, the God of Israel, I beg you, tell your servant." And the LORD said, "He will come down." ¹²Then said David,

"Will the men of Kei'lah surrender me and my men into the hand of Saul?" And the LORD said, "They will surrender you." ¹³Then David and his men, who were about six hundred, arose and departed from Kei'lah, and they went wherever they could go. When Saul was told that David had escaped from Keilah, he gave up the expedition. ¹⁴And David remained in the strongholds in the wilderness, in the hill country of the wilderness of Ziph. And Saul sought him every day, but God did not give him into his hand.

David Eludes Saul in the Wilderness

15 And David was afraid because[u] Saul had come out to seek his life. David was in the wilderness of Ziph at Horesh. ¹⁶And Jonathan, Saul's son, rose, and went to David at Horesh, and strengthened his hand in God. ¹⁷And he said to him, "Fear not; for the hand of Saul my father shall not find you; you shall be king over Israel, and I shall be next to you; Saul my father also knows this." ¹⁸And the two of them made a covenant before the LORD; David remained at Horesh, and Jonathan went home.

19 Then the Ziphites went up to Saul at Gib'e-ah, saying, "Does not David hide among us in the strongholds at Horesh, on the hill of Hachi'lah, which is south of Jeshi'mon? ²⁰Now come down, O king, according to all your heart's desire to come down; and our part shall be to surrender him into the king's hand." ²¹And Saul said, "May you be blessed by the LORD; for you have had compassion on me. ²²Go, make yet more sure; know and see the place where his haunt is, and who has seen him there; for it is told me that he is very cunning. ²³See therefore, and take note of all the lurking places where he hides, and come back to me with sure information. Then I will go with you; and if he is in the land, I will search him out among all the thousands of Judah." ²⁴And they arose, and went to Ziph ahead of Saul.

Now David and his men were in the wilderness of Maon, in the Ar'abah to the south of Jeshi'mon.

23:1–29 David and his men move from place to place throughout southern Judah. Despite information on his whereabouts leaking to Saul, he takes each step at God's direction and is kept safe by his Providence. For the location of several sites in this chapter, see map: *David, The Early Days* at 1 Sam 21.

23:1 Keilah: Three miles south of Adullam (22:1), not far from Philistine territory.

23:2 inquired: By means of the priest Abiathar. See note on 22:13.

23:6 ephod: A decorated liturgical vestment worn by the high priest, having a breastpiece containing the sacred lots, Urim and Thummim (Ex 28:5–30). Simpler linen ephods were worn by other priests (22:18).

23:7 God has given him: Wishful thinking on Saul's part, as 23:14 will indicate.

23:12 They will surrender you: Quite possibly out of fear rather than treachery. News of the massacre in Nob (22:19) would have made the Keilahites think twice about harboring David from the rabid hatred of Saul.

23:13 six hundred: The popularity of David continues to grow (up 50 percent from 22:2).

23:14 wilderness of Ziph: Rugged highlands 20 miles south of Jerusalem, below Hebron.

23:16 strengthened his hand: With words of encouragement and support and possibly with material provisions as well. Jonathan recognizes that running and hiding from Saul would be an exhausting trial of faith for David, who knows the Lord's plan but who might be tempted to doubt it in the midst of difficult circumstances.

23:17 next to you: Jonathan acknowledges David's kingship and is content to accept a subordinate role as the king's minister.

23:18 made a covenant: A renewal of the covenant ratified in 18:3.

23:19 among us: The revelation of David's location by the Ziphites is the background for Ps 54.

23:23 sure information: Saul demands actionable intelligence so that his army can locate David without having to chase him all over the Judean wilderness.

23:24 Maon: Eight miles southeast of Hebron.

---

[u] Or *saw that.*

²⁵And Saul and his men went to seek him. And David was told; therefore he went down to the rock which is ᵛ in the wilderness of Maon. And when Saul heard that, he pursued after David in the wilderness of Maon. ²⁶Saul went on one side of the mountain, and David and his men on the other side of the mountain; and David was making haste to get away from Saul, as Saul and his men were closing in upon David and his men to capture them, ²⁷when a messenger came to Saul, saying, "Make haste and come; for the Philis′tines have made a raid upon the land." ²⁸So Saul returned from pursuing after David, and went against the Philis′tines; therefore that place was called the Rock of Escape. ²⁹ᵂ And David went up from there, and dwelt in the strongholds of En-ge′di.

David Spares Saul's Life

24 When Saul returned from following the Philis′tines, he was told, "Behold, David is in the wilderness of En-ge′di." ²Then Saul took three thousand chosen men out of all Israel, and went to seek David and his men in front of the Wildgoats′ Rocks. ³And he came to the sheepfolds by the way, where there was a cave; and Saul went in to relieve himself. Now David and his men were sitting in the innermost parts of the cave. ⁴And the men of David said to him, "Here is the day of which the Lord said to you, 'Behold, I will give your enemy into your hand, and you shall do to him as it shall seem good to you.'" Then David arose and stealthily cut off the skirt of Saul's robe. ⁵And afterward David's heart struck him, because he had cut off Saul's skirt. ⁶He said to his men, "The Lord forbid that I should do this thing to my lord, the Lord's anointed, to put forth my hand against him, seeing he is the Lord's anointed." ⁷So David persuaded his men with these words, and did not permit them to attack Saul. And Saul rose up and left the cave, and went upon his way.

8 Afterward David also arose, and went out of the cave, and called after Saul, "My lord the king!" And when Saul looked behind him, David bowed with his face to the earth, and did obeisance. ⁹And David said to Saul, "Why do you listen to the words of men who say, 'Behold, David seeks your hurt'? ¹⁰Behold, this day your eyes have seen how the Lord gave you today into my hand in the cave; and some bade me kill you, but Iˣ spared you. I said, 'I will not put forth my hand against my lord; for he is the Lord's anointed.' ¹¹See, my father, see the skirt of your robe in my hand; for by the fact that I cut off the skirt of your robe, and did not kill you, you may know and see that there is no wrong or treason in my hands. I have not sinned against you, though you hunt my life to take it. ¹²May the Lord judge between me and you, may the Lord avenge me upon you; but my hand shall not be against you. ¹³As the proverb of the ancients says, 'Out of the wicked comes forth wickedness'; but my hand shall not be against you. ¹⁴After whom has the king of Israel come out? After whom do you pursue? After a dead dog! After a flea! ¹⁵May the Lord therefore be judge, and give sentence between me and you, and see to it, and plead my cause, and deliver me from your hand."

16 When David had finished speaking these words to Saul, Saul said, "Is this your voice, my son David?" And Saul lifted up his voice and wept. ¹⁷He said to David, "You are more righteous than I; for you have repaid me good, whereas I have repaid you evil. ¹⁸And you have declared this day how you have dealt well with me, in that you did not kill me when the Lord put me into your hands. ¹⁹For if a man finds his enemy, will he let him go away safe? So may the Lord reward you with good for what you have done to me this day. ²⁰And now, behold, I know that you shall surely be king, and that the kingdom of Israel shall be established in your hand. ²¹Swear to me therefore by the Lord that you will not cut

---

24:1–22: 26:1–25.

23:27 raid: The timing of this Philistine invasion appears to be an act of divine Providence, for just as David is on the verge of being captured, a crisis of national security forces Saul to pull back from the pursuit and to order his troops elsewhere.

23:29 En-gedi: An oasis spring overlooking the western shore of the Dead Sea.

24:2 Wildgoats′ Rocks: In the vicinity of En-gedi, where wild ibexes roam the hills.

24:3 sheepfolds: Stone enclosures built to contain flocks and to protect them from thieves and wild animals during the night (Jn 10:1).

24:5 David's heart: Experiences a twinge of regret, since cutting the royal robe shows a measure of disrespect for the royal office. David knows that a king is anointed with the Spirit (16:13).

24:6 the Lord's anointed: A royal title in ancient Israel. See note on 2:10.

24:11 my father: I.e., father-in-law (18:27). **not kill you:** David will pass up a second opportunity to assassinate Saul in 26:7–12. • David's victory in the cave surpasses his victory over Goliath. For it is achieved, not with weapons and bloodshed, but by putting his resentment and anger to death. In sparing Saul's life, he deals many blows to the devil. We can likewise buffet the devil, enemy of peace and father of envy, when we make efforts at peace and hold resentment in check (St. John Chrysostom, *Homilies on David and Saul* 2).

24:13 wickedness: Finds no place in David's heart, which at this point is innocent (24:11), humble (24:8), and noble (24:6, 21–22).

24:14 dead dog ... flea: David is no more a threat to Saul than either of these harmless creatures.

24:16–22 Saul displays a surprising sense of guilt and remorse. It will not last long, for the king's heart will harden again, and the hunt for David will go on (26:2).

24:20 you shall surely be king: Saul recognizes the inevitable, but he is not yet ready to surrender the crown to David.

ᵛGk: Heb *and dwelt.*
ᵂCh 24:1 in Heb.
ˣGk Syr Tg: Heb *you.*

off my descendants after me, and that you will not destroy my name out of my father's house." ²²And David swore this to Saul. Then Saul went home; but David and his men went up to the stronghold.

Death of Samuel

25 Now Samuel died; and all Israel assembled and mourned for him, and they buried him in his house at Ra'mah.

David and Abigail

Then David rose and went down to the wilderness of Par'an. ²And there was a man in Maon, whose business was in Carmel. The man was very rich; he had three thousand sheep and a thousand goats. He was shearing his sheep in Carmel. ³Now the name of the man was Nabal, and the name of his wife Ab'igail. The woman was of good understanding and beautiful, but the man was churlish and ill-behaved; he was a Ca'lebite. ⁴David heard in the wilderness that Nabal was shearing his sheep. ⁵So David sent ten young men; and David said to the young men, "Go up to Carmel, and go to Nabal, and greet him in my name. ⁶And thus you shall salute him: 'Peace be to you, and peace be to your house, and peace be to all that you have. ⁷I hear that you have shearers; now your shepherds have been with us, and we did them no harm, and they missed nothing, all the time they were in Carmel. ⁸Ask your young men, and they will tell you. Therefore let my young men find favor in your eyes; for we come on a feast day. Please, give whatever you have at hand to your servants and to your son David.'"

9 When David's young men came, they said all this to Nabal in the name of David; and then they waited. ¹⁰And Nabal answered David's servants, "Who is David? Who is the son of Jesse? There are many servants nowadays who are breaking away from their masters. ¹¹Shall I take my bread and my water and my meat that I have killed for my shearers, and give it to men who come from I do not know where?" ¹²So David's young men turned away, and came back and told him all this. ¹³And David said to his men, "Every man belt on his sword!" And every man of them belted on his sword; David also belted on his sword; and about four hundred men went up after David, while two hundred remained with the baggage.

14 But one of the young men told Ab'igail, Nabal's wife, "Behold, David sent messengers out of the wilderness to salute our master; and he railed at them. ¹⁵Yet the men were very good to us, and we suffered no harm, and we did not miss anything when we were in the fields, as long as we went with them; ¹⁶they were a wall to us both by night and by day, all the while we were with them keeping the sheep. ¹⁷Now therefore know this and consider what you should do; for evil is determined against our master and against all his house, and he is so ill-natured that one cannot speak to him."

18 Then Ab'igail made haste, and took two hundred loaves, and two skins of wine, and five sheep ready dressed, and five measures of parched grain, and a hundred clusters of raisins, and two hundred cakes of figs, and laid them on donkeys. ¹⁹And she said to her young men, "Go on before me; behold, I come after you." But she did not tell her husband Nabal. ²⁰And as she rode on the donkey, and came down under cover of the mountain, behold, David and his men came down toward her; and she met them. ²¹Now David had said, "Surely in vain have I guarded all that this fellow has in the wilderness, so that nothing was missed of all that belonged to him; and he has returned me evil for good. ²²God do so to David ʸ and more also, if by morning I leave so much as one male of all who belong to him."

23 When Ab'igail saw David, she made haste, and alighted from the donkey, and fell before David on her face, and bowed to the ground. ²⁴She fell

---

24:22 the stronghold: The cave hideout of Adullam (22:1, 4–5).

25:1 Samuel died: After a lifetime of service as the Lord's prophet and the last of Israel's judges (3:19–20; 7:15–17). Samuel must have been widely admired among the people since representatives of every Israelite tribe come to pay their respects at his passing. The notice of his death prepares for upcoming events in 28:3–25. **Ramah:** Samuel's hometown in the hill country of Ephraim (1:1; 7:17). **wilderness of Paran:** In the Sinai Peninsula. Because it lies at such a distance from the events that follow, some scholars prefer to follow the Greek LXX, which reads: "the wilderness of Maon" (in southern Canaan).

25:2–44 The story behind David's marriage to Abigail. Not only is she pious, beautiful, and sensible, but the Lord directs her steps to intervene and thus prevent David from making a terrible mistake (25:32–34).

25:2 Maon: Eight miles south of Hebron in southern Canaan. **Carmel:** Just north of Maon.

25:3 Nabal: The Hebrew means "fool" (alluded to in 25:25). Though probably not his birth name, it is a fitting nickname for the man, since he shows himself to be godless, senseless, and tactless. **Abigail:** United with Nabal in marriage but the antithesis of him in every other respect. **Calebite:** A descendant of Caleb, a hero of the Conquest generation whose family settled in the region of Hebron (Josh 14:13–14).

25:8 feast day: Sheep shearing is a celebrated event and a traditional time of generosity. Taking advantage of the day, David politely asks for provisions in return for his earlier favor, namely, he and his men formed a "wall" of protection between desert marauders and Nabal's grazing flocks (25:16).

25:10 breaking away: Insinuates that David is little more than a runaway slave, i.e., a man of no importance or distinction.

25:13 his sword: David, enraged by the rudeness of Nabal, plans to avenge the insult with a massacre.

25:18 Abigail made haste: Executing a plan to placate David's anger and compensate him and his men for their kindness. She is successful on both counts (25:32–35).

25:22 God do so to David: A conditional self-curse. See note on Ruth 1:17.

ʸ Gk Compare Syr: Heb *the enemies of David.*

at his feet and said, "Upon me alone, my lord, be the guilt; please let your handmaid speak in your hearing, and hear the words of your handmaid. 25Let not my lord regard this ill-natured fellow, Nabal; for as his name is, so is he; Nabal^z is his name, and folly is with him; but I your handmaid did not see the young men of my lord, whom you sent. 26Now then, my lord, as the LORD lives, and as your soul lives, seeing the LORD has restrained you from bloodguilt, and from taking vengeance with your own hand, now then let your enemies and those who seek to do evil to my lord be as Nabal. 27And now let this present which your servant has brought to my lord be given to the young men who follow my lord. 28Please forgive the trespass of your handmaid; for the LORD will certainly make my lord a sure house, because my lord is fighting the battles of the LORD; and evil shall not be found in you so long as you live. 29If men rise up to pursue you and to seek your life, the life of my lord shall be bound in the bundle of the living in the care of the LORD your God; and the lives of your enemies he shall sling out as from the hollow of a sling. 30And when the LORD has done to my lord according to all the good that he has spoken concerning you, and has appointed you prince over Israel, 31my lord shall have no cause of grief, or pangs of conscience, for having shed blood without cause or for my lord taking vengeance himself. And when the LORD has dealt well with my lord, then remember your handmaid."

32 And David said to Ab'igail, "Blessed be the LORD, the God of Israel, who sent you this day to meet me! 33Blessed be your discretion, and blessed be you, who have kept me this day from bloodguilt and from avenging myself with my own hand! 34For as surely as the LORD the God of Israel lives, who has restrained me from hurting you, unless you had made haste and come to meet me, truly by morning there had not been left to Nabal so much as one male." 35Then David received from her hand what she had brought him; and he said to her, "Go up in peace to your house; see, I have listened to your voice, and I have granted your petition."

36 And Ab'igail came to Nabal; and behold, he was holding a feast in his house, like the feast of a king. And Nabal's heart was merry within him, for he was very drunk; so she told him nothing at all until the morning light. 37And in the morning, when the wine had gone out of Nabal, his wife told him these things, and his heart died within him, and he became as a stone. 38And about ten days later the LORD struck Nabal; and he died.

39 When David heard that Nabal was dead, he said, "Blessed be the LORD who has avenged the insult I received at the hand of Nabal, and has kept back his servant from evil; the LORD has returned the evil-doing of Nabal upon his own head." Then David sent and wooed Ab'igail, to make her his wife. 40And when the servants of David came to Ab'igail at Carmel, they said to her, "David has sent us to you to take you to him as his wife." 41And she rose and bowed with her face to the ground, and said, "Behold, your handmaid is a servant to wash the feet of the servants of my lord." 42And Ab'igail made haste and rose and mounted on a donkey, and her five maidens attended her; she went after the messengers of David, and became his wife.

Ahino-am of Jezreel

43 David also took Ahin'o-am of Jezre'el; and both of them became his wives. 44Saul had given Michal his daughter, David's wife, to Palti the son of La'ish, who was of Gallim.

25:26 as Nabal: Abigail hints at the demise of her husband.

25:29 bundle of the living: An allusion to "the book of the living" (Ps 69:28), evoking the common practice of wrapping personal treasures in a cloth for safekeeping. **your enemies:** Likened to a stone that is flung from a slingshot and then forgotten. Notice that Nabal will become "as a stone" in 25:37.

25:43–44 Accumulating wives is considered a sign of growing wealth and influence. In the Books of Samuel, it is an indication that David is rising toward kingship (2 Sam 3:1–5).

25:43 Jezreel: A village of Judah (Josh 15:56).

25:44 Michal: Will return to David after Saul's death (2 Sam 3:13–16).

^z That is *fool.*

WORD STUDY

A Sure House (25:28)

Bayit ne'eman (Heb.): designates an "enduring dynasty". By "house" is meant a family line of successors, and by "sure" is meant one that is faithful and reliable as well as one that is lasting and stable. The rise of two such houses is foretold in 1 Samuel. The first is a *priestly* dynasty that will replace the faithless house of Eli (1 Sam 2:35), and the second is a *royal* dynasty that will replace the faithless house of Saul (1 Sam 25:28). The idea is that Yahweh will raise up two faithful houses (for Zadok the priest and David the king) on the ruins of two fallen houses that collapsed under the weight of sin (that of Eli the priest and Saul the first king). The promise to David resonates throughout the Books of Samuel, as the words of Abigail anticipate the founding of the Davidic covenant, when God will swear an oath to establish the "house" of David and make it "sure" forever (2 Sam 7:11–17; cf. Ps 89:3–4; 132:11–12).

David Again Spares Saul's Life

26 Then the Ziphites came to Saul at Gib′e-ah, saying, "Is not David hiding himself on the hill of Hachi′lah, which is on the east of Jeshi′mon?" ²So Saul arose and went down to the wilderness of Ziph, with three thousand chosen men of Israel, to seek David in the wilderness of Ziph. ³And Saul encamped on the hill of Hachi′lah, which is beside the road on the east of Jeshi′mon. But David remained in the wilderness; and when he saw that Saul came after him into the wilderness, ⁴David sent out spies, and learned of a certainty that Saul had come. ⁵Then David rose and came to the place where Saul had encamped; and David saw the place where Saul lay, with Abner the son of Ner, the commander of his army; Saul was lying within the encampment, while the army was encamped around him.

6 Then David said to Ahim′-elech the Hittite, and to Jo′ab's brother Abi′shai the son of Zeru′iah, "Who will go down with me into the camp to Saul?" And Abishai said, "I will go down with you." ⁷So David and Abi′shai went to the army by night; and there lay Saul sleeping within the encampment, with his spear stuck in the ground at his head; and Abner and the army lay around him. ⁸Then said Abi′shai to David, "God has given your enemy into your hand this day; now therefore let me pin him to the earth with one stroke of the spear, and I will not strike him twice." ⁹But David said to Abi′shai, "Do not destroy him; for who can put forth his hand against the LORD's anointed, and be guiltless?" ¹⁰And David said, "As the LORD lives, the LORD will strike him; or his day shall come to die; or he shall go down into battle and perish. ¹¹The LORD forbid that I should put forth my hand against the LORD's anointed; but take now the spear that is at his head, and the jar of water, and let us go." ¹²So David took the spear and the jar of water from Saul's head; and they went away. No man saw it, or knew it, nor did any awake; for they were all asleep, because a deep sleep from the LORD had fallen upon them.

13 Then David went over to the other side, and stood afar off on the top of the mountain, with a great space between them; ¹⁴and David called to the army, and to Abner the son of Ner, saying, "Will you not answer, Abner?" Then Abner answered, "Who are you that calls to the king?" ¹⁵And David said to Abner, "Are you not a man? Who is like you in Israel? Why then have you not kept watch over your lord the king? For one of the people came in to destroy the king your lord. ¹⁶This thing that you have done is not good. As the LORD lives, you deserve to die, because you have not kept watch over your lord, the LORD's anointed. And now see where the king's spear is, and the jar of water that was at his head."

17 Saul recognized David's voice, and said, "Is this your voice, my son David?" And David said, "It is my voice, my lord, O king." ¹⁸And he said, "Why does my lord pursue after his servant? For what have I done? What guilt is on my hands? ¹⁹Now therefore let my lord the king hear the words of his servant. If it is the LORD who has stirred you up against me, may he accept an offering; but if it is men, may they be cursed before the LORD, for they have driven me out this day that I should have no share in the heritage of the LORD, saying, 'Go, serve other gods.'* ²⁰Now therefore, let not my blood fall to the earth away from the presence of the LORD; for the king of Israel has come out to seek my life,ᵃ like one who hunts a partridge in the mountains."

21 Then Saul said, "I have done wrong; return, my son David, for I will no more do you harm, because my life was precious in your eyes this day; behold, I have played the fool, and have erred exceedingly." ²²And David made answer, "Here is the spear, O king! Let one of the young men come over and fetch it. ²³The LORD rewards every man for his righteousness and

---

26:1-25: 24:1-22.

26:1-25 Events in chap. 26 parallel events in chap. 24, most notably when David passes up a chance to take Saul's life. Refusing to take violent action against Yahweh's anointed shows David's utmost respect for the office of the king (compare 24:6 with 26:11).

26:1 the Ziphites: Once again they supply Saul with intelligence on the location of David's hideout (as in 23:19). **Jeshimon:** Apparently the Judean wilderness, west of the Dead Sea.

26:5 Abner: Saul's cousin and chief military commander (14:50). David will taunt him for leaving Saul vulnerable to assassination (26:13-16).

26:6 Ahim-elech the Hittite: The only mention of him in the Bible. He is probably a mercenary fighting for David's cause. **Abishai:** One of David's nephews, the son of his sister

Zeruiah (1 Chron 2:16). Later he is made the commander of an elite guard unit (2 Sam 23:18).

26:10 the LORD will strike: God will take care of eliminating David's enemies, as illustrated in the recent Nabal incident (25:38-39).

26:12 sleep from the LORD: Again the Lord is active in taking David's side and shielding him from harm. See note on 23:27.

26:19 the heritage: The land of Canaan, given to Israel as an inheritance. See word study: *Inheritance* at Josh 13:7. **serve other gods:** Exile from the land would force David to live and worship among pagans. The assumption is that Israel is the only place consecrated for the worship of Yahweh.

26:20 partridge: The Hebrew means "caller". It well describes David, who is calling out to Saul's camp from a distance (26:14).

26:21 return, my son: The invitation is refused. David knows that Saul is too unstable to be trusted. At this point the two men go their separate ways and will never see each other again (26:25).

ᵃ Gk: Heb *a flea* (as in 24:14).
*26:19, *Go, serve other gods:* They did not consider the possibility of worshiping Yahweh, the God of Israel, in a foreign land.

his faithfulness; for the Lord gave you into my hand today, and I would not put forth my hand against the Lord's anointed. ²⁴Behold, as your life was precious this day in my sight, so may my life be precious in the sight of the Lord, and may he deliver me out of all tribulation." ²⁵Then Saul said to David, "Blessed be you, my son David! You will do many things and will succeed in them." So David went his way, and Saul returned to his place.

David Goes to King Achish in Gath

27 And David said in his heart, "I shall now perish one day by the hand of Saul; there is nothing better for me than that I should escape to the land of the Philis′tines; then Saul will despair of seeking me any longer within the borders of Israel, and I shall escape out of his hand." ²So David arose and went over, he and the six hundred men who were with him, to A′chish the son of Ma′och, king of Gath. ³And David dwelt with A′chish at Gath, he and his men, every man with his household, and David with his two wives, Ahin′o-am of Jezre′el, and Ab′igail of Carmel, Nabal's widow. ⁴And when it was told Saul that David had fled to Gath, he sought for him no more.

5 Then David said to A′chish, "If I have found favor in your eyes, let a place be given me in one of the country towns, that I may dwell there; for why should your servant dwell in the royal city with you?" ⁶So that day A′chish gave him Zik′lag; therefore Zik′lag has belonged to the kings of Judah to this day. ⁷And the number of the days that David dwelt in the country of the Philis′tines was a year and four months.

8 Now David and his men went up, and made raids upon the Gesh′urites, the Girzites, and the Amal′ekites; for these were the inhabitants of the land from of old, as far as Shur, to the land of Egypt. ⁹And David struck the land, and left neither man nor woman alive, but took away the sheep, the oxen, the donkeys, the camels, and the garments, and came back to A′chish. ¹⁰When A′chish asked, "Against whom**ᵇ** have you made a raid today?" David would say, "Against the Neg′eb of Judah," or "Against the Negeb of the Jerah′meelites," or, "Against the Negeb of the Kenites." ¹¹And David saved neither man nor woman alive, to bring tidings to Gath, thinking, "Lest they should tell about us, and say, 'So David has done.'" Such was his custom all the while he dwelt in the country of the Philis′tines. ¹²And A′chish trusted David, thinking, "He has made himself utterly abhorred by his people Israel; therefore he shall be my servant always."

28 In those days the Philis′tines gathered their forces for war, to fight against Israel. And A′chish said to David, "Understand that you and your men are to go out with me in the army." ²David said to A′chish, "Very well, you shall know what your servant can do." And Achish said to David, "Very well, I will make you my bodyguard for life."

Saul Consults a Medium at En-dor

3 Now Samuel had died, and all Israel had mourned for him and buried him in Ra′mah, his own city. And Saul had put the mediums and the wizards out of the land. ⁴The Philis′tines assembled, and came and encamped at Shu′nem; and Saul gathered all Israel, and they encamped at Gilbo′a. ⁵When Saul saw the army of the Philis′tines, he was afraid, and his heart trembled greatly. ⁶And when Saul inquired of the Lord, the Lord did not answer him, either by dreams, or by U′rim, or by prophets. ⁷Then Saul said to his servants, "Seek out for me a woman who is a medium, that I may go to her and inquire of her." And his servants said to him, "Behold, there is a medium at En-dor."

8 So Saul disguised himself and put on other garments, and went, he and two men with him; and

---

27:1–12 David pretends to defect to the Philistines, but his real aim is to escape the wrath of Saul. The strategy is both cunning and effective, as is the deceitful front he is forced to maintain during his stay (27:8–12).

27:1 perish one day: David is tired of life as a fugitive and begins to despair of surviving the hostile pursuit of Saul.

27:2 Gath: One of the five main cities of the Philistines (6:17). The city ruler accepts David and his men as a military asset (28:1) whose skills on the battlefield are a matter of common knowledge (29:5).

27:5 country towns: David wants to move away from Gath so that he and his fighters can operate with minimal supervision from the Philistines. His words of flattery toward Achish are a ploy to implement this ulterior plan.

27:6 Ziklag: A Philistine border town in southwest Canaan. Israelite kings continued to claim it as royal property in later times.

27:8–12 David misleads Achish about his military expeditions. He professes to make raids on Israel and its allies, but in fact he is plundering and weakening Israel's enemies.

27:8 Geshurites: Lived south of the Philistines. They had remained unconquered since the time of Joshua (Josh 13:2).

Girzites: Otherwise unknown. **Amalekites:** Nomads of the Sinai Peninsula.

27:10 Negeb: The arid region stretching over the deep south of Canaan. **Jerahmeelites:** Descendants of Judah through his son Hezron (1 Chron 2:3–9). **Kenites:** See note on Judg 1:16.

28:2 my bodyguard: An offer made on the condition that David proves himself in battle.

28:3 Samuel had died: This happened earlier, before David took up residence among the Philistines (25:1). **mediums … wizards:** Saul had followed the Torah in outlawing all forms of occultism and witchcraft in Israel (Lev 19:31; 20:27) (CCC 2116–17). See note on Deut 18:9–14.

28:4 Shunem: Over 15 miles southwest of the Sea of Galilee in the Jezreel valley. **Gilboa:** A mountain that overlooks the Jezreel valley from the south.

28:6 dreams … Urim … prophets: None of these acceptable channels of divine revelation yielded information about the outcome of the Philistine conflict. The Lord's eerie silence is a judgment on Saul for his stubbornness (28:15–18). See note on 14:41.

28:7 En-dor: Southwest of Mt. Tabor in lower Galilee.

28:8–19 Saul consults the witch of Endor in search of knowledge about the future. The visit ends in disappointment, however, for when a séance conjures up the deceased spirit

---

ᵇGk Vg: Heb lacks *whom.*

they came to the woman by night. And he said, "Divine for me by a spirit, and bring up for me whomever I shall name to you." [9]The woman said to him, "Surely you know what Saul has done, how he has cut off the mediums and the wizards from the land. Why then are you laying a snare for my life to bring about my death?" [10]But Saul swore to her by the LORD, "As the LORD lives, no punishment shall come upon you for this thing." [11]Then the woman said, "Whom shall I bring up for you?" He said, "Bring up Samuel for me." [12]When the woman saw Samuel, she cried out with a loud voice; and the woman said to Saul, "Why have you deceived me? You are Saul." [13]The king said to her, "Have no fear; what do you see?" And the woman said to Saul, "I see a god coming up out of the earth." [14]He said to her, "What is his appearance?" And she said, "An old man is coming up; and he is wrapped in a robe." And Saul knew that it was Samuel, and he bowed with his face to the ground, and did obeisance.

15 Then Samuel said to Saul, "Why have you disturbed me by bringing me up?" Saul answered, "I am in great distress; for the Philis'tines are warring against me, and God has turned away from me and answers me no more, either by prophets or by dreams; therefore I have summoned you to tell me what I shall do." [16]And Samuel said, "Why then do you ask me, since the LORD has turned from you and become your enemy? [17]The LORD has done to you as he spoke by me; for the LORD has torn the kingdom out of your hand, and given it to your neighbor, David. [18]Because you did not obey the voice of the LORD, and did not carry out his fierce wrath against Am'alek, therefore the LORD has done this thing to you this day. [19]Moreover the LORD will give Israel also with you into the hand of the Philis'tines; and tomorrow you and your sons shall be with me; the LORD will give the army of Israel also into the hand of the Philistines."

20 Then Saul fell at once full length upon the ground, filled with fear because of the words of Samuel; and there was no strength in him, for he had eaten nothing all day and all night. [21]And the woman came to Saul, and when she saw that he was terrified, she said to him, "Behold, your handmaid has listened to you; I have taken my life in my hand, and have listened to what you have said to me. [22]Now therefore, you also listen to your handmaid; let me set a morsel of bread before you; and eat, that you may have strength when you go on your way." [23]He refused, and said, "I will not eat." But his servants, together with the woman, urged him; and he listened to their words. So he arose from the earth, and sat upon the bed. [24]Now the woman had a fatted calf in the house, and she quickly killed it, and she took flour, and kneaded it and baked unleavened bread of it, [25]and she put it before Saul and his servants; and they ate. Then they rose and went away that night.

The Philistines Reject David

29 Now the Philis'tines gathered all their forces at A'phek; and the Israelites were encamped by the fountain which is in Jezre'el. [2]As the lords of the Philis'tines were passing on by hundreds and by thousands, and David and his men were passing on in the rear with A'chish, [3]the commanders of the Philis'tines said, "What are these Hebrews doing here?" And A'chish said to the commanders of the Philistines, "Is not this David, the servant of Saul, king of Israel, who has been with me now for days and years, and since he deserted to me I have found no fault in him to this day." [4]But the commanders of the Philis'tines were angry with him; and the commanders of the Philistines said to him, "Send the man back, that he may return to the place to which you have assigned him; he shall not go down with us to battle, lest in the battle he become an adversary to us. For how could this fellow reconcile himself to his lord? Would it not be with the heads of the men here? [5]Is not this David, of whom they sing to one another in dances,

'Saul has slain his thousands,
and David his ten thousands'?"

29:5: 18:7; 21:11.

---

of Samuel, the king receives nothing but comfortless words of doom. Necromancy, the occultic art of communicating with the dead, is condemned as an abomination in the Mosaic Law (Deut 18:9–13). The episode also reveals that belief in life after death was not unusual in ancient Israel. See note on 28:3.

28:9 my death: Mediums are subject to capital punishment by stoning (Lev 20:27).

28:13 out of the earth: I.e., out of the depths of Sheol, the realm of the dead (CCC 633). See word study: *Sheol* at Num 16:30.

28:14 robe: Saul recognizes Samuel's attire from the incident in 15:27.

28:18 against Amalek: Saul failed to destroy the Amalekites as the Lord instructed (15:1–9). This is the transgression that disqualified Saul from continuing as king over Israel (15:23).

28:19 shall be with me: Saul and his sons will be among the dead the very next day (31:2–4). Note that Samuel, a prophet in life (3:20), continues to prophesy in death (Sir 46:20).

28:24 fatted calf: A feast marks the end of Saul's career just as a sacrificial meal marked its beginning (9:22–24).

29:1 Aphek: Near the northern extremity of Philistine territory. This is the same place the Philistines mustered for war in 4:1.

29:3 these Hebrews: The commanders are not convinced of David's loyalty, which is still untested. The concern that "Hebrews" might switch their allegiance in battle and turn against the Philistines is justified by the earlier incident in 14:21. **no fault in him:** Achish is naïve to the point of gullibility. He still has no idea that David is playing a game of deception.

29:4 the place: The town of Ziklag (27:6).

29:5 Saul has slain: Lyrics from an Israelite war song (18:7; 21:11).

6 Then A'chish called David and said to him, "As the LORD lives, you have been honest, and to me it seems right that you should march out and in with me in the campaign; for I have found nothing wrong in you from the day of your coming to me to this day. Nevertheless the lords do not approve of you. ⁷So go back now; and go peaceably, that you may not displease the lords of the Philis'tines." ⁸And David said to A'chish, "But what have I done? What have you found in your servant from the day I entered your service until now, that I may not go and fight against the enemies of my lord the king?" ⁹And A'chish made answer to David, "I know that you are as blameless in my sight as an angel of God; nevertheless the commanders of the Philis'-tines have said, 'He shall not go up with us to the battle.' ¹⁰Now then rise early in the morning with the servants of your lord who came with you; and start early in the morning, and depart as soon as you have light." ¹¹So David set out with his men early in the morning, to return to the land of the Philis'tines. But the Philistines went up to Jezre'el.

David Avenges the Destruction of Ziklag

30 Now when David and his men came to Zik'lag on the third day, the Amal'ekites had made a raid upon the Neg'eb and upon Ziklag. They had overcome Ziklag, and burned it with fire, ²and taken captive the women and all^c who were in it, both small and great; they killed no one, but carried them off, and went their way. ³And when David and his men came to the city, they found it burned with fire, and their wives and sons and daughters taken captive. ⁴Then David and the people who were with him raised their voices and wept, until they had no more strength to weep. ⁵David's two wives also had been taken captive, Ahin'o-am of Jezre'el, and Ab'igail the widow of Nabal of Carmel. ⁶And David was greatly distressed; for the people spoke of stoning him, because all the people were bitter in soul, each for his sons and daughters. But David strengthened himself in the LORD his God.

7 And David said to Abi'athar the priest, the son of Ahim'elech, "Bring me the ephod." So Abiathar brought the ephod to David. ⁸And David inquired of the LORD, "Shall I pursue after this band? Shall I overtake them?" He answered him, "Pursue; for you shall surely overtake and shall surely rescue." ⁹So David set out, and the six hundred men who were with him, and they came to the brook Be'sor, where those stayed who were left behind. ¹⁰But David went on with the pursuit, he and four hundred men; two hundred stayed behind, who were too exhausted to cross the brook Be'sor.

11 They found an Egyptian in the open country, and brought him to David; and they gave him bread and he ate, they gave him water to drink, ¹²and they gave him a piece of a cake of figs and two clusters of raisins. And when he had eaten, his spirit revived; for he had not eaten bread or drunk water for three days and three nights. ¹³And David said to him, "To whom do you belong? And where are you from?" He said, "I am a young man of Egypt, servant to an Amal'ekite; and my master left me behind because I fell sick three days ago. ¹⁴We had made a raid upon the Neg'eb of the Cher'ethites and upon that which belongs to Judah and upon the Negeb of Caleb; and we burned Zik'lag with fire." ¹⁵And David said to him, "Will you take me down to this band?" And he said, "Swear to me by God, that you will not kill me, or deliver me into the hands of my master, and I will take you down to this band."

16 And when he had taken him down, behold, they were spread abroad over all the land, eating and drinking and dancing, because of all the great spoil they had taken from the land of the Phi-lis'tines and from the land of Judah. ¹⁷And David struck them from twilight until the evening of the next day; and not a man of them escaped, except four hundred young men, who mounted camels and fled. ¹⁸David recovered all that the Amal'e-kites had taken; and David rescued his two wives. ¹⁹Nothing was missing, whether small or great, sons or daughters, spoil or anything that had been taken; David brought back all. ²⁰David also captured all the flocks and herds; and the people drove those cattle before him,^d and said, "This is David's spoil."

29:8 what have I done?: David pretends to be offended by the order to disengage. In his heart, however, he is prob-ably relieved to escape the moral dilemma of fighting against his own beloved Israel. **the enemies of my lord:** The words are deliberately vague. Achish understands David to mean the Israelites, but the reader knows that David has in mind the enemies of Israel and King Saul (whom he addresses as "my lord" in 24:8 and 26:17).

29:11 Jezreel: Site of the upcoming battle, nearly 40 miles northeast of Aphek.

30:1 Ziklag: The town given to David and his men (27:6). **Amalekites:** Nomads of the Sinai Peninsula and longtime ene-mies of Israel (Ex 17:16). Taking the citizens of Ziklag captive is probably in retaliation for David's raid in 27:8. **Negeb:** The arid region that stretches over the deep south of Canaan.

30:5 two wives: Married while David was on the run from Saul (25:42–43).

30:7 Abiathar: High priest of Israel. See note on 22:20. **the ephod:** The priestly vestment where the sacred lots are stored. See note on 23:6.

30:9 brook Besor: About 13 miles south of Ziklag.

30:10 too exhausted: David's men have been traveling on foot for three days (30:1). The march is more than 60 miles from Aphek (29:1) to the Besor brook (30:9).

30:14 Cherethites: Migrants from the island of Crete asso-ciated with the Philistines (Ezek 25:16). David will later recruit select Cherethites to serve among his royal bodyguards (2 Sam 8:18).

30:17 twilight: Probably the darkness just before daybreak. The word is translated "dawn" in Job 7:4 and Ps 119:147.

---

^c Gk: Heb lacks *and all*.
^d Cn: Heb *they drove before those cattle*.

21 Then David came to the two hundred men, who had been too exhausted to follow David, and who had been left at the brook Be'sor; and they went out to meet David and to meet the people who were with him; and when David drew near to the people he saluted them. ²²Then all the wicked and base fellows among the men who had gone with David said, "Because they did not go with us, we will not give them any of the spoil which we have recovered, except that each man may lead away his wife and children, and depart." ²³But David said, "You shall not do so, my brothers, with what the LORD has given us; he has preserved us and given into our hand the band that came against us. ²⁴Who would listen to you in this matter? For as his share is who goes down into the battle, so shall his share be who stays by the baggage; they shall share alike." ²⁵And from that day forward he made it a statute and an ordinance for Israel to this day.

26 When David came to Zik'lag, he sent part of the spoil to his friends, the elders of Judah, saying, "Here is a present for you from the spoil of the enemies of the LORD"; ²⁷it was for those in Bethel, in Ra'moth of the Neg'eb, in Jat'tir, ²⁸in Aro'er, in Siphmoth, in Eshtemo'a, ²⁹in Racal, in the cities of the Jerah'meelites, in the cities of the Kenites, ³⁰in Hormah, in Borash'an, in A'thach, ³¹in He'bron, for all the places where David and his men had roamed.

The Death of Saul and His Sons

31 Now the Philis'tines fought against Israel; and the men of Israel fled before the Philistines, and fell slain on Mount Gilbo'a. ²And the Philis'tines overtook Saul and his sons; and the Philistines slew Jonathan and Abin'adab and Mal"chishu'a, the sons of Saul. ³The battle pressed hard upon Saul, and the archers found him; and he was badly wounded by the archers. ⁴Then Saul said to his armor-bearer, "Draw your sword, and thrust me through with it, lest these uncircumcised come and thrust me through, and make sport of me." But his armor-bearer would not; for he feared greatly. Therefore Saul took his own sword, and fell upon it. ⁵And when his armor-bearer saw that Saul was dead, he also fell upon his sword, and died with him. ⁶Thus Saul died, and his three sons, and his armor-bearer, and all his men, on the same day together. ⁷And when the men of Israel who were on the other side of the valley and those beyond the Jordan saw that the men of Israel had fled and that Saul and his sons were dead, they forsook their cities and fled; and the Philis'tines came and dwelt in them.

8 On the next day, when the Philis'tines came to strip the slain, they found Saul and his three sons fallen on Mount Gilbo'a. ⁹And they cut off his head, and stripped off his armor, and sent messengers throughout the land of the Philis'tines, to carry the good news to their idols^e and to the people. ¹⁰They put his armor in the temple of Ash'taroth; and they fastened his body to the wall of Beth-shan. ¹¹But when the inhabitants of Ja'besh-gil'ead heard what the Philis'tines had done to Saul, ¹²all the valiant men arose, and went all night, and took the body of Saul and the bodies of his sons from the wall of Beth-shan; and they came to Ja'besh and burnt them there. ¹³And they took their bones and buried them under the tamarisk tree in Ja'besh, and fasted seven days.

31:1–13: 2 Sam 1:6–10; 1 Chron 10:1–12.

30:23 the LORD has given: David attributes the success of the recovery mission to God. Not only did the Lord assure him that the expedition would prosper (30:8), but the hand of divine Providence is evident in the fact that none of the family members are killed (30:2) and none of the plundered property is missing (30:19). David thus reasons that an equal distribution of spoil is in order, since no one can claim to have "taken" for himself what the Lord has "given" to all.

30:26–31 Spoils of the raid are parceled out to several towns in southern Judah. On the one hand, this is a gesture of thanks for assisting David in his flight from Saul. On the other, it is a political move to win Judah's support for David and facilitate his ascent to the throne (2 Sam 2:4).

30:31 Hebron: In southern Judah, nearly 20 miles south of Jerusalem. Hebron will become David's first royal capital (2 Sam 2:3; 5:1–5).

31:1–13 Saul, the tragic figure of 1 Samuel, comes to his tragic end. His self-destructive behavior culminates in an act of suicide (31:4), which is followed by the violent abuse of his corpse (31:9–10). The death of Saul occurred ca. 1010 B.C.

31:1 Mount Gilboa: About 20 miles southwest of the Sea of Galilee. It overlooks the Jezreel valley from the south.

31:2 the sons of Saul: Three of his four sons are slain in the battle (1 Chron 8:33). The lone survivor, Ish-bosheth (also called Eshbaal), will make a bid for kingship after Saul's death (2 Sam 2:8–10).

31:4 uncircumcised: A derogatory epithet for Philistines (14:6).

31:9 his head: Carried off and put on display in the Philistine temple of Dagon, according to 1 Chron 10:10. **news to their idols:** Triumph in the battle is (wrongly) taken as a sign that the gods of the Philistines have prevailed over the God of Israel.

31:10 Ashtaroth: Canaanite goddesses. See note on Judg 2:13. **Beth-shan:** Five miles east of Mt. Gilboa in the direction of the Jordan valley.

31:11 Jabesh-gilead: An Israelite settlement east of the Jordan. Warriors of Jabesh risk their lives to retrieve the body of Saul in gratitude for the time Saul rushed to their defense against the Ammonites (11:1–11). See note on 11:1.

31:12 burnt them: Cremation was not usual Israelite practice. Perhaps it was called for in this instance, where the bodies in question were shamefully abused and disfigured.

31:13 seven days: A traditional period of mourning for the dead (Gen 50:10; Jud 16:24; Sir 22:12).

---

^eGk Compare 1 Chron 10:9: Heb *to the house of their idols.*

STUDY QUESTIONS
1 Samuel

Chapter 1

For understanding

1. **1:2.** From what standard does polygamy deviate? Why was it tolerated in early biblical history? Whom did Elkanah most likely marry first? In Hebrew, what do the wives' names mean?
2. **1:3.** How does the title "LORD of hosts" describe Yahweh? Where is Shiloh, and what function did it serve?
3. **1:11.** In the Bible, what kind of promise is a vow? What was the only way married women in Israel could be released from a vow? Allegorically, how is Hannah a type of the Church at prayer? On a moral level, what moved God to answer her prayer? According to St. John Chrysostom, how does vigilance at prayer benefit us? How does this passage imply that Samuel is to be dedicated to Yahweh as a Nazirite? In what way is Samuel like Samson and St. John the Baptist?
4. **1:20.** What are two possible meanings of the Hebrew word *shemu'el*? What eight parallels exist between the Samuel story and the Pentateuch that suggest that Samuel is a new Moses? What expectation lies behind these parallels?

For application

1. **1:6–7.** Families often provide occasion for personal rivalries. In your experience, how do rivalries tend to begin, and what provocations are usually involved? How do you believe the Lord wants you to behave when provoked (e.g., when blamed for a perceived fault)?
2. **1:11.** Read the note for this verse. If you have ever made a conditional promise to the Lord in return for some favor, what was the outcome? How quickly did you fulfill your promise? Why is bargaining with God not always a good idea?
3. **1:12–15.** Think of a time when, like Hannah, you "poured out your soul before the Lord" because of a difficult situation. What was your approach to prayer? What spiritual helps did you use (e.g., books, certain devotions)? What did you learn about yourself and your relationship with God from your prayer?
4. **1:27.** What are some examples of prayers you made that were answered favorably? What did you do in thanksgiving for them?

Chapter 2

For understanding

1. **2:1–10.** As a prayer of praise, what does Hannah's Song celebrate? What is the theme of the song? How is that thematic pattern worked out through the book? How does Hannah's Song, which appears at the beginning of the Books of Samuel, parallel David's Song, which appears at the end? To what other biblical poems is Hannah's Song linked?
2. **2:10.** For whom was the title "his anointed" initially used, and how is it used here? How was the term translated "anointed" (Heb. *mashiah*) used in early Judaism?
3. **2:22.** What is known about the activities and responsibilities of female ministers who served in the Israelite sanctuary? What do later sources say of the women who served in the Second Temple? What are the consecrated women at Shiloh acting like here?
4. **2:31–36.** What does the oracle in these verses announce? When will the end come? In the context of 1 Samuel, what other fall does the fall of the priestly house of Eli mirror? According to St. Augustine, what does the end of the priestly house of Eli prefigure allegorically?
5. **2:35.** Whose house will be raised up in fulfillment of this prophecy? What will the Zadokite line of Aaronic priests constitute? What does Christian faith recognize as the fulfillment of this oracle? How is this most clearly stated in the Book of Hebrews?

For application

1. **2:2.** Why is praise of God one of the highest forms of prayer? If *God* does not need our praise, who does? Why?
2. **2:17.** Look up paragraphs 2118 through 2120 in the *Catechism*. What is sacrilege? Why is it an offense against the first commandment of the Decalogue?
3. **2:22–25.** What responsibility does a parent have for the behavior of his children when they are small, when they are teenagers, and when they are adults? In a situation like Eli's, where his adult children as priests are under his direct authority as high priest, what is his responsibility for their misbehavior?
4. **2:29–30.** What are some ways that modern parents have of honoring their children above the Lord? What honor does the Lord deserve? In Catholic understanding, how does the Lord honor those who honor him?

Chapter 3

For understanding

1. **3:3.** What lamp is referred to in this verse? What is perhaps the temple referred to here? Where is the Ark of God veiled from sight? From where does Yahweh speak?
2. **3:2–14.** In his call to be a prophet, what does Samuel receive in his first encounter with the Lord? Why does a new chapter in salvation history begin with Samuel's acceptance of his prophetic vocation?
3. **3:17.** What kind of formula is "may God do so to you"? What does it invoke, and how may its nature have been specified?
4. **3:19.** Of what is the Lord's presence in Samuel's life a sign? On what will success and failure in doing the Lord's will depend? What causes Samuel to be recognized as a true prophet and spokesman for God?

For application

1. **3:7.** In the context of this verse, what does "knowing the Lord" mean? How would you describe your "knowledge" of the Lord?
2. **3:9.** Eli offers Samuel some excellent spiritual advice. How do you discern when the Lord is speaking, and how do you listen for his voice? If you are unsure, what are you doing to learn how to listen to the Lord? For example, what spiritual tools are you using?
3. **3:11–15.** Considering Samuel's position, and the message of the Lord about the fate of Eli and his house, why might Eli have been afraid to pass the message on to him? If you had been in Samuel's place, how willing would you have been to inform Eli of impending doom?
4. **3:18.** What do you think of Eli's reply? What do you think Eli should have done in response? How does God warn us today when our wrongdoing or our inaction merits punishment? Can you think of any examples where he has actually issued such warnings to the modern world?

Chapter 4

For understanding

1. **4:1–11.** What are these verses about? What setbacks do the Israelites suffer, and what are they made to experience in this catastrophe?
2. **4:3.** Of what was the Ark of the Covenant a representation? While it proved devastating to Israel's enemies in the past, what is the problem with Israel's attitude toward its use in this battle, and why?
3. **4:21.** What does the name Ichabod mean? What does it memorialize? How long did the priestly line of Eli continue through Ichabod's brother Ahitub?
4. **Word Study: Glory (4:22).** In what various ways can the word *kabod*, often translated "glory", be used in Scripture? What does it mean when it refers to the glory of God? Since the Hebrew noun "glory" (*kabod*) is related to the verb "be heavy" (*kabed*), how is it likely the Israelites understood the glory of the Lord, and what would that explain in 1 Samuel with regard to the Philistines?

For application

1. **4:3.** How would you describe the confidence that the Israelites place in the Ark of the Covenant? How might respect for religious objects devolve into spiritual presumption or even superstition? What does CCC 1676 have to say on this subject?
2. **4:11.** Suppose that a major Christian site, such as St. Peter's in Rome, were desecrated or destroyed. What would be the impact on the faith of the Church at large? On your own? In what do Christians place their ultimate hope?
3. **4:21.** Read the note for this verse. How does the name of the child reflect the despair of his mother? If you have children, what motivated you to select the names you did for them? According to CCC 2156–59, what is the importance of a Christian name?

Chapter 5

For understanding

1. **5:1–12.** Where is the captured ark taken, and to what does its location lead? What do the plagues that ravaged Philistia recall? In both cases, upon whom do the judgments of God come?
2. **5:1.** Where is Ashdod? Of what league is it a part? To what god is it home, and of what is he the god?
3. **5:3.** Although capture of the ark seems to imply that Dagon is stronger than Yahweh, what is the truth of the matter as revealed by the idol's position before the ark?

For application

1. **5:5.** The *Catechism* (2110) describes superstition as "in some sense ... a perverse excess of religion". How does the behavior of the priests of Dagon in this verse resemble superstitious behavior with which you are familiar? Given the definition of superstition in CCC 2111, how serious a matter do you think superstition is?
2. **5:6–12.** What, if anything, do the Philistines learn from their experience with the Ark of God? What do they seem not to have learned? How does that compare with what happens when people flock to churches during a disaster but return to their old ways once the situation has passed?
3. **5:6–7.** What does it mean to *profane* a religious object? What connection do you see between these verses and what St. Paul says about the consequences of failure to discern the body of the Lord (1 Cor 11:29–30)? In addition to those that Paul mentions, what other consequences might ensue?

Chapter 6

For understanding

1. **6:7.** What is the idea behind calling for two milk cows upon which a yoke has never been placed? Why take their calves away from them? About what is their lowing perhaps a protest?
2. **6:9.** What does the name Beth-shemesh mean? Although several locations in ancient Canaan bear this name, which one is meant here? To whom was it home?
3. **6:19.** Why would the Lord slay some of the men—Israelites—of Beth-shemesh for looking into the ark?
4. **6:21.** What is the translation of the name Kiriath-jearim? Where is it located? How long does the ark remain there?

For application

1. **6:2.** Read the note for this verse. What forms of divination occur in our culture (see CCC 2116)? Why do people in our "technologically sophisticated" age continue to practice it? Why are Christians forbidden to engage in it?

2. **6:3.** At shrines such as Lourdes, pilgrims sometimes leave personal or medical items as votive offerings. What motivates them to do that? How different is their motive from that of the Philistine diviners?
3. **6:9.** The diviners propose a test to see if the plagues are caused by God or by chance. What are some methods you use to determine whether a course of action is according to God's will? How do you evaluate the results?
4. **6:20.** Of what are the people of Beth-shemesh afraid? How is their reaction like that of the Philistines before the Ark of God? Is their fear of the Lord a virtue (as Scripture indicates it should be) or something else?

Chapter 7

For understanding
1. **7:3–4.** How do the Israelites respond to Samuel's preaching of repentance? What helps establish Samuel as one of the great intercessors in Israel?
2. **7:3.** What does returning to the Lord "with all your heart" signify? What are the Ashtaroth? To whom is exclusive allegiance stipulated in the Deuteronomic covenant?
3. **7:6.** What is symbolic about drawing water and pouring it out before the Lord? What does Samuel provide as judge of Israel? Who are the last judges in biblical history?
4. **7:12.** How is the name Ebenezer translated? To whom is the boulder propped up as a memorial and named Ebenezer? Of what is it a memorial? What reversal in the story does its location mark?

For application
1. **7:3.** What is a "divided heart"? What do Sir 2:12–13 and Jas 1:7 have to say about praying with a divided heart? How does Samuel's direction to the house of Israel apply to the way you should pray?
2. **7:4.** Why would Israel, who knows that the Lord is its only God, worship the Baals and the Ashtaroth as well? What are some of the ways people have of "hedging their bets", spiritually, when it comes to seeking divine help?
3. **7:9.** According to 1 Sam 7:8–10 the answer to Samuel's intercessory prayer is swift. What is your experience with intercessory prayer? To how many answered prayers can you point? What happens to your faith when your prayer seems to go unanswered?
4. **7:12.** Samuel erects a stone as a memorial of answered prayer. How do you memorialize prayers that God has answered for you? What are some spiritual benefits of doing that?

Chapter 8

For understanding
1. **8:1–22.** What crisis moves Israel to clamor for a king? To what does the demand for a Gentile model of government amount? How do scholars often view these verses? Why might their hypothesis be open to question?
2. **8:5.** Why is kingship not wrong in itself, according to Scripture? What, then, is the problem here?
3. **8:9.** What does the Lord have in mind in telling Israelites about the "ways of the king"? What are four ways in which the burdens of a monarchy will outweigh its blessings?
4. **8:10.** What Hebrew wordplay does the text set up for the story that follows?

For application
1. **8:7.** What is there about human nature that makes it tend to resist the reign of God? What is the danger to men when God allows them to have things their own way?
2. **8:10–17.** Samuel lists only the drawbacks of a monarchical system of government; what are some of the benefits? What are some of the drawbacks and benefits of our system of government?
3. **8:18.** What is the wisdom in a parent allowing a child to experience the consequences of his actions rather than protecting him from them? How does God act like a parent to us when we choose to act sinfully?
4. **8:19–20.** What is the implied criticism of the system of judges in the people's reply to Samuel's warning? How does this amount to a criticism of God? What are the dangers in our being just like everyone else?

Chapter 9

For understanding
1. **9:1–2.** What do these verses introduce? From a human standpoint, what are Saul's credentials for leadership? Why do none of these natural qualifications carry weight with the Lord? What are we to notice about the lineage of Saul and Samuel, both of whom are God's answer to requests?
2. **9:9.** What is a "seer"? Why would anyone consult a seer? What is the purpose of the parenthetical explanation?
3. **9:12.** What is the "high place" referred to in this verse? Once Solomon builds the Jerusalem Temple, what will happen to sanctuaries like this?
4. **9:16.** What does the Hebrew term *nagid* mean? How is it used later to describe Solomon, and how is it used here? What will be the top priority for Saul's reign? How are the words that Yahweh speaks to Samuel similar to those he spoke to Moses, and how is the situation different?
5. **9:20.** Since the question about "all that is desirable" in this verse is slightly obscure, what, in view of the context, are two possible interpretations of its meaning?

For application
1. **9:2.** Why do you think studies show that tall, good-looking people are preferred for leadership positions or attain celebrity status more readily than short, plain people? If you had to promote a subordinate to a leadership position, what kind of person would you choose? What do you think God looks for in a leader of his people?

2. **9:8.** Read the note for this verse. What similar custom do Catholics observe when requesting church services at baptisms, weddings, and funerals? What does 1 Cor 9:8–11 say in this regard?
3. **9:21.** Why do you think Saul emphasizes his low status in response to Samuel's offer of "all that is desirable in Israel?" Is he being genuinely humble, or is some other consideration at work?

Chapter 10

For understanding
1. **10:1.** How is oil administered in the rite of anointing of priests, prophets, and kings? Of what is anointing a sign?
2. **10:5.** What does the name Gibeath-elohim mean, and to what does it probably refer? How would prophets in Israel minister? What is Samuel's role in a company of prophets? How would they behave when seized by the Spirit of God?
3. **10:6.** What does the Spirit of God do to leaders and deliverers in Israel? What is suggested by the expression "be turned into another man"? What do scholars often imagine happened to Saul?
4. **10:25.** With what does Samuel, like Moses, provide the kings of Israel? Where is Samuel's scroll kept?

For application
1. **10:1.** Read the note for this verse. What is the use of sacred chrism in the administration of Baptism? in Confirmation? in Holy Orders? Which of these sacraments makes the person a Christian?
2. **10:6.** What effect does the Holy Spirit have on the soul of a person who is validly baptized? According to CCC 1830, what are the gifts of the Holy Spirit supposed to accomplish in the moral life of a Christian?
3. **10:10–11.** Have you ever known anyone who has undergone a profound religious conversion? If so, what changes have you noticed in his behavior and in the reactions of others to these changes? Has your own behavior been changed because of the action of the Holy Spirit in your life?

Chapter 11

For understanding
1. **11:1.** Who is Nahash the Ammonite, and what does his name mean? Where is Ammon and to whom is its ancestry traced back? Where is Jabesh-gilead, and what may have been Saul's connection with it? What kind of treaty do the townspeople propose to Ammonite overlords?
2. **11:14.** What does the expression "there renew the kingdom" probably mean?
3. **11:15.** When is public recognition of Saul's kingship formally ratified? What kind of prowess do the Israelites want in a king? According to the Greek LXX, who performs the rite of coronation, and how does it affect the period of judges?

For application
1. **11:2.** Modern revolutionary armies sometimes rape or mutilate the people they are attacking. What is their purpose? What is the Church's teaching on the dignity of the human person? Do such tactics accord with it?
2. **11:6.** What does St. Paul mean when he advises, "Be angry but do not sin" (Eph 4:26)? What kinds of situations arouse a spirit of righteous anger in you? Does your anger result in any kind of positive action, or does it disappear after a while?
3. **11:7.** This verse speaks of the "dread of the LORD" falling on the people whom Saul threatened. What is the difference between the *dread* of the Lord that Saul inspires and the *fear* of the Lord that Scripture espouses?

Chapter 12

For understanding
1. **12:1–25.** What does Samuel's farewell speech affirm about Samuel himself, and of what does it accuse Israel? Although Samuel's career as a judge is ending, why is this not a retirement speech?
2. **12:11.** Who are Jerubbaal, Barak, and Jephthah? Why is it right for Samuel to rank himself among them?
3. **12:12.** According to Samuel, what does the vote for a king really express, and what is it despite?
4. **12:14.** What will observance of the Deuteronomic covenant keep alive? Between what is the choice between the blessings and the curses really a choice?

For application
1. **12:14.** Read the note for this verse. How does the choice between covenant blessings and curses apply to us today? What are the concrete, temporal blessings we should expect from loyalty to God, and what are the curses we should expect for disloyalty?
2. **12:20–21.** What effect should the sins of your past have on your spiritual future? What are some of the "vain things" you have pursued in the past that you found could not profit or save you?
3. **12:22.** How does Samuel's promise to the people of Israel apply to the Church in this century? What moral challenges do the People of God now face, and how should we respond to Samuel's encouragement not to fear?

Chapter 13

For understanding
1. **13:1.** What words have been lost from the Hebrew text? What help is the Greek LXX in filling in the blanks? What does the historian Josephus contend about the length of Saul's reign? What does Paul specify about it; and, on the apostle's reckoning, when would Saul have been king?

2. **13:9.** How is Saul's behavior a double act of disobedience? According to the Torah, what must the king do, and what could only the Levitical priests do?
3. **13:14.** What does Saul's disobedience mean he is denied? What is Saul allowed to retain for the time being? What will happen when he defies the Lord a second time? What is the significance of the advance reference to David? According to St. Augustine, what does the change from Saul to David foreshadow, allegorically?
4. **13:21.** What is a *pim*? What do the exorbitant prices for servicing Israelite farm equipment mean that the Philistines are doing?

For application
1. **13:5-7.** What is your response in times of spiritual warfare when it seems that the odds are stacked against you? Do you, as the people of Israel did, run for the caves and holes to hide, or do you follow Jesus (even if trembling)?
2. **13:8-9.** Following on the previous question, what do you do when God seems to delay or be silent at the very time you are losing support, patience, or other spiritual and personal resources? What often happens when you give up on prayer and take matters into your own hands?
3. **13:11-12.** Given Saul's excuse to Samuel for disobeying the latter's command to wait, what do you think Saul's real motive was? What is rationalization? What are some occasions on which you have rationalized a decision to act on your own rather than wait for God to act?
4. **13:14.** Read the note for v. 14. What do you think of the severity of the penalty for this one act of disobedience? Why is God not being unjust in warning that the penalty for one mortal sin is eternal punishment? (Hint: refer to CCC 1855-59.)

Chapter 14

For understanding
1. **14:3.** Who is Ahijah? What does Saul take him into his service to do? Where does Ahijah's brother Ahimelech minister? What is the ephod, and how is it worn?
2. **14:18.** Although the Hebrew text states that the item requested is the ark, how do important manuscripts of the Greek LXX read? What three reasons indicate that the Greek wording might be the original?
3. **14:21.** What possibility exists that Hebrews and Israelites might be two distinct groups? What could explain the Hebrews' presence in the land? According to Scripture, what is the relation between the two groups?
4. **14:41.** What are the Urim and the Thummim? Who has custody of them?

For application
1. **14:6.** According to the note for this verse, Jonathan's proposal is an example of heroic trust in God despite the odds. What are some acts of trust that you have made despite the circumstances of your life? How can such acts be examples of the virtue of prudence?
2. **14:10-11.** What is the tone of the Philistines' remark about Jonathan and his armor bearer? How does their attitude toward Hebrews validate Jonathan's belief that the Lord has given them into his hands?
3. **14:19-20.** Read the note for v. 19. According to the text, why does Saul change his mind about seeking the Lord's guidance? What does Saul's change of mind reveal about his character?
4. **14:43.** Even though Jonathan has inadvertently violated his father's oath, he admits his action without excusing it. How is this an example of the cardinal virtue of fortitude? Although we teach our children always to tell the truth, do our actions always accord with our advice?

Chapter 15

For understanding
1. **15:3.** What does "utterly destroy" mean here? As stipulated in Deuteronomy, what does this wartime policy require Israel to do? What does strict application of the law forbid?
2. **15:11.** To what does the use of the plural "commandments" in the Lord's rebuke stand in contrast? How does this detail hint at the reason why Saul is rejected as king?
3. **15:22.** What does the Lord regard as more important, sacrifice or obedience? Of what is the separation of moral life from liturgical life a contradiction? What, according to Scripture, makes worship an empty and vain gesture?
4. **15:29.** Although Scripture often speaks of God in a human way or as experiencing human emotions, what do other passages like this one insist about him? What does Scripture affirm about God even while describing him in anthropomorphic terms? What do theologians mean by the term "divine accommodation"? According to St. Gregory of Nyssa, what warning does God's repentance over Saul give to those who grow insolent through prosperity?

For application
1. **15:1-3.** These verses lead into one of what Pope Benedict XVI calls the "dark sayings of the Bible". In your own Scripture reading, how do you deal with these "dark sayings"? How do they fit into your understanding of what the word of God reveals to us about his love and our salvation?
2. **15:11.** The note for this verse refers to a "pattern of disobedience" to God's commands. How does a pattern of actions form a person's character? In the record of Saul's behavior that you have read so far, what details indicate a *pattern* of self-will? As a spiritual parent, how would you recommend that such a pattern be corrected?
3. **15:22-23.** *Why* is obedience better than sacrifice? How are rebellion and stubbornness like the sins of divination and idolatry? What is the internal link between these sins?
4. **15:29.** The note for this verse provides several examples of how Scripture speaks of God in anthropomorphic terms. Can you think of other examples? How do such terms influence your mental image of God and your personal relationship with him? If that mental image is negative (e.g., of the "wrathful God of the Old Testament"), what are some Old Testament passages that present a positive image?

Chapter 16

For understanding
1. **16:4.** Where is Bethlehem in relation to Jerusalem? In addition to being the hometown of David, whose birthplace is it anticipated to be? How does the evangelist Matthew draw attention to this?
2. **16:11.** Why does the Lord often bypass the wiser and stronger of the world, who appear more qualified to accomplish great things? In part, what is this intended to show?
3. **16:13.** What is the effect of the Spirit of the Lord upon David? What action symbolizes the anointing of the Spirit? How is the presence of the Spirit in David different from his presence in earlier figures? What does the Spirit descending on and abiding with David anticipate?
4. **16:14.** What evil spirit torments Saul? What ability of David gets him a position at court and in what capacity? What does the sending of an evil spirit "from the LORD" mean here? What biblical doctrine does the expression also underline, and to what polytheistic beliefs does it stand in contrast?

For application
1. **16:1.** Why does the Lord correct Samuel for grieving over Saul? How might grief over the fate of a loved one impede you from taking necessary action?
2. **16:3.** Why do you think the Lord directs Samuel to act but says that he will fill in the details only later? How is the Lord's direction to Samuel similar to his call to Abram to go to an unnamed country "that I will show you" (Gen 12:1)? What does the Lord want from you when you pray for direction?
3. **16:6–12.** How do you evaluate the character of persons with whom you want to associate? What role does appearance make in your assessment? What does it mean to base your judgment "on the heart" as the Lord does?
4. **16:14.** Read paragraph 1673 in the *Catechism*. Although the two overlap, how would you distinguish between a psychological and a spiritual problem? What indications would lead you to determine that the problem is primarily spiritual in nature?

Chapter 17

For understanding
1. **17:4.** What is Gath? How tall is "six cubits and a span"? Why do many scholars think that Goliath was actually six and a half feet tall? Either way, why is Goliath's height seen as colossal?
2. **17:35.** How does David's life as a good shepherd prefigure that of Jesus, the Good Shepherd? According to St. Caesarius of Arles, how is David, who smote the lion and the bear, allegorically a type of Christ?
3. **17:41–54.** From a human standpoint, what makes the duel between David and Goliath a mismatch at every level? Yet why is the mighty Philistine felled? What is the lesson for Israel? According to St. Augustine, what does this scene depict? What do the five stones represent? In contrast to Goliath, on what does David rely? What is significant about Goliath being felled by a stone hurled at his forehead?
4. **17:49.** In what way does Goliath's fall resemble the fall of the Philistine god Dagon before the ark?

For application
1. **17:4–11.** What "insurmountable" enemies do you face? What makes them look so fearsome? What, at bottom, causes you to fear them?
2. **17:16.** What is Goliath's aim in repeating his challenge morning and evening for forty days? What effect does a chronic problem have on a person's confidence in God? How might such a strategy of the devil be thwarted?
3. **17:38–39.** Although David disdains armor, on what kind of protection is he relying? According to Eph 6:10–17, what kind of armor do we need?
4. **17:47.** If the spiritual battle is the Lord's, what is our part in it? How should we act when it appears that the battle is against us?

Chapter 18

For understanding
1. **18:1–30.** With whom does David's popularity both soar and plummet? By whom is David loved? What is Saul's attitude at first, and how does it change? According to St. Melito of Sardis, where do we see the mystery of the Lord prefigured?
2. **18:3.** What is the covenant Jonathan makes with David? In Israel, as in the ancient Near East, what do covenants create? Thus, what does David consider Jonathan to be?
3. **18:4.** Of what is Jonathan's act of stripping himself of his robe, armor, sword, bow, and girdle symbolic? What has Jonathan somehow learned about David?
4. **18:17–27.** What does Saul pretend to desire? Why is his affection more apparent than real? How does Saul's attempt to rid himself of David ultimately backfire?

For application
1. **18:1–3.** What do you look for in a friendship? How would you describe the difference between an acquaintance with whom you are on good terms and a real friend?
2. **18:8–9.** Read paragraphs 2538–40 in the *Catechism* on the capital sin of envy. Of what are you most likely to experience envy—another's success, possessions, relationships? What can you do to eliminate this sin from your life?
3. **18:17–22.** Many people use relationships to manipulate others' fate. Have you ever been so manipulated or tried to maneuver others to achieve your aims? On reflection, what do you think of the ethics of such activity?

Chapter 19

For understanding
1. **19:6.** What will the demented Saul do, as he has done earlier with Jonathan?
2. **19:12.** What is the backdrop for David's prayers in Ps 59? From this point forward, what does David become?
3. **19:17.** Why does Michal lie to her father?

For application
1. **19:12.** The note for this verse mentions Ps 59, in which the Psalmist prays for deliverance from those who lie in wait to kill him. Have you ever needed protection or deliverance from evil? How earnestly have you sought the Lord for it? How has he provided it?
2. **19:17.** According to CCC 2488, the right to the communication of the truth "requires us in concrete situations to judge whether or not it is appropriate to reveal the truth to someone who asks for it". What is Saul's right to the communication of truth here? What is the morality of lying to protect someone's life (including one's own)?
3. **19:22–24.** God sometimes provides help in surprising ways. What is the most surprising intervention he has made in your life? How did it influence your trust in the Lord?

Chapter 20

For understanding
1. **20:5.** What part of the month does the New Moon indicate? How was it celebrated in ancient Israel?
2. **20:6.** What attitude does the author of 1 Samuel take toward David's patently untrue excuse to Saul? How does Scripture handle narrating the sins of men? What does St. Augustine say about why God's judgment is revealed or concealed in Scripture?
3. **20:8.** Why does David ask Jonathan to deal kindly with him? How is the Hebrew term *ḥesed* translated in v. 14 and then in v. 15?
4. **20:42.** Why do David and Jonathan swear "in the name of the LORD"? How will David honor his pledge to Jonathan years later?

For application
1. **20:8.** Read the note for this verse. Has your loyalty toward family or friends been tested in the recent or even remote past? What behavior on your part did the testing involve? Did your behavior strengthen or weaken your relationship with God?
2. **20:15.** What does the word "house" mean in this verse? How can loyalty toward friends apply to their families?
3. **20:23.** To what extent or in what way is the Lord "between" you and your closest friends? In other words, how potentially helpful or harmful are these friendships to your relationship with God?

Chapter 21

For understanding
1. **21:1.** Where is Nob? Why is it called the "city of priests"? What is stationed there? Who is Ahimelech, and what is his relationship to Eli?
2. **21:4.** What is the "holy bread" mentioned here? As what is it known? Who is permitted to eat it, and what does Ahimelech do for David and his men? When does Jesus appeal to this precedent? Why would Ahimelech specify that David's men have kept themselves from women?
3. **21:7.** What does Doeg the Edomite turn out to be? For which psalm is Doeg's treachery the background? From whom are Edomites descended?
4. **21:13.** Why does David feign insanity before the Philistines? From what is David trying to escape?

For application
1. **21:4.** What is the point of restricting lay people's contact with liturgical objects such as chalices, ciboria, and anything that houses the Eucharistic species? How do such restrictions enhance respect for the holiness of the Eucharist?
2. **21:5.** What contrasts do you note about ancient and modern attitudes toward sexual activity in this passage? Between married couples, when does sexual expression enhance personal holiness, and when does it hinder it?
3. **21:7.** Read Ps 52, alluded to in the note for this verse. How would you apply the psalm to yourself? For example, in what do you place most of your trust for your own welfare?

Chapter 22

For understanding
1. **22:1.** Where is the cave of Adullam? Whom does David, a fugitive and outlaw, begin to gather to himself in that hideout? For which psalms is David's time in this hideout the backdrop?
2. **22:3.** Where is Mizpeh? Where is Moab? Why does David travel here? What is David's probable family connection with Moab?
3. **22:13.** Why is Saul's accusation of Ahimelech baseless? How has David tricked Ahimelech? How would he have inquired of God for David?
4. **22:20.** Who is the lone survivor of the priestly line of Eli? What does David do for him? Why does Solomon later expel him from the priesthood?

Study Questions

For application
1. **22:1.** In Ps 142, alluded to in the note for this verse, the psalmist complains that he has nowhere to hide and that no one takes notice of him. Have you ever felt abandoned or persecuted by others or even by God? How would you pray at such times, and what would be the tone of your prayer?
2. **22:13.** If you have ever been falsely accused, how serious was the accusation? In such a situation, when is it appropriate for you to defend yourself, and when is it better to exercise the virtue of meekness and leave your defense to the Lord (as Moses and Jesus did)?
3. **22:17.** Why do Saul's servants refuse his order to kill the priests of Nob? What are some examples of physical attacks on clerical persons that have occurred in recent years? Why are such attacks made out of contempt for the clerical office considered more serious than physical attacks made out of dislike for the person?

Chapter 23

For understanding
1. **23:1–29.** Where do David and his men move about? How does David take each step, and how is he kept safe?
2. **23:16.** How does Jonathan strengthen David's hand? What does Jonathan know about David's trials?
3. **23:27.** Why is the timing of the Philistine raid upon Israel apparently an act of divine Providence?

For application
1. **23:10–11.** David seeks the Lord's guidance by means of the ephod with its sacred lots. What tools do you use to seek the Lord's guidance? For what indications do you look to determine his leading (as opposed to your own preference)?
2. **23:16–18.** What encouragement in your faith do you receive from fellow Christians? Acting on the example of David and Jonathan, what agreements might it be possible for you to make in order to give and receive such encouragement—for example, by forming small sharing groups?
3. **23:27.** Read the note for this verse. CCC 303 says that divine Providence is both concrete and immediate; have you experienced it as such? What is the difference between a mere coincidence and a providential act?

Chapter 24

For understanding
1. **24:3.** What are the sheepfolds mentioned here?
2. **24:5.** Why does David feel a twinge of regret for cutting off a fringe of Saul's robe? What does David know about the king's anointing?
3. **24:11.** According to St. John Chrysostom, what other victory does David's victory in the cave surpass? Why? What does David's sparing of Saul's life accomplish, spiritually? What application does Chrysostom make of this for us?

For application
1. **24:4.** According to the *Catechism* (2264–65), when would killing someone become a legitimate act of self-defense? Does the urging of David's men to kill the unsuspecting Saul amount to a legitimate act of self-defense?
2. **24:6.** What does David's respect for "the LORD's anointed" say about his character? What risk might he be taking with his men by rejecting their urge to harm Saul?
3. **24:12.** What does David say is the right way to get revenge against Saul? According to the Sermon on the Mount (Mt 5:22–25, 44), what should the Christian do when faced with the desire for vengeance?

Chapter 25

For understanding
1. **25:1.** What does Samuel spend a lifetime of service doing? What indicates that Samuel must have been widely admired among the people? Where is the wilderness of Paran? Why do some scholars prefer to follow the Greek LXX rendering of the "wilderness of Maon"?
2. **25:3.** What does the Hebrew name Nabal mean? Why is it a fitting nickname for the man? What is Abigail like? What is a Calebite?
3. **Word Study: A Sure House (25:28).** What does the Hebrew phrase *bayit ne'eman* designate? What is meant by a "sure house"? Which are the two such houses mentioned in 1 Samuel, and what is the idea behind them? What do the words of Abigail anticipate?
4. **25:29.** To what is "the bundle of the living" an allusion, and what common practice does it evoke? What does Abigail mean by wishing that David's enemies be flung out from the hollow of a sling? What are we to notice about Nabal in this regard?
5. **25:43–44.** Of what is the accumulation of wives a sign? In the Books of Samuel, what does it indicate?

For application
1. **25:10–11.** How reasonable is Nabal's answer to David's servants, given David's status as an outlaw? According to the note for v. 8, what should Nabal have done? According to CCC 1937, what is God's will with regard to sharing goods?
2. **25:21–22.** What do David's words reveal about his temper? Why does Jesus link anger with the fifth commandment of the Decalogue (Mt 5:22)?
3. **25:24–31.** What are the arguments Abigail uses in her speech to David to placate him? Where does she position herself? What do you think she means by "when the LORD has dealt well with my lord" in v. 31?
4. **25:37–38.** Although the text attributes Nabal's death to the Lord, what natural cause do you think hastened his death? What happens to a person when his "heart dies within him"? How is the virtue of hope an antidote?

Chapter 26

For understanding
1. **26:1–25.** What events do those in this chapter parallel? What does David's refusal to take violent action against Saul show about him?
2. **26:5.** Who is Abner? About what will David taunt him?
3. **26:19.** What is the heritage referred to here? What would exile from the land force David to do? What assumption is active here?

For application
1. **26:6–11.** If David has no intention of harming Saul, what is the purpose of infiltrating Saul's camp? Who or what does he expect will deal with Saul's life? When we are wronged, to whom should we look for vindication?
2. **26:19.** Commenting on the Our Father, the *Catechism* (2795) notes that sin "has exiled us from the land of the covenant", which is heaven. How are we to return to it?
3. **26:24.** According to CCC 2258 and following, why is human life precious to God? What gives man his dignity as a person, and what end does God have in mind for him (CCC 356–57)?

Chapter 27

For understanding
1. **27:1–12.** What does David pretend to do, and what is his real aim? How successful are this strategy and the deceitful front he is forced to maintain?
2. **27:5.** Why does David want to move away from Gath? Why does he flatter Achish?
3. **27:10.** Where is the Negeb? Who are the Jerahmeelites?

For application
1. **27:1.** In the previous chapter, David complained of a forced exile that would compel him to worship other gods, yet now he chooses a self-imposed exile for his own and his retainers' personal safety. Has necessity of some kind ever required you to move your home to another location? Did that move separate you from any attachment or relationship? Did you regard the move as permanent or temporary?
2. **27:8–12.** Read the note for these verses. By plundering and weakening Israel's enemies, how is David strengthening his future position against the Philistines? How commendable do you find his ruthlessness?

Chapter 28

For understanding
1. **28:3.** When did Samuel die? What does Saul accomplish in outlawing the mediums and wizards from the land?
2. **28:6.** For what is Saul looking from the acceptable means of divine revelation? What does the Lord's eerie silence constitute?
3. **28:8–19.** Why does Saul consult the witch of Endor? How does the visit end? What does the Mosaic Law say about necromancy? What does the episode also reveal about belief in life after death?
4. **28:18.** Why does the ghost of Samuel mention Saul's failure against Amalek?

For application
1. **28:1–2.** David's reply to Achish's offer is deliberately ambiguous. What does Achish think he means, and what do you (as the reader) think David means? By equivocating in this way, is David violating the eighth commandment of the Decalogue? (See CCC 2489.)
2. **28:6–7.** What do you do when you seek the Lord for guidance and he seems to be silent? Do you pray harder, adopt Saul's solution, give up, or take matters into your own hands?
3. **28:8–11.** Why does the Church condemn all forms of divination and magic? How are these practices contrary to the first commandment of the Decalogue? Have you ever dabbled in them, even if only in jest? What are some of the spiritual dangers of dabbling in the occult?

Chapter 29

For understanding
1. **29:1.** Where is Aphek? What happened there earlier in the book?
2. **29:3.** Why are the Philistine commanders not convinced of David's loyalty? What is the attitude of Achish?
3. **29:8.** What is David's response to the request of Achish to stay out of the battle? What is probably his real attitude? What is the difference between what Achish understands in David's words and what the reader understands?

For application
1. **29:3.** According to the note for this verse, Achish is naïve to the point of being gullible. If you have ever been tricked by someone you trusted, what did the betrayal do to your self-confidence? What did it do to your ability to trust others?
2. **29:6–7.** Suppose you were in the position of laying off an employee you valued. How would you announce the layoff in such a way as to soften the blow? What encouragement toward finding another job might you want to provide?
3. **29:8.** If you were in the position of the employee being laid off, how would you respond to the notice? How would you cope with your fears, disappointment, feelings of rejection, or anger toward your employer?

Chapter 30

For understanding
1. **30:14.** Who are the Cherethites? What will David later do with them?
2. **30:23.** To whom does David attribute the success of his mission? How is the hand of divine Providence made evident in this expedition? How does David thus reason about the distribution of the spoils?
3. **30:26–31.** How are the spoils of the raid parceled out? What might have motivated David's gesture toward southern Judah?
4. **30:31.** Where is Hebron? What will it become?

For application
1. **30:1–6.** People whose homes have been burglarized often say they feel personally violated. How might a victim of such a crime imitate David and strengthen himself in the Lord?
2. **30:23.** How often do you forget to thank the Lord for answered prayer? How important is gratitude in the spiritual life? What are some of the ways you have of expressing it?

Chapter 31

For understanding
1. **31:1–13.** What happens to Saul in this chapter? In what does his self-destructive behavior culminate? When does the death of Saul occur?
2. **31:9.** Where is Saul's head taken, and what is done with it? What is triumph in battle wrongly taken to mean by the Philistines?
3. **31:11.** Where is Jabesh-gilead? What do the warriors of Jabesh do for Saul?
4. How common in Israel is the practice of cremation? Why is it probably called for in this case?

For application
1. **31:4.** What seems to have been Saul's primary motive for his suicide? What does paragraph 2282 of the *Catechism* say about the moral responsibility of the one committing suicide?
2. **31:9.** Read the note for this verse. According to Samuel's prophecy in 28:16–19, what is the Lord's role in Saul's death? How do you understand Samuel's statement in 28:16 that "the Lord has turned from you and become your enemy"? What would cause the Lord to be anyone's enemy?

INTRODUCTION TO THE SECOND BOOK OF SAMUEL

Author and Date Little is known for certain about the authorship and date of the Books of Samuel. Jewish rabbinic tradition considers 2 Samuel to be the work of the prophets Nathan and Gad, both of whom appear in the book (7:2–4; 12:1–15; 24:11–14) and both of whom are credited with writing chronicles about the reign of King David (1 Chron 29:29–30). The ascription to Nathan and Gad could well be correct, at least in identifying the origins of the story in 2 Samuel, but it remains doubtful that such a tradition will be proven. The only source document explicitly mentioned by the narrator is the "Book of Jashar" (see 1:18). Nevertheless, contemporary scholarship hypothesizes that several written sources have been drawn together to form the bulk of 2 Samuel. Among these, scholars speak of a history of David's rise to kingship (1 Sam 16—2 Sam 5), a narrative about the Ark of the Covenant (1 Sam 4–6 along with 2 Sam 6), a court history that details the royal succession from David to Solomon (2 Sam 9—1 Kings 2), and an appendix (2 Sam 21–24). Whatever dates of composition may be assigned to such sources, it appears that the compiler of 2 Samuel must have lived in the period of the divided monarchy after 930 B.C. It is likewise reasonable to suppose that a later editor put the finishing touches on the Books of Samuel in the exilic period, sometime after 586 B.C. For additional information, see Introduction to 1 Samuel: *Author and Date*.

Title The Books of Samuel have appeared under different names over the centuries. The Hebrew title *Shemu᾽el*, "Samuel", was given to the whole story of 1 and 2 Samuel, which was originally a single book instead of two separate volumes. The Greek translation of the Hebrew Bible, known as the Septuagint, was the first to divide the text of Samuel into two books, labeling them "First and Second Kingdoms". Saint Jerome adopted this same division but altered the headings to "First and Second Kings". Modern editions of the Bible typically revert to using the Hebrew title but follow the Greek and Latin tradition of printing the text as two distinct books.

Place in the Canon Second Samuel occupies the same position in the Jewish and Christian canons of Scripture, although the former regards it as one of the "Former Prophets" and the latter designates it as one the "Historical Books". See introduction to 1 Samuel: *Place in the Canon*.

Structure Second Samuel covers three successive phases in the life of King David, followed by a carefully composed appendix. **(1)** The early chapters document the *triumphs* of David (1:1—10:19). These consist of the political, spiritual, and military victories that solidify David's rule over Judah in the south, over Israel in the north, and over several border states surrounding Palestine. **(2)** The central chapters present us with the *transgressions* of David (11:1—12:31). These are the king's ill-fated decisions to commit adultery and to attempt a cover-up, which involves him in murder. **(3)** The latter chapters of the book witness David pressed down by a multitude of *troubles* in the aftermath of his sin (13:1—20:26). These come in the form of family strife, political intrigue, and temporary exile from Jerusalem. **(4)** The appendix to the book preserves a sampling of David's poetry in the midst of additional stories about David (21:1—24:25), arranged in the form of a literary chiasm (the pattern a-b-c-c'-b'-a').

Content and Themes Second Samuel spans most of the kingship of David, who stands at the midpoint of salvation history between Abraham and Jesus Christ. Scripture remembers him as Israel's most admirable king, the one who restores Yahweh to the center of national life and who transforms his struggling nation into a kingdom of international prominence. This achievement is partly the result of intelligent leadership but mainly the result of the Lord's blessing. Both dimensions of David's life, the political and the spiritual, constitute the threads that tie together the main elements of the story line.

(1) At one level, 2 Samuel reads like David's *political biography*. It shows him to be a master politician with a flair for diplomacy and military leadership. His first major success is to unite the twelve tribes under his leadership after long centuries of intertribal tension and conflict. This he accomplishes in two stages: first, he gains the loyalty of his own tribe, Judah (2:1–4), and then he forges a covenant of kingship with the remaining tribes from the north (5:1–5). With a level of national solidarity achieved, David moves to establish a royal capital. His city of choice is Jerusalem, strategically located between Judah in the south and the majority of Israel up north (5:6–12). From this base of operations, he launches a series of campaigns against hostile nations encircling Israel (8:1–14). The successful subjugation of these neighboring states brings wealth to his small empire (8:7–8, 10) and peace to his borders (7:1). This enables David to focus on forming a working government with advisory and cabinet positions (8:16–18; 20:23–26). Part of David's success must be credited, not only to his aptitude for organization and leadership, but also to his charismatic personality. In times of political upheaval, nearly every member of his administration remains loyal to the king (15:15–18, 21), and even in times of dangerous combat, his elite warriors have no qualms about risking their own lives to protect the life of the king and to fulfill his every wish (21:15–17; 23:13–17).

(2) At another level, 2 Samuel reads like David's *spiritual biography*. For behind the props of David's public life is the story of his personal relationship with God. Early on, we see a deeply religious man who is prayerful, obedient, and zealous for the Lord. David seeks Yahweh's guidance on important matters (2:1; 5:19, 23); with joy and celebration he moves the Ark of the Covenant to his capital city (6:1–19); he blesses his people in the name of the Lord (6:18, 20; 19:39); and eventually he is pressed with a desire to build a Temple worthy of the God of Israel (7:2–5). At one point, David even speaks with a clear conscience about his "righteousness" in the sight of the Lord (22:21). Small wonder that a man of such ardent spiritual commitment would be blessed by the Lord with such extraordinary success (5:12; 8:6, 14; 22:21–46). But David also shows himself to be a human figure. He, too, struggles to be faithful, and at one tragic moment, he lands himself in serious sin. Idleness leads him to lust (11:2); passion drives him to commit adultery (11:4); and a fear of the consequences moves him to arrange for the murder of an innocent man (11:14–15). This is abominable behavior, to be sure, and the narrator makes no attempt to excuse him. Still, David refuses to wallow in sin and is quick to confess his wrongdoing and seek forgiveness (12:13; 24:10, 17). He is not exempt from the Lord's discipline, however. In many ways, the second half of the book is a painful display of David enduring one hardship after another as punishment for his crimes. From these David emerges a more humble man as he learns to trust in God's plan for his life (16:10–12) and to yearn for God's mercy for his failings (24:14).

Christian Perspective Second Samuel prepares the way for Jesus Christ by presenting us with David, the ideal king. In various ways, David is a type of the Messiah to come: he is righteous before the Lord (22:21–25); he reigns as the Lord's "anointed" (22:51); he suffers at the hands of his own people (chaps. 15–18); and in the midst of bitter testing, his closest friends remain loyal, although one of them betrays him (15:12, 15–21, 31). More importantly, the covenant of kingship that Yahweh establishes with David is the bedrock of New Testament teaching about Christ and the kingdom of God. The Lord's pledge to David is to build him an everlasting dynasty and to make his royal offspring the son of Yahweh and the builder of a glorious Temple (see Nathan's oracle in 7:8–16). Jesus is the messianic fulfillment of this ancient Davidic covenant: he is grafted into David's royal line (Mt 1:1–16); he is chosen to sit on David's throne (Lk 1:32–33); he is proclaimed the Son of God and King of Israel (Mt 16:16; Jn 1:49); and he builds the living Temple of God from his faithful disciples (Mt 16:18; 1 Pet 2:4–10). According to the very earliest Christian preaching, this is all in fulfillment of the Lord's oath to David (Acts 2:22–36).

OUTLINE OF THE SECOND BOOK OF SAMUEL

1. David's Triumphs (chaps. 1–10)
    A. David Laments Saul and Jonathan (chap. 1)
    B. David Reigns over Judah (chaps. 2–4)
    C. David Reigns over All Israel (chap. 5)
    D. David Moves the Ark to Jerusalem (chap. 6)
    E. The Davidic Covenant (chap. 7)
    F. David Conquers Nations (chaps. 8–10)

2. David's Transgressions (chaps. 11–12)
    A. David Sins: Adultery and Murder (chap. 11)
    B. David Repents: Nathan's Parable and the Death of a Child (chap. 12)

3. David's Troubles (chaps. 13–20)
    A. Amnon's Incest and Death (13:1–33)
    B. Absalom's Exile and Return (13:34—14:33)
    C. Absalom's Revolt and Death (chaps. 15–18)
    D. David's Return to Jerusalem (chap. 19)
    E. Sheba's Revolt (chap. 20)

4. Appendix (chaps. 21–24)
   A. Saul's Bloodguilt (21:1–14)
   B. David and the Philistines (21:15–22)
   C. David's Poetry (22:1—23:7)
   D. David's Mighty Warriors (23:8–39)
   E. David's Sinful Census (24:1–25)

THE SECOND BOOK OF
SAMUEL

David Mourns Saul and Jonathan

1 After the death of Saul, when David had returned from the slaughter of the Amal′ekites, David remained two days in Zik′lag; ²and on the third day, behold, a man came from Saul's camp, with his clothes torn and earth upon his head. And when he came to David, he fell to the ground and did obeisance. ³David said to him, "Where do you come from?" And he said to him, "I have escaped from the camp of Israel." ⁴And David said to him, "How did it go? Tell me." And he answered, "The people have fled from the battle, and many of the people also have fallen and are dead; and Saul and his son Jonathan are also dead." ⁵Then David said to the young man who told him, "How do you know that Saul and his son Jonathan are dead?" ⁶And the young man who told him said, "By chance I happened to be on Mount Gilbo′a; and there was Saul leaning upon his spear; and behold, the chariots and the horsemen were close upon him. ⁷And when he looked behind him, he saw me, and called to me. And I answered, 'Here I am.' ⁸And he said to me, 'Who are you?' I answered him, 'I am an Amal′ekite.' ⁹And he said to me, 'Stand beside me and slay me; for anguish has seized me, and yet my life still lingers.' ¹⁰So I stood beside him, and slew him, because I was sure that he could not live after he had fallen; and I took the crown which was on his head and the armlet which was on his arm, and I have brought them here to my lord."

11 Then David took hold of his clothes, and tore them; and so did all the men who were with him; ¹²and they mourned and wept and fasted until evening for Saul and for Jonathan his son and for the people of the Lord and for the house of Israel, because they had fallen by the sword. ¹³And David said to the young man who told him, "Where do you come from?" And he answered, "I am the son of a sojourner, an Amal′ekite." ¹⁴David said to him, "How is it you were not afraid to put forth your hand to destroy the Lord's anointed?" ¹⁵Then David called one of the young men and said, "Go, fall upon him." And he struck him so that he died. ¹⁶And David said to him, "Your blood be upon your head; for your own mouth has testified against you, saying, 'I have slain the Lord's anointed.'"

David's Lamentation

17 And David lamented with this lamentation over Saul and Jonathan his son, ¹⁸and he said it[a] should be taught to the people of Judah; behold, it is written in the Book of Jashar.[b] He said:

¹⁹"Your glory, O Israel, is slain upon your high
  places!
  How are the mighty fallen!
²⁰Tell it not in Gath,
  publish it not in the streets of Ash′kelon;
lest the daughters of the Philis′tines rejoice,
  lest the daughters of the uncircumcised exult.

1:6-10: 1 Sam 31:1–13; 1 Chron 10:1–12.

1:1-16 David receives news of Saul's death, confirmed by the delivery of the king's crown and royal armpiece (1:10). However, the story of his demise is suspicious and ultimately incriminating. Saul committed suicide in 1 Sam 31:4, but here the messenger fabricates a tale intended to make himself look like a hero (1:9-10). Apparently the messenger has come to David with the expectation of reward (4:10); instead, he utters his own death sentence (1:16).
1:1 Amalekites: A nomadic people of the Sinai Peninsula. Only days earlier, David made a strike against the Amalekites in retaliation for taking his family and fellow townspeople captive (1 Sam 30:1-20). **Ziklag:** The current residence of David and his followers (1 Sam 27:6). It lies on the border between Judah and Philistia in southwest Canaan.
1:2 clothes torn ... earth: Expressions of extreme distress (Gen 37:34; 1 Sam 4:12).
1:6 Mount Gilboa: About 20 miles southwest of the Sea of Galilee. It was the site of Israel's recent defeat by the Philistines (1 Sam 31:1).

1:10 I took the crown: Evidently the Amalekite found the slain king before the Philistines decapitated his corpse (1 Sam 31:8-9).
1:14 the Lord's anointed: A title for the kings of Israel, who are anointed with oil and the power of the Spirit (1 Sam 16:13; CCC 695). David has profound respect for the office of the king and a holy fear of harming the Lord's representative (1 Sam 24:6). The Amalekite has no such respect, and it costs him his life (1:15). See note on 1 Sam 2:10.
1:16 blood be upon your head: An idiom for bearing the guilt of bloodshed (3:28-29; Deut 19:10; Josh 2:19; Mt 27:25).
1:18 Book of Jashar: A collection of epic Hebrew poetry that commemorates significant events in the early history of Israel. Little else is known about this ancient work, which has since been lost, except that another excerpt appears in Josh 10:12-13.
1:19-27 David's song of lament for Saul and Jonathan. Its thematic refrain is the downfall of the "mighty" (1:19, 25, 27). David likewise sings a lament at the death of Abner (3:33-34).
1:19 Your glory: Or "The gazelle". Either way, the reference is to King Saul.
1:20 Gath ... Ashkelon: Prominent cities of the Philistines. See note on Judg 3:3.

---

[a] Gk: Heb *the Bow*.
[b] Or *The upright*.

²¹"You mountains of Gilbo'a,
 let there be no dew or rain upon you,
 nor upsurging of the deep!ᶜ
For there the shield of the mighty was defiled,
 the shield of Saul, not anointed with oil.

²²"From the blood of the slain,
 from the fat of the mighty,
the bow of Jonathan turned not back,
 and the sword of Saul returned not empty.

²³"Saul and Jonathan, beloved and lovely!
 In life and in death they were not divided;
they were swifter than eagles,
 they were stronger than lions.

²⁴"You daughters of Israel, weep over Saul,
 who clothed you daintily in scarlet,
 who put ornaments of gold upon your apparel.

²⁵"How are the mighty fallen
 in the midst of the battle!

"Jonathan lies slain upon your high places.
²⁶ I am distressed for you, my brother Jonathan;
 very pleasant have you been to me;
 your love to me was wonderful,
 passing the love of women.*

²⁷"How are the mighty fallen,
 and the weapons of war perished!"

David Anointed King of Judah

2 After this David inquired of the LORD, "Shall I go up into any of the cities of Judah?" And the LORD said to him, "Go up." David said, "To which shall I go up?" And he said, "To He'bron." ²So David went up there, and his two wives also, Ahin'o-am of Jezre'el, and Ab'igail the widow of Nabal of Carmel. ³And David brought up his men who were with him, every one with his household; and they dwelt in the towns of He'bron. ⁴And the men of Judah came, and there they anointed David king over the house of Judah.

When they told David, "It was the men of Ja'besh-gil'ead who buried Saul," ⁵David sent messengers to the men of Ja'besh-gil'ead, and said to them, "May you be blessed by the LORD, because you showed this loyalty to Saul your lord, and buried him! ⁶Now may the LORD show mercy and faithfulness to you! And I will do good to you because you have done this thing. ⁷Now therefore let your hands be strong, and be valiant; for Saul your lord is dead, and the house of Judah has anointed me king over them."

Ish-bosheth Made King of Israel

8 Now Abner the son of Ner, commander of Saul's army, had taken Ish-bo'sheth† the son of Saul, and brought him over to Ma"hana'im; ⁹and he made him king over Gilead and the Ash'urites and Jezre'el and E'phraim and Benjamin and all Israel. ¹⁰Ish-bo'sheth, Saul's son, was forty years old when he began to reign over Israel, and he reigned two years. But the house of Judah followed David. ¹¹And the time that David was king in He'bron over the house of Judah was seven years and six months.

The Battle of Gibeon

12 Abner the son of Ner, and the servants of Ish-bo'sheth the son of Saul, went out from Ma"hana'im to Gib'eon. ¹³And Jo'ab the son of Zeru'iah, and the servants of David, went out and met them

---

1:21 no dew or rain upon you: May reflect the ancient belief that a hero's death could trigger drought and famine. **not anointed with oil:** Oil was rubbed on leather shields to slick the surface and to act as a preservative (Is 21:5).

1:26 my brother: In view of the covenant of brotherhood previously sealed between David and Jonathan. Legal kinship rather than biological kinship underlies this language. See note on 1 Sam 18:3. **passing the love of women:** Jonathan was a dear and loyal friend to David (1 Sam 18:1; 20:17). The statement, so imbued with emotion, should not be generalized to mean that bonds of personal friendship are necessarily stronger or deeper than the bonds of marital love.

1:27 weapons of war: A poetic depiction of Saul and Jonathan, both of whom were skilled fighters and military strategists.

2:1 Hebron: The leading city of Judah at this time, almost 20 miles south of Jerusalem. It serves as David's royal capital for more than seven years (5:5). Caleb and his family settled in Hebron at the time of the Conquest (Josh 14:13–15), although the city was known to the Patriarchs long before this (Gen 13:18; 35:27).

2:4 anointed David: A public ceremony is conducted to formalize the private anointing of David by Samuel (1 Sam 16:13). **house of Judah:** The southern tribe of Judah, along with the Simeonites who dwell among them (Josh 19:1). **Jabesh-gilead:** An Israelite settlement east of the Jordan. David praises the city for its loyalty to Saul (1 Sam 31:11–13) and invites the people to acknowledge him as Saul's royal successor (2:7). David apparently failed to win their support as long as Ish-bosheth (Saul's son) was ruling the Transjordan (2:8–9).

2:8 Abner: Saul's cousin and chief military officer (1 Sam 14:50). **Ish-bosheth:** Saul's only surviving son, also called "Eshbaal" (1 Chron 8:33). The name is a derogatory epithet that means "man of shame." Abner's attempt to make Ish-bosheth the successor to Saul was doomed from the outset, for the Lord had already declared Saul unworthy of a dynasty (1 Sam 13:13–14). **Mahanaim:** East of the Jordan, isolated from Philistine threats in the west. For a short time it served as the capital of northern Israel. The name in Hebrew means "two armies" or "two camps" (Gen 32:2).

2:9 all Israel: Ish-bosheth claims the loyalty of the northern tribes settled east and west of the Jordan.

2:12 Gibeon: Roughly six miles northwest of Jerusalem.

2:13 Joab: David's chief military officer (8:16). **the pool:** Archaeologists have uncovered a giant water reservoir in Gibeon, measuring more than 80 feet deep and more than 35 feet in diameter. It was thus known as "the great pool" at Gibeon (Jer 41:12).

ᶜCn: Heb *fields of offerings.*
*1:26: Vulgate adds, "As the mother loves her only son, so did I love you."
†2:8, *Ish-bosheth:* "Man of shame." The name was really Ish-baal, "Man or servant of Baal," but the writer could not bring himself to pronounce so profane a name, especially as it belonged to an Israelite; cf. 1 Chron 8:33; 9:39, where the name is given as Esh-baal.

at the pool of Gib′eon; and they sat down, the one on the one side of the pool, and the other on the other side of the pool. ¹⁴And Abner said to Jo′ab, "Let the young men arise and play* before us." And Joab said, "Let them arise." ¹⁵Then they arose and passed over by number, twelve for Benjamin and Ish-bo′sheth the son of Saul, and twelve of the servants of David. ¹⁶And each caught his opponent by the head, and thrust his sword in his opponent's side; so they fell down together. Therefore that place was called Hel′-kath-hazzu′rim,ᵈ which is at Gib′eon. ¹⁷And the battle was very fierce that day; and Abner and the men of Israel were beaten before the servants of David.

18 And the three sons of Zeru′iah were there, Jo′ab, Abi′shai, and As′ahel. Now Asahel was as swift of foot as a wild gazelle; ¹⁹and As′ahel pursued Abner, and as he went he turned neither to the right hand nor to the left from following Abner. ²⁰Then Abner looked behind him and said, "Is it you, As′ahel?" And he answered, "It is I." ²¹Abner said to him, "Turn aside to your right hand or to your left, and seize one of the young men, and take his spoil." But As′ahel would not turn aside from following him. ²²And Abner said again to As′ahel, "Turn aside from following me; why should I strike you to the ground? How then could I lift up my face to your brother Jo′ab?" ²³But he refused to turn aside; therefore Abner struck him in the belly with the butt of his spear, so that the spear came out at his back; and he fell there, and died where he was. And all who came to the place where As′ahel had fallen and died, stood still.

24 But Jo′ab and Abi′shai pursued Abner; and as the sun was going down they came to the hill of Ammah, which lies before Giah on the way to the wilderness of Gib′eon. ²⁵And the Benjaminites gathered themselves together behind Abner, and became one band, and took their stand on the top of a hill. ²⁶Then Abner called to Jo′ab, "Shall the sword devour for ever? Do you not know that the end will be bitter? How long will it be before you bid your people turn from the pursuit of their brethren?" ²⁷And Jo′ab said, "As God lives, if you had not spoken, surely the men would have given up the pursuit of their brethren in the morning." ²⁸So Jo′ab blew the trumpet; and all the men stopped, and pursued Israel no more, nor did they fight any more.

29 And Abner and his men went all that night through the Ar′abah; they crossed the Jordan, and marching the whole forenoon they came to Ma″hana′im. ³⁰Jo′ab returned from the pursuit of Abner; and when he had gathered all the people together, there were missing of David's servants nineteen men besides As′ahel. ³¹But the servants of David had slain of Benjamin three hundred and sixty of Abner's men. ³²And they took up As′ahel, and buried him in the tomb of his father, which was at Bethlehem. And Jo′ab and his men marched all night, and the day broke upon them at He′bron.

Abner Defects to David

3 There was a long war between the house of Saul and the house of David; and David grew stronger and stronger, while the house of Saul became weaker and weaker.

2 And sons were born to David at He′bron: his first-born was Amnon, of Ahin′o-am of Jezre′el; ³and his second, Chil′e-ab, of Ab′igail the widow of Nabal of Carmel; and the third, Ab′salom the son of Ma′acah the daughter of Talmai king of Ge′shur; ⁴and the fourth, Adoni′jah the son of Haggith; and the fifth, Shephati′ah the son of Abi′tal; ⁵and the sixth, Ith′re-am of Eglah, David's wife. These were born to David in He′bron.

6 While there was war between the house of Saul and the house of David, Abner was making himself strong in the house of Saul. ⁷Now Saul

---

3:2–5: 1 Chron 3:1–4.

2:14 play before us: A form of combat entertainment is meant.

2:15 twelve … twelve: The 24-man duel is a way of settling the conflict without the need for war on a larger scale. However, since none of the warriors survives, there is no clear victor and a fierce battle ensues anyway (2:17).

2:18 Zeruiah: One of David's sisters (1 Chron 2:16). The brothers Joab, Abishai, and Asahel are thus David's nephews.

2:21 Turn aside: Already defeated, Abner wants a truce that will end the violence (2:22, 26).

2:28 blew the trumpet: A signal to disengage the enemy. See word study: *Trumpet* at Judg 6:34.

2:32 Bethlehem: Five miles south of Jerusalem. It is the hometown of David and his family (1 Sam 17:12).

3:1 long war: Lasts at least the two years David has to contend with Ish-bosheth (2:10).

3:2–5 David fathers six sons by six wives during his time in Hebron. This is not surprising, since the multiplication of wives was customary among the monarchs of the ancient Near East. Neither is it commendable, however, since Deuteronomy disallows this very thing for the kings of Israel (Deut 17:14–17). Notice that the author of 2 Samuel simply describes the situation without endorsing or even evaluating the morality of David's actions. See note on 1 Sam 20:6.

3:3 Geshur: A small kingdom east of the Sea of Galilee. David's union with Maacah may have been a political marriage that helped to cement an alliance between King Talmai and the house of Judah.

3:7 my father's concubine: Taking one of Saul's lesser wives is a political move more than an act of passion or lust. Abner, in typical Near Eastern fashion, is making a public bid for the throne of the house of Saul. Later, Absalom will use sexual aggression in a plot to usurp the royal authority of David (16:21–22).

ᵈThat is *the field of sword-edges.*
*2:14, *play:* He meant "do battle." The idea was to settle the matter by a fight between two select groups of soldiers.

had a concubine, whose name was Rizpah, the daughter of Ai'ah; and Ish-bo'sheth said to Abner, "Why have you gone in to my father's concubine?" [8]Then Abner was very angry over the words of Ish-bo'sheth, and said, "Am I a dog's head of Judah? This day I keep showing loyalty to the house of Saul your father, to his brothers, and to his friends, and have not given you into the hand of David; and yet you charge me today with a fault concerning a woman. [9]God do so to Abner and more also, if I do not accomplish for David what the Lord has sworn to him, [10]to transfer the kingdom from the house of Saul, and set up the throne of David over Israel and over Judah, from Dan to Be'er-she'ba." [11]And Ish-bo'sheth could not answer Abner another word, because he feared him.

12 And Abner sent messengers to David at He'bron, [e] saying, "To whom does the land belong? Make your covenant with me, and behold, my hand shall be with you to bring over all Israel to you." [13]And he said, "Good; I will make a covenant with you; but one thing I require of you; that is, you shall not see my face, unless you first bring Michal, Saul's daughter, when you come to see my face." [14]Then David sent messengers to Ish-bo'sheth Saul's son, saying, "Give me my wife Michal, whom I betrothed at the price of a hundred foreskins of the Philis'tines." [15]And Ish-bo'sheth sent, and took her from her husband Pal'ti-el the son of La'ish. [16]But her husband went with her, weeping after her all the way to Bahu'rim. Then Abner said to him, "Go, return"; and he returned.

17 And Abner conferred with the elders of Israel, saying, "For some time past you have been seeking David as king over you. [18]Now then bring it about; for the Lord has promised David, saying, 'By the hand of my servant David I will save my people Israel from the hand of the Philis'tines, and from the hand of all their enemies.'" [19]Abner also spoke to Benjamin; and then Abner went to tell David at He'bron all that Israel and the whole house of Benjamin thought good to do.

20 When Abner came with twenty men to David at He'bron, David made a feast for Abner and the men who were with him. [21]And Abner said to David, "I will arise and go, and will gather all Israel to my lord the king, that they may make a covenant with you, and that you may reign over all that your heart desires." So David sent Abner away; and he went in peace.

Abner Is Killed by Joab

22 Just then the servants of David arrived with Jo'ab from a raid, bringing much spoil with them. But Abner was not with David at He'bron, for he had sent him away, and he had gone in peace. [23]When Jo'ab and all the army that was with him came, it was told Joab, "Abner the son of Ner came to the king, and he has let him go, and he has gone in peace." [24]Then Jo'ab went to the king and said, "What have you done? Behold, Abner came to you; why is it that you have sent him away, so that he is gone? [25]You know that Abner the son of Ner came to deceive you, and to know your going out and your coming in, and to know all that you are doing."

26 When Jo'ab came out from David's presence, he sent messengers after Abner, and they brought him back from the cistern of Sirah; but David did not know about it. [27]And when Abner returned to He'bron, Jo'ab took him aside into the midst of the gate to speak with him privately, and there he struck him in the belly, so that he died, for the blood of As'ahel his brother. [28]Afterward, when David heard of it, he said, "I and my kingdom are for ever guiltless before the Lord for the blood of Abner the son of Ner. [29]May it fall upon the head of Jo'ab, and upon all his father's house; and may the house of Joab never be without one who has

---

3:9 **God do so to Abner:** A conditional self-curse. See note on Ruth 1:17. **the Lord has sworn:** An oath not previously mentioned. Transfer of royal power from Saul to David can be traced back to the words of Samuel in 1 Sam 13:14; 15:28.

3:10 **Dan to Beer-sheba:** The full extent of Israelite territory from north to south. David is destined to unite all the tribes of Israel under the mantle of his kingship (5:1–5).

3:12–16 Abner shifts his allegiance from Ish-bosheth to David. This is surprising, given his loyalty to Saul over the years (3:8) and his attempt to perpetuate Saul's kingdom (2:8-9). It must have dawned on him that Ish-bosheth, weak and unassertive, was no match for David and his unstoppable rise to power.

3:12 **Hebron:** David's initial capital in southern Judah. See note on 2:1.

3:13 **Michal:** Given to David in marriage (1 Sam 18:27) but then given to another man (1 Sam 25:44).

3:17 **you have been seeking:** David has long been popular among the tribes, even among those closest to the late King Saul (1 Sam 18:1–5, 16, 20).

3:18 **save my people:** David will be a political savior to Israel, securing the borders of the country and giving the Lord's people rest from surrounding enemy threats (5:17–25; 7:1; 8:1–14). **Philistines:** Hostile neighbors of Israel in southwest Canaan. See note on Judg 3:3.

3:19 **Benjamin:** The tribe of Saul and his son Ish-bosheth (1 Sam 9:1–2).

3:21 **make a covenant:** The plan is carried out in 5:1–5.

3:22–30 Joab's assassination of Abner. The narrative stresses the innocence and ignorance of David in the face of this treachery: the king sends Abner away "in peace" (3:23), and he does not even "know" that Joab is plotting Abner's demise behind his back (3:26). David can thus exclaim that he is "guiltless before the Lord" (3:28).

3:27 **for the blood:** Joab regards himself an "avenger of blood", a kinsman responsible for bringing justice to the perpetrator who killed his brother Asahel (3:30, referring to 2:23). Taking life for life as retribution for murder was customary in ancient tribal societies (Num 35:19–21).

---

[e] Gk: Heb *where he was.*

a discharge, or who is leprous, or who holds a spindle, or who is slain by the sword, or who lacks bread!" ³⁰So Jo'ab and Abi'shai his brother slew Abner, because he had killed their brother As'ahel in the battle at Gib'eon.

31 Then David said to Jo'ab and to all the people who were with him, "Tear your clothes, and put on sackcloth, and mourn before Abner." And King David followed the bier. ³²They buried Abner at He'bron; and the king lifted up his voice and wept at the grave of Abner; and all the people wept. ³³And the king lamented for Abner, saying,

"Should Abner die as a fool dies?
³⁴Your hands were not bound,
    your feet were not fettered;
as one falls before the wicked
    you have fallen."

And all the people wept again over him. ³⁵Then all the people came to persuade David to eat bread while it was yet day; but David swore, saying, "God do so to me and more also, if I taste bread or anything else till the sun goes down!" ³⁶And all the people took notice of it, and it pleased them; as everything that the king did pleased all the people. ³⁷So all the people and all Israel understood that day that it had not been the king's will to slay Abner the son of Ner. ³⁸And the king said to his servants, "Do you not know that a prince and a great man has fallen this day in Israel? ³⁹And I am this day weak, though anointed king; these men the sons of Zeru'iah are too hard for me. The LORD repay the evildoer according to his wickedness!"

Ish-bosheth Is Assassinated

4 When Ish-bo'sheth, Saul's son, heard that Abner had died at He'bron, his courage failed, and all Israel was dismayed. ²Now Saul's son had two men who were captains of raiding bands; the name of the one was Ba'anah, and the name of the other Re'chab, sons of Rimmon a man of Ben-

jamin from Be-er'oth (for Be-eroth also is reckoned to Benjamin; ³the Be-er'othites fled to Gitta'im, and have been sojourners there to this day).

4 Jonathan, the son of Saul, had a son who was crippled in his feet. He was five years old when the news about Saul and Jonathan came from Jezre'el; and his nurse took him up, and fled; and, as she fled in her haste, he fell, and became lame. And his name was Mephib'osheth.

5 Now the sons of Rimmon the Be-er'othite, Re'chab and Ba'anah, set out, and about the heat of the day they came to the house of Ish-bo'sheth, as he was taking his noonday rest. ⁶And behold, the doorkeeper of the house had been cleaning wheat, but she grew drowsy and slept; so Re'chab and Ba'anah his brother slipped in.ᶠ ⁷When they came into the house, as he lay on his bed in his bedchamber, they struck him, and slew him, and beheaded him. They took his head, and went by the way of the Ar'abah all night, ⁸and brought the head of Ish-bo'sheth to David at He'bron. And they said to the king, "Here is the head of Ish-bosheth, the son of Saul, your enemy, who sought your life; the LORD has avenged my lord the king this day on Saul and on his offspring." ⁹But David answered Re'chab and Ba'anah his brother, the sons of Rimmon the Be-er'othite, "As the LORD lives, who has redeemed my life out of every adversity, ¹⁰when one told me, 'Behold, Saul is dead,' and thought he was bringing good news, I seized him and slew him at Zik'lag, which was the reward I gave him for his news. ¹¹How much more, when wicked men have slain a righteous man in his own house upon his bed, shall I not now require his blood at your hand, and destroy you from the earth?" ¹²And David commanded his young men, and they killed them, and cut off their hands and feet, and hanged them beside the pool at He'bron. But they took the head of Ish-bo'sheth, and buried it in the tomb of Abner at Hebron.

3:35 God do so: A conditional self-curse. See note on Ruth 1:17.

3:39 repay the evildoer: Exasperated with his unruly nephews, David surrenders them to Yahweh for judgment. It is clear from his words that David disapproves of violence as a means to secure his rule over Israel. See note on 2:18.

4:1–12 Ish-bosheth's captains turn against him and become his assassins. David considers this action uncalled for, and so, instead of rewarding them, he orders their death (4:12). The tribal descent of these men (Benjaminites, 4:2–3) shows that even Saul's own tribe is eager to recognize the kingship of David. The way is now clear for David to rule over all Israel, for his three chief rivals have now been eliminated (Saul, Abner, and Ish-bosheth).

4:2 Be-eroth: A Gibeonite settlement that was given to the Benjaminites (Josh 18:25).

4:3 Gittaim: Location unknown. Perhaps the flight to Gittaim is connected with Saul's violence against the Gibeonites mentioned in 21:2.

4:4 Mephibosheth: Son of Jonathan and grandson of Saul, also called "Meribbaal" (1 Chron 8:34). His name probably means "from the mouth of shame". This brief introduction of Mephibosheth, which relates the boyhood accident that left him handicapped, prepares for his appearances later in the book (9:1–13; 16:1–4; 19:24–30).

4:7 the Arabah: The Jordan valley (2:29; Deut 1:1).

4:9 redeemed my life: David has often experienced God's protection and deliverance. With the Lord at his side, he has no need of sinister politics to succeed in the royal mission assigned to him. According to 4:8, Rechab and Baanah wrongly assume that God is using them to fulfill his plans for David.

4:10 slew him: The Amalekite messenger whose fabricated tale about Saul's death angered David (1:1–16).

4:12 cut ... hanged: Dismembering and displaying the bodies of the slain is a gruesome part of Near Eastern warfare (Josh 10:26; 1 Sam 31:9).

ᶠ Gk: Heb ⁶*And they came here into the middle of the house fetching wheat; and they struck him in the belly; and Rechab and Baanah his brother escaped.*

David Anointed King of All Israel

5 *Then all the tribes of Israel came to David at He′bron, and said, "Behold, we are your bone and flesh. ²In times past, when Saul was king over us, it was you that led out and brought in Israel; and the LORD said to you, 'You shall be shepherd of my people Israel, and you shall be prince over Israel.'" ³So all the elders of Israel came to the king at He′bron; and King David made a covenant with them at Hebron before the LORD, and they anointed David king over Israel. ⁴David was thirty years old when he began to reign, and he reigned forty years. ⁵At He′bron he reigned over Judah seven years and six months; and at Jerusalem he reigned over all Israel and Judah thirty-three years.

Jerusalem Is Made Capital of the Kingdom

6 And the king and his men went to Jerusalem against the Jeb′usites, the inhabitants of the land, who said to David, "You will not come in here, but the blind and the lame† will ward you off"—thinking, "David cannot come in here." ⁷Nevertheless David took the stronghold of Zion, that is, the city of David. ⁸And David said on that day, "Whoever would strike the Jeb′usites, let him get up the water shaft to attack the lame and the blind, who are hated by David's soul." Therefore it is said, "The blind and the lame shall not come into the house." ⁹And David dwelt in the stronghold, and called it the city of David. And David built the city round about from the Millo inward. ¹⁰And David became greater and greater, for the LORD, the God of hosts, was with him.

11 And Hiram king of Tyre sent messengers to David, and cedar trees, also carpenters and masons who built David a house. ¹²And David perceived that the LORD had established him king over Israel, and that he had exalted his kingdom for the sake of his people Israel.

13 And David took more concubines and wives from Jerusalem, after he came from He′bron; and

---

5:1–3: 1 Chron 11:1–3.   **5:4, 5:** 1 Chron 3:4.   **5:6–10:** 1 Chron 11:4–9.   **5:11–12:** 1 Chron 14:1, 2.

5:1–5 David reaches the summit of royal power to which God has called him. No longer a charismatic leader of loyal militiamen (1 Sam 22:1–2), or even the king of an entire tribe such as Judah (2:4), he is now the uncontested ruler of all Israel. This is the true beginning of the united monarchy, the golden age of OT history when all twelve tribes stand united under a single king of Israel. It will last less than 100 years, spanning the reigns of David and Solomon, after which the northern tribes will break away from the house of David and the turbulent days of the divided monarchy will begin (see 1 Kings 12).

5:1 Hebron: David's first capital in southern Judah. See note on 2:1. **your bone and flesh:** I.e., your kinsfolk (19:12).

5:2 led out ... brought in: A reference to David's military leadership during the days of Saul (1 Sam 18:5, 13, 30).

5:3 covenant: The northern tribes swear an oath of allegiance to seal their acceptance of David's kingship. The obligations entailed by this covenant would be fitted into the larger framework of the Deuteronomic covenant, which made provision for royal government in Israel (Deut 17:14–20). **anointed:** The third time David receives a ceremonial anointing as king. The first was in 1 Sam 16:13, the second in 2:4.

5:4 forty years: David's reign spans from about 1010 to 970 B.C. See chart: *Old Testament Chronology* at 1 Sam 13.

5:6 Jerusalem: The ancient city known as "Salem" (Gen 14:18) and for a time called "Jebus" (Josh 18:28). David makes Jerusalem both the political and spiritual capital of Israel, first, by choosing it as the place of his royal residence and administration (5:9–11) and, second, by making it the host city for the Ark of the Covenant (6:12–19). The selection of this site for the seat of Israel's government was strategically motivated, for it sat on neutral ground between the tribal territories of Judah and Benjamin, and its more-or-less central location in Canaan made it well suited for David's rule over all Israel, north and south. Jerusalem was captured by David about 1004 B.C. and revered as the royal city even into NT times (Mt 5:35). **Jebusites:** One of the peoples of ancient Canaan who survived the Israelite conquest of the land. They have long proven to be stiff opposition for the tribes of Judah (Josh 15:63) and Benjamin (Judg 1:21). **the blind and the lame:** Taunting words of Jebusites who think the city is so well fortified against attack that even handicapped persons could successfully defend it.

5:7 Zion: The first mention of this location in the Bible. It refers to the southeastern ridge of ancient Jerusalem called the Ophel. The site was naturally defensible, being flanked by deep valleys, and had a natural water supply at the base of its eastern slope called the Gihon Spring. Occasionally the name "Zion" is extended to mean the city of Jerusalem as a whole (Ps 147:12; Is 2:3). It is also used metaphorically to designate the redeemed People of God (Is 51:16; 62:11–12). • According to the NT, Zion is a prophetic sign of heaven, the eternal elevation where angels and saints forever worship the Lord (Heb 12:22; Rev 14:1). **the city of David:** Another name for the Zion fortress.

5:8 water shaft: The meaning of the Hebrew is uncertain. **(1)** Many envision a "tunnel" or secret passageway that gave the Jebusites access to the Gihon Spring without the risk of venturing outside the citadel walls in times of siege. If this is correct, David is urging his men to crawl up the underground shaft and to launch a surprise attack on the stronghold from within. **(2)** Others take it to mean "throat" or "windpipe", in which case David is urging his men to use lethal force against the defenders of the Jebusite fortress. The idea would be that David wants them dead rather than crippled or maimed. **into the house:** Into the Lord's Temple. The restriction mentioned here is otherwise unknown.

5:9 the Millo: Perhaps stone terraces that supported buildings on the upper slope of the Zion ridge.

5:11 Hiram: Sends contractors and supplies from Phoenicia to construct a royal residence for David on Zion. Similar arrangements will be made for Solomon and the building of the Jerusalem Temple (1 Kings 5:1–12). **Tyre:** One of the main seaports of ancient Phoenicia (modern Lebanon).

5:13 more ... wives: Beyond the seven wives David already has (3:2–5, 14–15). **more sons:** A total of 17 sons are named in 2 Samuel. The expanded list in 1 Chron 3:1–9 names 19 sons born to David's wives, not counting other children born to his concubines.

---

*5:1: The two chapters 5–6 represent the climax of David's career with the establishment of Jerusalem as the political and religious center of Israel.
†5:6, *the blind and the lame:* The meaning is, that the place was so strong that it could be defended even by the blind and the lame. But David took it by a stratagem, his men climbing secretly up a shaft from the spring Gihon. The place was ideal for a capital city.

more sons and daughters were born to David. ¹⁴And these are the names of those who were born to him in Jerusalem: Sham′mu-a, Shobab, Nathan, Solomon, ¹⁵Ib′har, Eli′shu-a, Ne′pheg, Japhi′a, ¹⁶Elish′ama, Eli′ada, and Eliph′elet.

Philistine Attack Repulsed

17 When the Philis′tines heard that David had been anointed king over Israel, all the Philistines went up in search of David; but David heard of it and went down to the stronghold. ¹⁸Now the Philis′tines had come and spread out in the valley of Reph′aim. ¹⁹And David inquired of the LORD, "Shall I go up against the Philis′tines? Will you give them into my hand?" And the LORD said to David, "Go up; for I will certainly give the Philistines into your hand." ²⁰And David came to Ba′al-pera′zim, and David defeated them there; and he said, "The LORD has broken through𝓰 my enemies before me, like a bursting flood." Therefore the name of that place is called Ba′al-pera′zim.ʰ ²¹And the Philis′tines left their idols there, and David and his men carried them away.

22 And the Philis′tines came up yet again, and spread out in the valley of Reph′aim. ²³And when David inquired of the LORD, he said, "You shall not go up; go around to their rear, and come upon them opposite the balsam trees. ²⁴And when you hear the sound of marching in the tops of the balsam trees, then bestir yourself; for then the LORD has gone out before you to strike the army of the Philis′tines." ²⁵And David did as the LORD commanded him, and struck the Philis′tines from Ge′ba to Gezer.

David Brings the Ark to Jerusalem

6 David again gathered all the chosen men of Israel, thirty thousand. ²And David arose and went with all the people who were with him from Ba′ale-ju′dah, to bring up from there the ark of God, which is called by the name of the LORD of hosts who sits enthroned on the cherubim. ³And they carried the ark of God upon a new cart, and brought it out of the house of Abin′adab which was on the hill; and Uzzah and Ahi′o,ⁱ the sons of Abinadab, were driving the new cartʲ ⁴with the ark of God; and Ahi′oⁱ went before the ark. ⁵And David and

---

5:14–16: 1 Chron 3:5–8; 14:3–7.   **5:17–21:** 1 Chron 14:8–12.   **5:22–25:** 1 Chron 14:13–16.   **6:1–11:** 1 Chron 13:1–14.

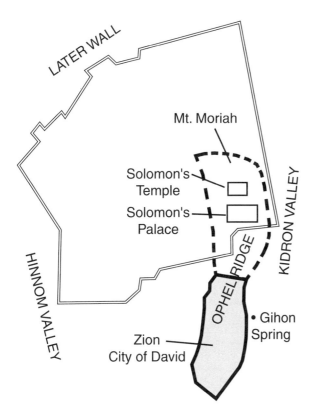

Zion, The City of David

5:17 Philistines: Hostile neighbors of Israel in southwest Canaan. See note on Judg 3:3. **the stronghold:** Probably the cave of Adullam (1 Sam 22:1–5) rather than the Zion stronghold just mentioned (5:7, 9).

5:18 valley of Rephaim: Begins a few miles southwest of Jerusalem and slopes downward toward Philistine territory.

5:19 inquired of the LORD: Perhaps by means of the sacred lots, Urim and Thummim.

5:21 their idols: Amulets or figurines believed to ensure success on the battlefield. David's men gather up these pagan cult objects in order to burn them (1 Chron 14:12).

5:24 marching: The sound of treetops rustling in the wind is the sound of Yahweh and his hosts moving into battle against the enemies of Israel.

6:1–23 David stations the Ark of the Covenant in Jerusalem. He thereby makes his capital a holy city and the spiritual center of Israelite worship. This episode resumes the story of the ark that left off at 1 Sam 7:2. For allusions to this historic event in the NT, see essay: *Mary, Ark of the Covenant* at Lk 1.

6:1 thirty thousand: A formidable military escort. It matches the number of soldiers from Israel who fell in battle the day the Ark of the Covenant was captured by the Philistines (see 1 Sam 4:10–11).

6:2 Baale-judah: Another name for Kiriath-jearim (Josh 15:9). **LORD of hosts:** On this title, see note on 1 Sam 1:3. **enthroned:** The Ark of the Covenant is an earthy representation of Yahweh's throne. See note on Ex 25:10.

6:3–8 The transport of the ark is irregular to the point of irreverent. It is wheeled along atop a new oxcart (6:3), when it should have been carried with poles on the shoulders of the Levites (Deut 10:8). Worse, Uzzah reaches out to steady the ark (6:6), even though physical contact with it is strictly forbidden (Num 4:15). Careless neglect of the Torah thus sparks a lethal blast of divine wrath against Uzzah (1 Chron 15:13). For similar instances where violators of liturgical law are struck dead, see Lev 10:1–2 and Num 16:1–40.

6:3 a new cart: The Philistines used a new oxcart when they returned the ark to Israel in 1 Sam 6:7. **house of Abinadab:** The ark has been stationed there for 20 years (1 Sam 7:2), during which time it was neglected (1 Chron 13:3).

𝓰 Heb *paraz.*
ʰ That is *Lord of breaking through.*
ⁱ Or *and his brother.*
ʲ Compare Gk: Heb *the new cart, and brought it out of the house of Abinadab which was on the hill.*

all the house of Israel were making merry before the LORD with all their might, with songs[k] and lyres and harps and tambourines and castanets and cymbals.

6 And when they came to the threshing floor of Nacon, Uzzah put out his hand to the ark of God and took hold of it, for the oxen stumbled. [7]And the anger of the LORD was kindled against Uzzah; and God struck him there because he put forth his hand to the ark;[1] and he died there beside the ark of God. [8]And David was angry because the LORD had broken forth upon Uzzah; and that place is called Per'ez-uz'zah,[m] to this day. [9]And David was afraid of the LORD that day; and he said, "How can the ark of the LORD come to me?" [10]So David was not willing to take the ark of the LORD into the city of David; but David took it aside to the house of O'bed-e'dom the Gittite. [11]And the ark of the LORD remained in the house of O'bed-e'dom the Gittite three months; and the LORD blessed Obed-edom and all his household.

12 And it was told King David, "The LORD has blessed the household of O'bed-e'dom and all that belongs to him, because of the ark of God." So David went and brought up the ark of God from the house of Obed-edom to the city of David with rejoicing; [13]and when those who bore the ark of the LORD had gone six paces, he sacrificed an ox and a fatling. [14]And David danced before the LORD with all his might; and David was belted with a linen ephod. [15]So David and all the house of Israel brought up the ark of the LORD with shouting, and with the sound of the horn.

16 As the ark of the LORD came into the city of David, Michal the daughter of Saul looked out of the window, and saw King David leaping and dancing before the LORD; and she despised him in her heart. [17]And they brought in the ark of the LORD, and set it in its place, inside the tent which David had pitched for it; and David offered burnt offerings and peace offerings before the LORD. [18]And when David had finished offering the burnt offerings and the peace offerings, he blessed the people in the name of the LORD of hosts, [19]and distributed among all the people, the whole multitude of Israel, both men and women, to each a cake of bread, a portion of meat,[n] and a cake of raisins. Then all the people departed, each to his house.

20 And David returned to bless his household. But Michal the daughter of Saul came out to meet David, and said, "How the king of Israel honored himself today, uncovering himself today before the eyes of his servants' maids, as one of the vulgar fellows shamelessly uncovers himself!" [21]And David said to Michal, "It was before the LORD, who chose me above your father, and above all his house, to appoint me as prince over Israel, the people of the LORD—and I will make merry before the LORD. [22]I will make myself yet more contemptible than this, and I will be abased in your[o] eyes; but by the maids of whom you have spoken, by them I shall be held

---

6:12–19: 1 Chron 15:1—16:3.

6:8 broken forth: Recalls how Yahweh's power burst forth against the Philistines in 5:20.

6:9 How ... come to me?: Questions expressing fear and awe before the ark also appear in 1 Sam 4:8; 6:20.

6:10 Obed-edom: Probably the Levite named Obed-edom, who will serve as gatekeeper for the ark after its installation in Jerusalem (1 Chron 15:18, 24; 16:38). **Gittite:** Means "from the city of Gath". The location in question is more likely the Levitical city of Gath-rimmon (Josh 21:24–25) than the Philistine town of Gath (1 Sam 6:17).

6:11 blessed: A sign that the Lord's anger has subsided (6:7). Inferring from what follows (6:20–23), it seems that Obed-edom receives blessings of fertility on his family and flocks (cf. Gen 1:28; Ps 128:3–4).

6:12–19 The ark comes to Zion in liturgical procession. Curiously, it is David the king who assumes the role of head celebrant. Notice that David **(1)** performs *priestly actions* (animal sacrifices, 6:13, 17), **(2)** wears a *priestly vestment* (linen ephod, 6:14; 1 Sam 22:18), and **(3)** gives a *priestly benediction* (6:18; cf. Lev 9:22; Num 6:22–27). See notes on 1 Kings 8:63 and 2 Chron 1:6.

6:17 the tent: Pitched in Zion, the city of David, in southeast Jerusalem (1 Chron 15:1). It is important to distinguish this Davidic Tabernacle from the older, Mosaic Tabernacle.

At this time, the Mosaic sanctuary is stationed several miles north of Jerusalem in Gibeon, where the priests of Israel conduct a perpetual liturgy of sacrifice in accord with Levitical law (1 Chron 16:39–42; 2 Chron 1:3). The Davidic tent, however, stands in Zion as a temporary shelter for the Ark of the Covenant; here the Levites conduct a perpetual liturgy of praise and thanksgiving to the melody of psalms and musical instruments (1 Chron 16:4–37; 2 Chron 1:4). See essay: *David's New Liturgy* at 1 Chron 16.

6:19 a portion of meat: The Hebrew term, which occurs only here and at 1 Chron 16:3 in the Bible, has an uncertain etymology and meaning. Detecting some connection with fruit, scholars have proposed the meaning "a cake of dates" or "a measure of wine". The Greek LXX renders it "food cooked over a fire", although most take this to be conjectural rather than a clue to its original meaning. • The parallel account in Chronicles indicates that David sanctifies the occasion with songs of thanksgiving (1 Chron 16:7), in which case the distribution of food may be a thank offering of unleavened bread and cakes (Lev 7:12) and possibly wine (as in later times, Ps 116:13). If so, David's actions further recall the gestures of Melchizedek, priest and king of ancient Jerusalem who gave bread and wine to Abraham and his men and blessed them in the name of the Lord (Gen 14:18–20).

6:20 honored himself: A sarcastic rebuke. Michal is embarrassed by David's behavior and scolds him for acting indecently in public. Apparently the king has shed his royal robes and is dancing around in nothing but his linen garment (6:14).

---

[k] Gk 1 Chron 13:8: Heb *fir-trees*.
[1] 1 Chron 13:10: Heb uncertain.
[m] That is *The breaking forth upon Uzzah*.
[n] Vg: Heb uncertain.
[o] Gk: Heb *my*.

in honor." ²³And Michal the daughter of Saul had no child to the day of her death.

God's Promise to David

7 Now when the king dwelt in his house, and the LORD had given him rest from all his enemies round about, ²the king said to Nathan the prophet, "See now, I dwell in a house of cedar, but the ark of God dwells in a tent." ³And Nathan said to the king, "Go, do all that is in your heart; for the LORD is with you."

4 But that same night the word of the LORD came to Nathan, ⁵"Go and tell my servant David, 'Thus says the LORD: Would you build me a house to dwell in? ⁶I have not dwelt in a house since the day I brought up the sons of Israel from Egypt to this day, but I have been moving about in a tent for my dwelling. ⁷In all places where I have moved with all the sons of Israel, did I speak a word with any of the judges^p of Israel, whom I commanded to shepherd my people Israel, saying, "Why have you not built me a house of cedar?"' ⁸Now therefore thus you shall say to my servant David, 'Thus says the LORD of hosts, I took you from the pasture, from following the sheep, that you should be prince over my people Israel; ⁹and I have been with you wherever you went, and have cut off all your enemies from before you; and I will make for you a great name, like the name of the great ones of the earth. ¹⁰And I will appoint a place for my people Israel, and will plant them, that they may dwell in their own place, and be disturbed no more; and violent men shall afflict them no more, as formerly, ¹¹from the time that I appointed judges over my people Israel; and I will give you rest from all your enemies. Moreover the LORD declares to you that the LORD will make you a house. ¹²When your days are fulfilled and you lie down

---

7:1–29: 1 Chron 17:1–27.

6:23 no child: Indicates that Michal forfeits the blessing that David intends to give his wives (6:20). Likewise, her childlessness guarantees that the house of Saul has no chance of living on through David's royal line. See note on 1 Sam 13:14.

7:1 his house: David's royal residence in Zion, built with premium Phoenician lumber and craftsmanship (5:11). **rest from all his enemies:** Achieved by the wars of subjugation summarized in 8:1–14. Placing the discourses of chap. 7 before the events of chap. 8 is an example of dischronologized narrative, meaning the strict order of history is subordinated to the thematic interests of the historian. In this instance, the author's rearrangement of the story shows that David's concern for the Ark of the Covenant (2 Sam 6)—not his bravery on the battlefield (2 Sam 8)—is the expression of loyalty that called forth the Lord's covenant of everlasting kingship for David and his heirs (2 Sam 7). • Theologically, the attainment of "rest" from military conflict signals that conditions are ripe for Israel to begin construction on a national sanctuary, as indicated in Deut 12:10–11.

7:2 Nathan: One of David's court prophets (12:1–14). Eventually the prophet Nathan will help to secure Solomon's succession to David's throne (1 Kings 1:11–45) and will produce written accounts of the reigns of David and Solomon (1 Chron 29:29; 2 Chron 9:29). **tent:** The temporary shelter that houses the Ark of the Covenant on Mt. Zion. David thinks it wrong that he should dwell in a cedar palace while the Lord makes do with an outdoor canopy. See note on 6:17.

7:6 moving about: Or "walking about", as in Gen 3:8; Lev 26:12.

7:8–16 Nathan's oracle. It is the theological summit of 2 Samuel and the foundation of the Davidic covenant (23:5). See essay: *The Davidic Covenant.*

7:9 great name: Refers to the exaltation and propagation of a royal name by dynastic succession, which is what Yahweh pledges to David in 7:11–12. Historical testimony to this from outside the Bible was uncovered in northern Israel by archaeologists in the 1990s, who discovered an Aramaic inscription from the ninth century B.C. reporting the death of a king from the "house of David" (*Tell Dan Inscription*, line 8a). • The promise to David links back to promises made to Abraham: Yahweh had pledged to make his "name great" (Gen 12:2) by establishing a line of "kings" from among his descendants (Gen 17:6).

7:12 your offspring: The royal heir is Solomon (1 Chron 28:5–6), who is not yet born at this point in the story (12:24). The early Christians, without denying a preliminary reference to Solomon, read this as a messianic prophecy, as did numerous ancient Jews (e.g., Dead Sea Scrolls, 4Q174). **from your body:** The same words in Hebrew were spoken to Abraham regarding the birth of his heir, Isaac (Gen

WORD STUDY

House (7:11)

Bayit (Heb.): a noun, meaning "house" or "household", that is used more than 2000 times in the Hebrew Bible. Broadly speaking, it can refer to a place of residence or to a people of common descent. (1) As a *place*, a house is a walled dwelling that a family occupies as a home (Gen 19:2; Judg 11:34). If a king lives in the house, it is a royal palace (1 Kings 9:1); and if the family is wealthy, the term can denote the entire estate (Gen 39:4). Houses in the ancient world were also built for gods in the form of temples, such as the house of Dagon built by the Philistines (1 Sam 5:2) and the Temple of Yahweh built by Solomon (1 Kings 6:1). (2) Referring to *people*, a house is a family unit, whether small, such as the household of Noah (Gen 7:1), or large, such as the tribal family of Judah (2 Sam 2:4). A house can even encompass family descendants yet to be born (Deut 25:9), such as a dynasty of kings (1 Kings 12:26). Plays on the various meanings of this word underlie Nathan's oracle in 2 Sam 7:8–16: David, who dwells in a luxurious "house" (royal palace, 2 Sam 7:2), wants to build a suitable "house" for the Lord (Temple, 2 Sam 7:5), only to find out that Yahweh intends to build him a "house" of royal descendants (dynasty, 2 Sam 7:11), one of whom will be tasked with building the "house" of worship that David desires (Temple, 2 Sam 7:13) (CCC 2580).

---

^p1 Chron 17:6: Heb *tribes.*

The Davidic Covenant

The Davidic covenant is the latest and greatest of the Old Testament covenants. Following the steady buildup of covenants between God and his people over the centuries, beginning with Adam and continuing with Noah, Abraham, and Moses, the divine covenant with David brings the biblical story to a theological highpoint. Each of these ancient covenants helps to prepare the way for messianic times, but Jewish and Christian traditions agree that hopes for a coming Messiah are anchored most explicitly in the Lord's covenant with David.

NATHAN'S ORACLE

The foundation of the Davidic covenant is Nathan's oracle in 2 Sam 7:8–16, which responds to David's intention to build a sanctuary for Yahweh. Nathan reveals that the king's desire, although noble, is not part of God's plan for his life. Instead, something more wonderful is envisioned. What David wants to do for the Lord hardly compares to what the Lord wants to do for David. This divine plan can be summarized under four headings.

(1) *Dynasty*. Yahweh first pledges to build David a "house" (2 Sam 7:11). By this he means a dynasty, a hereditary line of royal successors, so that his kingdom and his throne will be "established for ever" (2 Sam 7:16). The house of David may have to be disciplined as times and circumstances demand, but the house of David will never be fully disowned like the house of Saul was when the Lord abandoned it on account of Saul's failings (2 Sam 7:14–15). David's dynasty will exercise an everlasting rule that is guaranteed by God.

(2) *Temple*. Yahweh's second pledge responds directly to David's desire to build a Temple (2 Sam 7:2). The king wishes to begin construction on a worthy sanctuary, but, according to Nathan, the privilege of building a "house" for the Lord will fall to David's royal "offspring" (2 Sam 7:12–13). This is an allusion to David's son and successor, King Solomon, who pulls together a massive workforce to construct the Jerusalem Temple after his father's death (1 Kings 6–8). The Temple thus serves as an architectural sign of the Davidic covenant.

(3) *Adoption*. Yahweh's third pledge is to create a father-son relationship between himself and David's royal offspring (2 Sam 7:14). It is a promise that the kings of David's line will be made sons of God by divine adoption. In this way, the covenant of kingship creates an especially close relationship between Yahweh and the anointed successors of David. It is implied in Ps 2:7 that the royal adoption of each king takes place on the day of his coronation.

(4) *Law for Mankind*. In response to the oracle, David senses that God, in pledging himself to these grandiose commitments, is initializing a plan to extend his blessings to the human race beyond Israel. What the Lord has revealed to him is nothing less than *torat ha-ʾadam*, "the law of mankind" (see note on 2 Sam 7:19). The Law of Moses was a gift for Israel alone; but the covenant arrangement promised to David is a gift for Israel and other nations alike. This becomes visible in the days of Solomon, who recruits Gentiles from Phoenicia to assist with building the Temple (1 Kings 5:6, 18), who implores Yahweh to answer the prayers of the Gentiles who direct their pleas toward his Temple (1 Kings 8:41–43), and who instructs inquiring Gentiles from many nations in the fundamentals of godly "wisdom" (1 Kings 4:34; 10:1–10, 24).

Nathan's oracle is worded as a divine promise, but its terms are guaranteed by divine oath. Whether a formal pledge is made on this occasion or afterward makes little difference. It is clear from other texts that Yahweh makes his commitments to David into a covenant (2 Sam 23:5; Sir 45:25; 47:11) by swearing an oath to David (Ps 89:3–4, 35–37; 132:11–12). And since God alone swears the oath, he alone assumes responsibility for its fulfillment. The Davidic covenant of kingship is an unconditional "grant", meaning that Yahweh takes upon himself the unilateral obligation to make good on his pledges, regardless of whether or not David's future line of successors proves worthy of this honor.

NEW TESTAMENT FULFILLMENT

The pledges made to David are provisionally realized in Solomon during the golden age of the united monarchy and, to a lesser extent, in the centuries that the Davidic dynasty ruled in Jerusalem. But definitive fulfillment awaits the coming of Jesus Christ. He is the Messiah grafted into David's dynastic line (Mt 1:1–16) and the one chosen by God to sit on David's throne "for ever" (Lk 1:32–33). Like David, Jesus is anointed by the Spirit (1 Sam 16:13; Acts 10:38), and, like Solomon, he offers the wisdom of God to the world (1 Kings 10:1–10; Mt 12:42). The Temple he builds is not a stone-and-cedar sanctuary in Jerusalem, but his body, the Church of living believers indwelt by the Spirit (Mt 16:18; Eph 2:19–22; 1 Pet 2:4–5). In the Resurrection, Jesus' humanity attains the royal adoption promised to David's offspring (Acts 13:33–34; Rom 1:3–4), and, at his Ascension, he commences his everlasting reign (Lk 1:33) as David's messianic Lord (Mk 12:35–37). Even now, he holds the key to the kingdom of David (Rev 3:7) and bears the distinction of being "King of Israel" (Jn 1:49) as well as "he who rises to rule the Gentiles" (Rom 15:12). According to the very first Christian sermon, all of this is the fulfillment of Yahweh's oath to David (Acts 2:29–35).

with your fathers, I will raise up your offspring after you, who shall come forth from your body, and I will establish his kingdom. [13]He shall build a house for my name, and I will establish the throne of his kingdom for ever. [14]I will be his father, and he shall be my son. When he commits iniquity, I will chasten him with the rod of men, with the stripes of the sons of men; [15]but I will not take[q] my merciful love from him, as I took it from Saul, whom I put away from before you. [16]And your house and your kingdom shall be made sure for ever before me; your throne shall be established for ever.'" [17]In accordance with all these words, and in accordance with all this vision, Nathan spoke to David.

David's Prayer

18 Then King David went in and sat before the Lord, and said, "Who am I, O Lord God, and what is my house, that you have brought me thus far? [19]And yet this was a small thing in your eyes, O Lord God; you have spoken also of your servant's house for a great while to come, and have shown me future generations,[r] O Lord God! [20]And what more can David say to you? For you know your servant, O Lord God! [21]Because of your promise, and according to your own heart, you have wrought all this greatness, to make your servant know it. [22]Therefore you are great, O Lord God; for there is none like you, and there is no God besides you, according to all that we have heard with our ears. [23]What other[s] nation on earth is like your people Israel, whom God went to redeem to be his people, making himself a name, and doing for them[t] great and terrible things, by driving out[u] before

his people a nation and its gods?[v] [24]And you established for yourself your people Israel to be your people for ever; and you, O Lord, became their God. [25]And now, O Lord God, confirm for ever the word which you have spoken concerning your servant and concerning his house, and do as you have spoken; [26]and your name will be magnified for ever, saying, 'The Lord of hosts is God over Israel,' and the house of your servant David will be established before you. [27]For you, O Lord of hosts, the God of Israel, have made this revelation to your servant, saying, 'I will build you a house'; therefore your servant has found courage to pray this prayer to you. [28]And now, O Lord God, you are God, and your words are true, and you have promised this good thing to your servant; [29]now therefore may it please you to bless the house of your servant, that it may continue for ever before you; for you, O Lord God, have spoken, and with your blessing shall the house of your servant be blessed for ever."*

David's Wars

8 After this David defeated the Philis'tines and subdued them, and David took Meth'eg-am'mah out of the hand of the Philistines.

2 And he defeated Moab, and measured them with a line, making them lie down on the ground; two lines he measured to be put to death, and one full line to be spared. And the Moabites became servants to David and brought tribute.

3 David also defeated Hadade'zer the son of Re'hob, king of Zobah, as he went to restore his power at the river Euphrates. [4]And David took from him a thousand and seven hundred horsemen,

---

7:14: Heb 1:5. **8:1–14:** 1 Chron 18:1–13.

15:4). • In Solomon we see a partial reflection of the future, for he does build the Temple, and at the start of his reign he is certainly praiseworthy. Nevertheless, Solomon only foreshadows the future coming of Christ. So some things are written as if they were predictions concerning Solomon, yet Holy Scripture, which also prophesies by historical events, outlines in him a pattern for the future (St. Augustine, *City of God* 17, 8).

7:14 his father ... my son: The royal adoption of the king by Yahweh (CCC 238, 441). See essay: *The Davidic Covenant.* **chasten:** The house of David will be disciplined by the Lord at various points in its history, most notably during the Babylonian conquest of Judah and Jerusalem in 586 B.C., which leaves the throne of David unoccupied for the final centuries of OT history (Jer 22:1–12; 36:30–31).

7:18 before the Lord: In front of the Ark of the Covenant in the Zion tent (6:17). **Who am I:** David is humbled and astonished at the mission assigned to him.

7:19 have shown me future generations: The RSV offers a loose interpretation of the Hebrew rather than a strict translation. The text literally says, "This is the law of mankind." David seems to think that God wants to use the covenant of kingship to extend his blessings beyond Israel to the wider human family. See essay: *The Davidic Covenant.*

8:1–14 David expands his kingdom by military conquest. He subdues neighboring states that border Israel on the north (Zobahites, Syrians), east (Moabites, Ammonites), south (Edomites, Amalekites), and west (Philistines). Survivors of these wars are made vassals subservient to the Davidic king, with the result that precious metals begin flowing into the royal treasuries in the form of plunder and political tribute (8:7–8, 10–12). David's small empire is thus growing in size and wealth.

8:1 Metheg-ammah: Reference unknown. The parallel passage in Chronicles reads "Gath and its villages" (1 Chron 18:1).

8:2 measured: Whatever the exact procedure, two-thirds of the Moabites are marked out for execution, and the remaining one third is reduced to political vassalage.

8:3 Hadadezer: Translates "Hadad is help". Hadad is the name of an ancient Semitic storm god. **Zobah:** In the vicinity of the Syrian city of Damascus. Friction between Israelites and Zobahites goes back to the days of Saul (1 Sam 14:47). **river Euphrates:** Its upper course flows from Syria into Mesopotamia. • David's interest in securing this area

---

[q]Gk Syr Vg 1 Chron 17:13: Heb *shall not depart.*
[r]Cn: Heb *this is the law for man.*
[s]Gk: Heb *one.*
[t]Heb *you.*
[u]Gk 1 Chron 17:21: Heb *for your land.*
[v]Heb *before your people, whom you redeemed for yourself from Egypt, nations and its gods.*
*7:1–29: The point of this prophecy is the establishment of David's dynasty. Hence God says he will build David a house (verse 11). David thanks him suitably in a formal prayer (verses 18–29).

and twenty thousand foot soldiers; and David hamstrung all the chariot horses, but left enough for a hundred chariots. [5]And when the Syrians of Damascus came to help Hadade'zer king of Zobah, David slew twenty-two thousand men of the Syrians. [6]Then David put garrisons in Ar'am of Damascus; and the Syrians became servants to David and brought tribute. And the LORD gave victory to David wherever he went. [7]And David took the shields of gold which were carried by the servants of Hadade'zer, and brought them to Jerusalem. [8]And from Betah and from Bero'thai, cities of Hadade'zer, King David took very much bronze.

9 When To'i king of Ha'math heard that David had defeated the whole army of Hadade'zer, [10]To'i sent his son Jo'ram to King David, to greet him, and to congratulate him because he had fought against Hadade'zer and defeated him; for Hadadezer had often been at war with Toi. And Joram brought with him articles of silver, of gold, and of bronze; [11]these also King David dedicated to the LORD, together with the silver and gold which he dedicated from all the nations he subdued, [12]from E'dom, Moab, the Am'monites, the Philis'tines, Am'alek, and from the spoil of Hadade'zer the son of Re'hob, king of Zobah.

13 And David won a name for himself. When he returned, he slew eighteen thousand E'domites[w] in the Valley of Salt. [14]And he put garrisons in E'dom; throughout all Edom he put garrisons, and all the E'domites became David's servants. And the LORD gave victory to David wherever he went.

David's Officers

15 So David reigned over all Israel; and David administered justice and equity to all his people. [16]And Jo'ab the son of Zeru'iah was over the army; and Jehosh'aphat the son of Ahi'lud was recorder; [17]and Zad'ok the son of Ahi'tub and Ahim'elech the son of Abi'athar were priests; and Serai'ah was secretary; [18]and Bena'iah the son of Jehoi'ada was over[x] the Cher'ethites and the Pel'ethites; and David's sons were priests.

David's Kindness to Mephibosheth

9 * And David said, "Is there still any one left of the house of Saul, that I may show him kindness

---

8:15–18: 2 Sam 20:23–26; 1 Chron 18:14–17.

---

appears to be motivated by the Abrahamic covenant, which envisioned the Promised Land stretching northward to the Euphrates (Gen 15:18; Deut 1:7–8; Josh 1:4).

8:6 the LORD gave victory: Divine assistance has been the secret of David's success from the very beginning (1 Sam 16:13; 17:45–47; 18:14).

8:9 Hamath: On the Orontes River in Syria, north of the Zobah kingdom (8:3).

8:11 dedicated to the LORD: Solomon will store these valuables in the Temple treasury (1 Kings 7:51). David, in accord with Deut 17:17, does not use the spoils of war to increase his personal wealth.

8:13 Valley of Salt: Near the southern end of the Dead Sea.

8:15–18 David takes advantage of peacetime to form a working government. His small administration is given charge over military operations (Joab), religious worship (Zadok, Ahimelech), record keeping and correspondence (Jehoshaphat, Seraiah), and the king's personal protection (Benaiah).

8:15 justice and equity: Defined as the "way of the LORD" in Gen 18:19 (where the same Hebrew word pair is translated "righteousness and justice"). Equivalent expressions in the ancient Near East are connected with royal proclamations given when a new king comes to the throne. It is an initiative of social justice that a new king enacts for the benefit of his subjects, especially the poor and oppressed among them (cancellation of debts, liberation of slaves, tax relief, returning mortgaged estates to original owners, etc.).

8:16 recorder: Probably in charge of state documents and archives.

8:17 priests: Religious leadership is the shared responsibility of two chief priests. **Zadok** is a descendant of Aaron's grandson Phinehas (1 Chron 6:50–53), with whom the Lord made a covenant of perpetual priesthood (Num 25:6–13). The identity of **Ahimelech**, on the other hand, is less than certain.

He is here designated the son of Abiathar, whom David agreed to shelter from the murderous rage of Saul (1 Sam 22:20–23), but there is reason to suspect that the names "Ahimelech" and "Abiathar" were switched around in the course of copying the book (e.g., David's priests are Zadok and Abiathar in 20:25, and Abiathar's father is named Ahimelech in 1 Sam 22:20). **secretary:** In charge of royal correspondence.

8:18 Cherethites … Pelethites: Foreign mercenaries hired to serve as David's bodyguards (15:18; 20:7). **David's sons:** Seventeen sons are named in the book (see 3:2–5; 5:14–15). **priests:** This is clearly stated in the Hebrew. Nevertheless, the Greek LXX translates this as "head court officials", and the parallel passage in 1 Chron 18:17 calls the sons of David his "chief officials". Since cultic and civic responsibilities often overlapped in the biblical world, there is no need to see these texts in conflict. Beyond that, it is clear that David himself acts in a priestly capacity (see note on 6:12–19), just as Solomon will do after him (1 Kings 3:15; 9:25). Perhaps the priestly ministry of David's sons is linked to Yahweh's oath to make the Davidic ruler "a priest for ever according to the order of Melchizedek" (Ps 110:4).

9:1–20:26 Chapters 9–20, together with 1 Kings 1–2, comprise what scholars call the "Court History" or "Succession Narrative". It is the story of David's sons wrangling for power and the chance to succeed him as king of Israel. Thematically, it mirrors the preceding chapters: just as three individuals (Saul, Abner, Ish-bosheth) were eliminated to make way for David's rise to kingship, so now three of David's sons (Amnon, Absalom, Adonijah) are eliminated to make way for Solomon's ascent to the throne. Many consider these chapters some of the finest specimens of historiography and vivid narration that survive from biblical antiquity. The author probably lived close in time and place to the events he records.

9:1 for Jonathan's sake: More than simply honoring the memory of his fallen companion (1 Sam 31:2), David honors his covenant obligations to Jonathan, which entailed showing love and loyalty to Jonathan's entire "house" (1 Sam 20:14–17). David makes good on this by treating Jonathan's first-born son, Mephibosheth, like one of his own sons, inviting him to live at the royal residence and to eat at the king's table (9:7, 11). For background, see notes on 1 Sam 18:3 and 20:8.

---

[w]Gk: Heb *returned from striking eighteen thousand Syrians.*
[x]Syr Tg Vg 20:23; 1 Chron 18:17: Heb lacks *was over.*
*9:1: 2 Sam 9—1 Kings 2 (except 2 Sam 21–24) is the account of the struggle for the succession to David's throne. It goes back to the early monarchy and is probably the oldest continuous prose narrative in the Old Testament.

for Jonathan's sake?" ²Now there was a servant of the house of Saul whose name was Zi'ba, and they called him to David; and the king said to him, "Are you Ziba?" And he said, "Your servant is he." ³And the king said, "Is there not still some one of the house of Saul, that I may show the kindness of God to him?" Zi'ba said to the king, "There is still a son of Jonathan; he is crippled in his feet." ⁴The king said to him, "Where is he?" And Zi'ba said to the king, "He is in the house of Ma'chir the son of Am'miel, at Lo-de'bar." ⁵Then King David sent and brought him from the house of Ma'chir the son of Am'miel, at Lo-de'bar. ⁶And Mephib'osheth the son of Jonathan, son of Saul, came to David, and fell on his face and did obeisance. And David said, "Mephibosheth!" And he answered, "Behold, your servant." ⁷And David said to him, "Do not fear; for I will show you kindness for the sake of your father Jonathan, and I will restore to you all the land of Saul your father; and you shall eat at my table always." ⁸And he did obeisance, and said, "What is your servant, that you should look upon a dead dog such as I?"

9 Then the king called Zi'ba, Saul's servant, and said to him, "All that belonged to Saul and to all his house I have given to your master's son. ¹⁰And you and your sons and your servants shall till the land for him, and shall bring in the produce, that your master's son may have bread to eat; but Mephib'osheth your master's son shall always eat at my table." Now Zi'ba had fifteen sons and twenty servants. ¹¹Then Zi'ba said to the king, "According to all that my lord the king commands his servant, so will your servant do." So Mephib'osheth ate at David'sʸ table, like one of the king's sons. ¹²And Mephib'osheth had a young son, whose name was Mica. And all who dwelt in Zi'ba's house became Mephib'osheth's servants. ¹³So Mephib'osheth dwelt in Jerusalem; for he ate always at the king's table. Now he was lame in both his feet.

The Ammonites and Syrians Are Defeated

10 After this the king of the Am'monites died, and Ha'nun his son reigned in his stead. ²And David said, "I will deal loyally with Ha'nun the son of Na'hash, as his father dealt loyally with me." So David sent by his servants to console him concerning his father. And David's servants came into the land of the Am'monites. ³But the princes of the Am'monites said to Ha'nun their lord, "Do you think, because David has sent comforters to you, that he is honoring your father? Has not David sent his servants to you to search the city, and to spy it out, and to overthrow it?" ⁴So Ha'nun took David's servants, and shaved off half the beard of each, and cut off their garments in the middle, at their hips, and sent them away. ⁵When it was told David, he sent to meet them, for the men were greatly ashamed. And the king said, "Remain at Jericho until your beards have grown, and then return."

6 When the Am'monites saw that they had become odious to David, the Ammonites sent and hired the Syrians of Beth-re'hob, and the Syrians of Zobah, twenty thousand foot soldiers, and the king of Ma'acah with a thousand men, and the men of Tob, twelve thousand men. ⁷And when David heard of it, he sent Jo'ab and all the host of the mighty men. ⁸And the Am'monites came out and drew up in battle array at the entrance of the gate; and the Syrians of Zobah and of Re'hob, and the men of Tob and Ma'acah, were by themselves in the open country.

9 When Jo'ab saw that the battle was set against him both in front and in the rear, he chose some of the picked men of Israel, and arrayed them against the Syrians; ¹⁰the rest of his men he put in the charge of Abi'shai his brother, and he arrayed them against the Am'monites. ¹¹And he said, "If the Syrians are too strong for me, then you shall help me; but if the Am'monites are too strong for you, then I will come and help you. ¹²Be of good courage, and let

---

10:1–19: 1 Chron 19:1–19.

9:2 Ziba: A former servant of Saul but now a supporter of David (16:1–4).

9:3 crippled: The result of a boyhood accident (4:4).

9:4 Machir: Caretaker of Mephibosheth and a supporter of David (17:27–29). **Lo-debar:** East of the Jordan River, not far from Saul's former capital of Mahanaim (2:8).

9:6 Mephibosheth: Grandson of Saul. See note on 4:4.

9:7 restore to you: The circumstances making this necessary are unclear. Either David has claimed Saul's landholdings as state property, or perhaps Ziba has simply appropriated the estate without contest.

9:12 Mica: Perpetuated the family line of Saul by having four sons (1 Chron 8:33–35).

10:1 king of the Ammonites: Nahash (1 Sam 11:1).

10:2 deal loyally: The Hebrew suggests that Israel has established a treaty covenant with the kingdom of Ammon.

10:3 the city: Rabbah, the Ammonite capital, over 20 miles east of the Jordan (11:1; 12:26).

10:4 shaved off: An insult to bearded Semites. Shaving was typically reserved for times of mourning (Is 15:2; Jer 41:5). **cut off their garments:** Naked from the waist down, the emissaries are mocked and humiliated like prisoners of war (Is 20:4).

10:5 Jericho: A place of relative isolation in the western Jordan valley.

10:6 Beth-rehob: North of Israel near the source of the Jordan River. **Zobah:** In the vicinity of the Syrian city of Damascus. **Maacah:** North of Israel near the source of the Jordan River. **Tob:** About 40 miles southeast of the Sea of Galilee.

10:7 the mighty men: David's elite warriors (23:8–39).

10:9–14 The Ammonite coalition flees and is forced to regroup (10:15). Had they chosen to engage, Israel would have had to fight on two fronts under the command of David's two nephews Joab and Abishai. See note on 2:18.

ʸGk: Heb *my*.

us play the man for our people, and for the cities of our God; and may the LORD do what seems good to him." ¹³So Jo'ab and the people who were with him drew near to battle against the Syrians; and they fled before him. ¹⁴And when the Am'monites saw that the Syrians fled, they likewise fled before Abi'shai, and entered the city. Then Jo'ab returned from fighting against the Ammonites, and came to Jerusalem.

15 But when the Syrians saw that they had been defeated by Israel, they gathered themselves together. ¹⁶And Hadade'zer sent, and brought out the Syrians who were beyond the Euphra'tes;ᶻ and they came to He'lam, with Shobach the commander of the army of Hadadezer at their head. ¹⁷And when it was told David, he gathered all Israel together, and crossed the Jordan, and came to He'lam. And the Syrians arrayed themselves against David, and fought with him. ¹⁸And the Syrians fled before Israel; and David slew of the Syrians the men of seven hundred chariots, and forty thousand horsemen, and wounded Shobach the commander of their army, so that he died there. ¹⁹And when all the kings who were servants of Hadade'zer saw that they had been defeated by Israel, they made peace with Israel, and became subject to them. So the Syrians feared to help the Am'monites any more.

David Commits Adultery with Bathsheba

11 *In the spring of the year, the time when kings go forth to battle, David sent Jo'ab, and his servants with him, and all Israel; and they ravaged the Am'monites, and besieged Rabbah. But David remained at Jerusalem.

2 It happened, late one afternoon, when David arose from his couch and was walking upon the roof of the king's house, that he saw from the roof a woman bathing; and the woman was very beautiful. ³And David sent and inquired about the woman. And one said, "Is not this Bathshe'ba, the daughter of Eli'am, the wife of Uri'ah the Hittite?" ⁴So David sent messengers, and took her; and she came to him, and he lay with her. (Now she was purifying herself from her uncleanness.) Then she returned to her house. ⁵And the woman conceived; and she sent and told David, "I am with child."

6 So David sent word to Jo'ab, "Send me Uri'ah the Hittite." And Joab sent Uriah to David. ⁷When Uri'ah came to him, David asked how Jo'ab was doing, and how the people fared, and how the war prospered. ⁸Then David said to Uri'ah, "Go down to your house, and wash your feet." And Uriah went out of the king's house, and there followed him a present from the king. ⁹But Uri'ah slept at the door of the king's house with all the servants of his lord, and did not go down to his house. ¹⁰When they told David, "Uri'ah did not go down to his house," David said to Uriah, "Have you not come from a journey? Why did you not go down to your house?" ¹¹Uri'ah said to David, "The ark and Israel and Judah dwell in booths; and my lord Jo'ab and the servants of my lord are camping in the open field; shall I then go to my house, to eat and to drink, and to lie with my wife?† As you live, and as your soul lives, I will not do this thing." ¹²Then David said to Uri'ah, "Remain here today also, and tomorrow I will let you depart."

11:1: 1 Chron 20:1.

10:16 Hadadezer: A prince of the kingdom of Zobah (8:3–5). **Helam:** Over 35 miles east of the Sea of Galilee.

10:19 made peace: I.e., surrendered and submitted to becoming vassals of Israel. See note on 8:1–14.

11:1–27 David falls headlong into serious sin. In the course of three days, he violates three of the Ten Commandments: he covets his neighbor's wife (11:2–3; Ex 20:17), he commits adultery (11:4; Ex 20:14), and he arranges for the killing of an innocent man (11:15; Ex 20:13). David also abuses his royal authority by commanding others to execute his sinister designs (11:4, 14–15). Predictably, the Lord is "displeased" by this wanton and reckless behavior (11:27) (CCC 2258, 2380, 2514).

11:1 spring: Between the end of the winter rains and the beginning of the harvest season. Within this window of opportunity, farmers are available to serve as fighters on military expeditions (1 Kings 20:26). **when kings go forth:** Appears to be a criticism of David, the king who elects to stay home and relax on his couch while the warriors of Israel march forth to war (11:2). **Joab:** David's nephew and chief military com-

mander (8:16). **Rabbah:** The Ammonite capital, over 20 miles east of the Jordan.

11:2 saw from the roof: A moment of idle curiosity leads to lust and then to adultery (11:4). • Desire is inflamed by the free reign of the eyes, and when unbridled eyes stare at another in idleness, the passion of lust is quickly kindled (St. Clement of Alexandria, *Christ the Educator* 3, 11, 77). **bathing:** A ritual cleansing from menstrual uncleanness (11:4; Lev 15:19–30).

11:3 inquired: On previous occasions, David inquired about the Lord's will for his life (2:1; 5:19, 23). Now, instead of seeking direction from God, he seeks information about a woman who has captivated his senses. **Bathsheba:** Several times designated the "woman" or "wife" of Uriah, emphasizing that she belongs, not to David, but to another man (11:5, 11, 26; 12:10, 15). **Uriah the Hittite:** A Gentile numbered among David's elite warriors (23:39). His name means "Yahweh is my light", suggesting he has come to worship the God of Israel.

11:5 I am with child: Alarming news that prompts David to scheme his way out of public humiliation and punishment.

11:8 a present: The Hebrew can mean a valued "portion" of something, such as food (Gen 43:34). If that is the sense here, it suggests David is trying to stage a romantic evening for Uriah and his wife in the hopes of hiding his sin.

11:11 The ark: Kept in a shelter in the Israelite war camp. See note on Josh 3:3. **lie with my wife?:** Sexual abstinence is a wartime discipline to keep soldiers in a state of ritual purity (1 Sam 21:4–5). Uriah refuses to ignore this code of military conduct while the siege of Rabbah is still in progress.

ᶻHeb *river*.

*11:1: The story of David's double crime shows how he, too, unlike other contemporary monarchs, was under the divine law, not above it, and how God draws good from evil, since it was Bathsheba's son who would succeed David.

†11:11: It was a religious law that soldiers should remain continent in time of war; cf. 1 Sam 21:4–5.

So Uriah remained in Jerusalem that day, and the next. ¹³And David invited him, and he ate in his presence and drank, so that he made him drunk; and in the evening he went out to lie on his couch with the servants of his lord, but he did not go down to his house.

David Has Uriah Killed

14 In the morning David wrote a letter to Jo'ab, and sent it by the hand of Uri'ah. ¹⁵In the letter he wrote, "Set Uri'ah in the forefront of the hardest fighting, and then draw back from him, that he may be struck down, and die." ¹⁶And as Jo'ab was besieging the city, he assigned Uri'ah to the place where he knew there were valiant men. ¹⁷And the men of the city came out and fought with Jo'ab; and some of the servants of David among the people fell. Uri'ah the Hittite was slain also. ¹⁸Then Jo'ab sent and told David all the news about the fighting; ¹⁹and he instructed the messenger, "When you have finished telling all the news about the fighting to the king, ²⁰then, if the king's anger rises, and if he says to you, 'Why did you go so near the city to fight? Did you not know that they would shoot from the wall? ²¹Who killed Abim'elech the son of Jerub'besheth? Did not a woman cast an upper millstone upon him from the wall, so that he died at The'bez? Why did you go so near the wall?' then you shall say, 'Your servant Uri'ah the Hittite is dead also.'"

22 So the messenger went, and came and told David all that Jo'ab had sent him to tell. ²³The messenger said to David, "The men gained an advantage over us, and came out against us in the field; but we drove them back to the entrance of the gate. ²⁴Then the archers shot at your servants from the wall; some of the king's servants are dead; and your servant Uri'ah the Hittite is dead

also." ²⁵David said to the messenger, "Thus shall you say to Jo'ab, 'Do not let this matter trouble you, for the sword devours now one and now another; strengthen your attack upon the city, and overthrow it.' And encourage him."

26 When the wife of Uri'ah heard that Uriah her husband was dead, she made lamentation for her husband. ²⁷And when the mourning was over, David sent and brought her to his house, and she became his wife, and bore him a son. But the thing that David had done displeased the LORD.

Nathan Condemns David, and God Punishes Him

12 And the LORD sent Nathan to David. He came to him, and said to him, "There were two men in a certain city, the one rich and the other poor. ²The rich man had very many flocks and herds; ³but the poor man had nothing but one little ewe lamb, which he had bought. And he brought it up, and it grew up with him and with his children; it used to eat of his morsel, and drink from his cup, and lie in his bosom, and it was like a daughter to him. ⁴Now there came a traveler to the rich man, and he was unwilling to take one of his own flock or herd to prepare for the wayfarer who had come to him, but he took the poor man's lamb, and prepared it for the man who had come to him." ⁵Then David's anger was greatly kindled against the man; and he said to Nathan, "As the LORD lives, the man who has done this deserves to die; ⁶and he shall restore the lamb fourfold, because he did this thing, and because he had no pity."

7 Nathan said to David, "You are the man. Thus says the LORD, the God of Israel, 'I anointed you king over Israel, and I delivered you out of the hand of Saul; ⁸and I gave you your master's house, and

---

11:21 Abimelech: Aspired to kingship but got himself killed by a falling millstone (Judg 9:50–54). David learned from this episode in the Book of Judges the dangers of trying to overthrow a walled city at close quarters. **Jerubbesheth:** Gideon, also called Jerubbaal (Judg 6:32). Here the name of the Canaanite god "Baal" is replaced with a form of the word "shame" (Heb., *bosheth*).

11:25 trouble you: Literally "be evil in your eyes", an expression also used in 11:27. **now one and now another:** As if the death of Uriah were a matter of happenstance rather than deliberate strategy.

11:27 the mourning: A period of seven days (Gen 50:10; Jud 16:24). **a son:** The narrative never gives him a name. He is only called "the child" (12:14, 15, 16, 18, etc.). **displeased the LORD:** Literally "was evil in the eyes of the LORD".

12:1–4 Nathan's parable. Using symbolic narration, in which David is the rich man, Uriah the poor man, and Bathsheba the beloved ewe lamb, Nathan dramatizes the incident in 11:2-4 and indicts the king for abusing his royal power and stealing what does not belong to him. David thinks it a real-life court case and angrily condemns the perpetrator (12:5-6), unaware that he is condemning himself (12:6) (CCC 2538). For another parable designed to elicit an irreversible oath from David, see 14:1-20.

12:3 eat ... drink ... lie: The very things Uriah refused to do with his wife in 11:11. **like a daughter:** The Hebrew

for "daughter" is *bath*—a subtle allusion to the name Bathsheba.

12:4 took: Represents how David "took" Bathsheba (11:4).

12:5 As the LORD lives: An oath formula, making David's pronouncement a binding pledge.

12:6 fourfold: The standard of restitution for stolen sheep in the Torah (Ex 22:1).

12:7 You are the man: The trap springs shut, and David is identified as the rich man of the parable (CCC 1736).

12:7-14 Nathan speaks the Lord's judgment on David and promises dark days ahead. The **sword** of violence (12:10), used against Uriah (12:9), will turn back against the house of David when three of the king's sons are slain (Amnon, 13:28-29; Absalom, 18:15; Adonijah, 1 Kings 2:24-25). Evil will rear its head in David's **own house** (12:11) when his own son Absalom stages a rebellion against him (chaps. 15-18). And another man will lie with David's **wives** in broad daylight (12:11) when Absalom unites himself with the king's royal harem in full view of Israel (16:21-22). David will learn from these hardships that suffering is the painful consequence of spurning the Lord (12:14).

12:8 your master's wives: In the biblical world, kings frequently acquire the royal harem of their predecessor. David's predecessor, King Saul, had at least one wife (1 Sam 14:50) and one concubine (3:7).

your master's wives into your bosom, and gave you the house of Israel and of Judah; and if this were too little, I would add to you as much more. ⁹Why have you despised the word of the LORD, to do what is evil in his sight? You have struck down Uri′ah the Hittite with the sword, and have taken his wife to be your wife, and have slain him with the sword of the Am′monites. ¹⁰Now therefore the sword shall never depart from your house, because you have despised me, and have taken the wife of Uri′ah the Hittite to be your wife.' ¹¹Thus says the LORD, 'Behold, I will raise up evil against you out of your own house; and I will take your wives before your eyes, and give them to your neighbor, and he shall lie with your wives in the sight of this sun. ¹²For you did it secretly; but I will do this thing before all Israel, and before the sun.'" ¹³David said to Nathan, "I have sinned against the LORD." And Nathan said to David, "The LORD also has put away your sin; you shall not die. ¹⁴Nevertheless, because by this deed you have utterly scorned the LORD,ᵃ the child that is born to you shall die." ¹⁵Then Nathan went to his house.

And the LORD struck the child that Uri′ah's wife bore to David, and it became sick. ¹⁶David therefore besought God for the child; and David fasted, and went in and lay all night upon the ground. ¹⁷And the elders of his house stood beside him, to raise him from the ground; but he would not, nor did he eat food with them. ¹⁸On the seventh day the child died. And the servants of David feared to tell him that the child was dead; for they said, "Behold, while the child was yet alive, we spoke to him, and he did not listen to us; how then can we say to him the child is dead? He may do himself some harm." ¹⁹But when David saw that his servants were whispering together, David perceived that the child was dead; and David said to his servants, "Is the child dead?" They said, "He is dead." ²⁰Then David arose from the earth, and washed, and anointed himself, and changed his clothes; and he went into the house of the LORD, and worshiped; he then went to his own house; and when he asked, they set food before him, and he ate. ²¹Then his servants said to him, "What is this thing that you have done? You fasted and wept for the child while it was alive; but when the child died, you arose and ate food." ²²He said, "While the child was still alive, I fasted and wept; for I said, 'Who knows whether the LORD will be gracious to me, that the child may live?' ²³But now he is dead; why should I fast? Can I bring him back again? I shall go to him, but he will not return to me."

Solomon Is Born

24 Then David comforted his wife, Bathshe′ba, and went in to her, and lay with her; and she bore a son, and he called his name Solomon. And the LORD loved him, ²⁵and sent a message by Nathan the prophet; so he called his name Jedidi′ah,ᵇ because of the LORD.

The Ammonites Crushed

26 Now Jo′ab fought against Rabbah of the Am′monites, and took the royal city. ²⁷And Jo′ab sent messengers to David, and said, "I have fought against Rabbah; moreover, I have taken the city of waters. ²⁸Now, then, gather the rest of the people together, and encamp against the city, and take it; lest I take the city, and it be called by my name." ²⁹So David gathered all the people together and went to Rabbah, and fought against it and took it. ³⁰And he took the crown of their kingᶜ from his head; the weight of it was a talent of gold, and in it was a precious stone; and it was placed on David's head.

12:26–31: 1 Chron 20:1–3.

📖 **12:13 I have sinned:** A sincere confession of guilt, as shown by the forgiveness that follows. • The depth of David's remorse at having betrayed the Lord is expressed in Ps 51, which was composed in the aftermath of his adulterous affair. **you shall not die:** An exemption is granted from capital punishment, which is the penalty for both adultery and murder in ancient Israel (Lev 20:10; Deut 22:22).

✠ **12:14 the child:** Designated to bear the consequences of David's sin. • Nathan's oracle illustrates a distinction between the *guilt* of sin and the temporal *punishment* that is due to sin. In this situation, the Lord remits David's guilt (12:13) but requires him to pay a debt of personal suffering that remains on account of his transgressions (12:14) (CCC 1472–73).

12:20 house of the LORD: Presumably the tent that David pitched to house the Ark of the Covenant on Zion (6:17). **worshiped:** David does homage to the will of God, even in a time of grief. He is not embittered by the Lord's discipline, nor does he allow suffering to destroy his faith in the goodness of God. For the loving purpose behind God's discipline, see note on Heb 12:5–6.

12:21 What is this . . . ?: The servants think it strange that David stops rather than starts these mourning rituals when he learns of the child's death.

12:23 I shall go to him: Death will eventually take David to the realm of the deceased. See word study: *Sheol* at Num 16:30.

12:24 Solomon: The tenth son born to David (1 Chron 3:1–5) and the designated heir to his throne (1 Kings 1:46). The name "Solomon" (*Shelomoh*) resembles the Hebrew word for "peace" (*shalom*), a connection noted in 1 Chron 22:9. **the LORD loved him:** Significant from a theological perspective, since divine love is the basis for divine election (Deut 7:6–9). To say that Solomon is loved by God is to suggest that he is chosen by God to be the next king of Israel, as indeed he is (1 Kings 1:29–30).

12:25 Jedidiah: Means "beloved of Yahweh".

12:26–31 The siege of Rabbah comes to an end. It formed the historical backdrop for the David and Bathsheba incident (11:1, 14–25).

12:30 their king: Some prefer to read the Hebrew as "Milcom", the name of the national god of the Ammonites (1 Kings 11:5). **talent of gold:** Estimated at 75 pounds. A crown of this size and weight probably rested on the top of an idol-statue of Milcom.

ᵃHeb *the enemies of the* LORD.
ᵇThat is *beloved of the* LORD.
ᶜOr *Milcom* See Zeph 1:5.

And he brought forth the spoil of the city, a very great amount. ³¹And he brought forth the people who were in it, and set them to labor with saws and iron picks and iron axes, and made them toil at^d the brick-kilns; and thus he did to all the cities of the Am′monites. Then David and all the people returned to Jerusalem.

Amnon Defiles Tamar

13 *Now Ab′salom, David's son, had a beautiful sister, whose name was Ta′mar; and after a time Amnon, David's son, loved her. ²And Amnon was so tormented that he made himself ill because of his sister Ta′mar; for she was a virgin, and it seemed impossible to Amnon to do anything to her. ³But Amnon had a friend, whose name was Jon′adab, the son of Shim′e-ah, David's brother; and Jonadab was a very crafty man. ⁴And he said to him, "O son of the king, why are you so haggard morning after morning? Will you not tell me?" Amnon said to him, "I love Ta′mar, my brother Ab′salom's sister." ⁵Jon′adab said to him, "Lie down on your bed, and pretend to be ill; and when your father comes to see you, say to him, 'Let my sister Ta′mar come and give me bread to eat, and prepare the food in my sight, that I may see it, and eat it from her hand.'" ⁶So Amnon lay down, and pretended to be ill; and when the king came to see him, Amnon said to the king, "Please let my sister Ta′mar come and make a couple of cakes in my sight, that I may eat from her hand."

7 Then David sent home to Ta′mar, saying, "Go to your brother Amnon's house, and prepare food for him." ⁸So Ta′mar went to her brother Amnon's house, where he was lying down. And she took dough, and kneaded it, and made cakes in his sight, and baked the cakes. ⁹And she took the pan and emptied it out before him, but he refused to eat. And Amnon said, "Send out every one from me." So every one went out from him. ¹⁰Then Amnon said to Ta′mar, "Bring the food into the chamber, that I may eat from your hand." And Tamar took the cakes she had made, and brought them into the chamber to Amnon her brother. ¹¹But when she brought them near him to eat, he took hold of her, and said to her, "Come, lie with me, my sister." ¹²She answered him, "No, my brother, do not force me; for such a thing is not done in Israel; do not do this wanton folly. ¹³As for me, where could I carry my shame? And as for you, you would be as one of the wanton fools in Israel. Now therefore, I beg you, speak to the king; for he will not withhold me from you." ¹⁴But he would not listen to her; and being stronger than she, he forced her, and lay with her.

15 Then Amnon hated her with very great hatred; so that the hatred with which he hated her was greater than the love with which he had loved her. And Amnon said to her, "Arise, be gone." ¹⁶But she said to him, "No, my brother; for this wrong in sending me away is greater than the other which you did to me."^e But he would not listen to her. ¹⁷He called the young man who served him and said, "Put this woman out of my presence, and bolt the door after her." ¹⁸Now she was wearing a long robe with sleeves; for thus were the virgin daughters of the king clad of old.^f So his servant put her out, and bolted the door after her. ¹⁹And Ta′mar put ashes on her head, and tore the long robe which she wore; and she laid her hand on her head, and went away, crying aloud as she went.

20 And her brother Ab′salom said to her, "Has Amnon your brother been with you? Now hold your peace, my sister; he is your brother; do not take this to heart." So Ta′mar dwelt, a desolate woman, in her brother Absalom's house. ²¹When King David heard of all these things, he was very angry. ²²But Ab′salom spoke to Amnon neither good nor bad; for Absalom hated Amnon, because he had forced his sister Ta′mar.

13:1–39 Tragedy strikes the house of David when two of the royal sons mimic the iniquity of their father, the one committing sexual sin (Amnon, 13:11–14), and the other committing murder (Absalom, 13:28–29). See note on 11:1–27.

13:1 Absalom: The third son born to David (3:3). Although very dear to his father (18:33), Absalom turns out to be the chief troublemaker of the royal family and the one who causes David the greatest heartache (chaps. 13–18). **Tamar:** A virgin daughter of David (13:2), here the victim of incestuous rape (13:10–14). **Amnon:** The first-born son of David (3:2), i.e., the crown prince who stands to inherit the kingdom of his father (cf. 2 Chron 21:3). His death in 13:29 will open the way for younger sons of David to contend for his throne (e.g., Absalom, chaps. 15–18; Adonijah, 1 Kings 1).

13:3 Jonadab: David's nephew, the son of his older brother Shimeah (or Shammah, 1 Sam 17:13).

13:12 not done in Israel: Sexual relations between a brother and his half sister is defined as incest by the Torah (Lev 18:9; Deut 27:22). **wanton folly:** The same Hebrew term is used for the rape of Dinah in Gen 34:7.

13:13 he will not withhold me: Not a real possibility (Lev 20:17), simply a desperate attempt to halt Amnon's advances. Others conjecture that David might have agreed to such a union on the basis of ancient precedent, namely, the marriage between Abraham and his half sister Sarah (Gen 20:12).

13:14 forced: The Hebrew verb, meaning "subdued" or "humbled", is often connected with the violence of rape (Gen 34:2; Deut 22:24; Judg 19:24; 20:5).

13:15 very great hatred: No sooner does Amnon defile Tamar than he despises her. This makes it clear beyond doubt that his supposed "love" for her was nothing more than lust.

13:16 this wrong: Normally, when a man rapes an unmarried woman, he is obligated to marry her without the possibility of divorce (Deut 22:28–29).

13:21 very angry: David is outraged by the rape of Tamar, and yet he fails to discipline Amnon or bring him to justice. As a result, Absalom will avenge the crime against his sister by slaying her assailant (13:28–29).

---

^dCn: Heb *pass through.*
^eCn Compare Gk Vg: Heb *No, for this great wrong in sending me away is (worse) than the other which you did to me.*
^fCn: Heb *clad in robes.*
*13:1: The first signs of dissension become visible.

Absalom Avenges His Sister

23 After two full years Ab'salom had sheepshearers at Ba'al-ha'zor, which is near E'phraim, and Absalom invited all the king's sons. ²⁴And Ab'salom came to the king, and said, "Behold, your servant has sheepshearers; please let the king and his servants go with your servant." ²⁵But the king said to Ab'salom, "No, my son, let us not all go, lest we be burdensome to you." He pressed him, but he would not go but gave him his blessing. ²⁶Then Ab'salom said, "If not, please let my brother Amnon go with us." And the king said to him, "Why should he go with you?" ²⁷But Ab'salom pressed him until he let Amnon and all the king's sons go with him. ²⁸Then Ab'salom commanded his servants, "Mark when Amnon's heart is merry with wine, and when I say to you, 'Strike Amnon,' then kill him. Fear not; have I not commanded you? Be courageous and be valiant." ²⁹So the servants of Ab'salom did to Amnon as Absalom had commanded. Then all the king's sons arose, and each mounted his mule and fled.

30 While they were on the way, tidings came to David, "Ab'salom has slain all the king's sons, and not one of them is left." ³¹Then the king arose, and tore his garments, and lay on the earth; and all his servants who were standing by tore their garments. ³²But Jon'adab the son of Shim'e-ah, David's brother, said, "Let not my lord suppose that they have killed all the young men the king's sons, for Amnon alone is dead, for by the command of Ab'salom this has been determined from the day he forced his sister Ta'mar. ³³Now therefore let not my lord the king so take it to heart as to suppose that all the king's sons are dead; for Amnon alone is dead."

34 But Ab'salom fled. And the young man who kept the watch lifted up his eyes, and looked, and behold, many people were coming from the Horona'im road𝓰 by the side of the mountain. ³⁵And Jon'adab said to the king, "Behold, the king's sons have come; as your servant said, so it has come about." ³⁶And as soon as he had finished speaking, behold, the king's sons came, and lifted up their voice and wept; and the king also and all his servants wept very bitterly.

Absalom Flees

37 But Ab'salom fled, and went to Talmai the son of Ammi'hud, king of Ge'shur. And David mourned for his son day after day. ³⁸So Ab'salom fled, and went to Ge'shur, and was there three years. ³⁹And the spiritʰ of the king longed to go forth to Ab'salom; for he was comforted about Amnon, seeing he was dead.

David Is Persuaded to Bring Absalom Back

14 Now Jo'ab the son of Zeru'iah perceived that the king's heart went out to Ab'salom. ²And Jo'ab sent to Teko'a, and fetched from there a wise woman, and said to her, "Pretend to be a mourner, and put on mourning garments; do not anoint yourself with oil, but behave like a woman who has been mourning many days for the dead; ³and go to the king, and speak thus to him." So Jo'ab put the words in her mouth.

4 When the woman of Teko'a came to the king, she fell on her face to the ground, and did obeisance, and said, "Help, O king." ⁵And the king said to her, "What is your trouble?" She answered, "Alas, I am a widow; my husband is dead. ⁶And your handmaid had two sons, and they quarreled with one another in the field; there was no one to part them, and one struck the other and killed him. ⁷And now the whole family has risen against your handmaid, and they say, 'Give up the man who struck his brother, that

---

13:23 two full years: More than sufficient time for David to deal with Amnon according to his crimes. **sheepshearers:** Wool harvesting is a time of celebration and feasting (1 Sam 25:2–8). **Baal-hazor:** Almost 15 miles north of Jerusalem.

13:26 let my brother Amnon go: As if Amnon, the heir apparent, would be treated as the guest of honor in David's place.

13:29 mule: Mules are ridden by members of the royal family (18:9; 1 Kings 1:33).

13:31 tore his garments: A gesture of extreme distress (Gen 37:34; 1 Sam 4:12).

13:34 Horonaim: A reference to Upper and Lower Bethhoron, northwest of Jerusalem.

13:37 Absalom fled: In fear of reprisal from his brothers. **Talmai:** Grandfather of Absalom and the ruler of the small kingdom of Geshur, east of the Sea of Galilee. It is no surprise that Absalom should seek asylum here, since his mother, Maacah, is the daughter of Talmai and a princess of Geshur (3:3).

14:1 Joab: David's nephew and chief military officer (8:16). **went out to Absalom:** The Hebrew can also mean that David's heart "was against Absalom". It is difficult to say which is intended: 13:39 suggests the former, while 14:24 favors the latter.

14:2 Tekoa: About ten miles south of Jerusalem and the hometown of the prophet Amos (Amos 1:1). **Pretend to be a mourner:** Joab, in staging this ruse, appears to be acting in the interests of the kingdom. So long as the heir apparent to David's throne is estranged from the royal family and living in exile, the stability and continuity of Israel's government is in jeopardy.

14:4–20 The tale of the Tekoa woman. Like Nathan's parable in 12:1–4, it is designed to elicit an irrevocable oath from David. In this case, it is meant to secure the safe return of Absalom from exile as well as legal protection for his life. By indicating that the surviving son is his father's "heir" (14:7), the tale assumes that Absalom is next in line for the throne, even though he is David's third son (3:3). David's second son, Chileab (3:3), either has died by this point in the story or is otherwise unsuited for kingship. • Parallels with the story of Cain and Abel are obvious and may be intended. Both focus on two sons (14:6; Gen 4:2) alone in a field (14:6; Gen 4:8), with one brother being killed by the other (14:6; Gen 4:8). And just as the culprit's life is endangered as a result (14:7; Gen 4:14), so a higher authority steps in to ensure his protection (David in 14:10–11; God in Gen 4:15).

14:7 that we may kill: Refers to the ancient custom of blood vengeance, a form of tribal justice in which the near kinsman of a slain victim (called "the avenger of blood") is called upon to hunt down the murderer and take his life in return (Num 35:19).

𝓰Cn Compare Gk: Heb *the road behind him.*
ʰGk: Heb *David.*

we may kill him for the life of his brother whom he slew'; and so they would destroy the heir also. Thus they would quench my coal which is left, and leave to my husband neither name nor remnant upon the face of the earth."

8 Then the king said to the woman, "Go to your house, and I will give orders concerning you." 9And the woman of Teko'a said to the king, "On me be the guilt, my lord the king, and on my father's house; let the king and his throne be guiltless." 10The king said, "If any one says anything to you, bring him to me, and he shall never touch you again." 11Then she said, "Please let the king invoke the LORD your God, that the avenger of blood slay no more, and my son be not destroyed." He said, "As the LORD lives, not one hair of your son shall fall to the ground."

12 Then the woman said, "Please let your handmaid speak a word to my lord the king." He said, "Speak." 13And the woman said, "Why then have you planned such a thing against the people of God? For in giving this decision the king convicts himself, inasmuch as the king does not bring his banished one home again. 14We must all die, we are like water spilt on the ground, which cannot be gathered up again; but God will not take away the life of him who devises¹ means not to keep his banished one an outcast. 15Now I have come to say this to my lord the king because the people have made me afraid; and your handmaid thought, 'I will speak to the king; it may be that the king will perform the request of his servant. 16For the king will hear, and deliver his servant from the hand of the man who would destroy me and my son together from the heritage of God.' 17And your handmaid thought, 'The word of my lord the king will set me at rest'; for my lord the king is like the angel of God to discern good and evil. The LORD your God be with you!"

18 Then the king answered the woman, "Do not hide from me anything I ask you." And the woman said, "Let my lord the king speak." 19The king said, "Is the hand of Jo'ab with you in all this?" The woman answered and said, "As surely as you live, my lord the king, one cannot turn to the right hand or to the left from anything that my lord the king has said. It was your servant Joab who bade me; it was he who put all these words in the mouth of your handmaid. 20In order to change the course of affairs your servant Jo'ab did this. But my lord has wisdom like the wisdom of the angel of God to know all things that are on the earth."

21 Then the king said to Jo'ab, "Behold now, I grant this; go, bring back the young man Ab'-salom." 22And Jo'ab fell on his face to the ground, and did obeisance, and blessed the king; and Joab said, "Today your servant knows that I have found favor in your sight, my lord the king, in that the king has granted the request of his servant." 23So Jo'ab arose and went to Ge'shur, and brought Ab'salom to Jerusalem. 24And the king said, "Let him dwell apart in his own house; he is not to come into my presence." So Ab'salom dwelt apart in his own house, and did not come into the king's presence.

25 Now in all Israel there was no one so much to be praised for his beauty as Ab'salom; from the sole of his foot to the crown of his head there was no blemish in him. 26And when he cut the hair of his head (for at the end of every year he used to cut it; when it was heavy on him, he cut it), he weighed the hair of his head, two hundred shekels by the king's weight. 27There were born to Ab'salom three sons, and one daughter whose name was Ta'mar; she was a beautiful woman.

David Forgives Absalom

28 So Ab'salom dwelt two full years in Jerusalem, without coming into the king's presence. 29Then Ab'salom sent for Jo'ab, to send him to the king; but Joab would not come to him. And he sent a second time, but Joab would not come. 30Then he said to his servants, "See, Jo'ab's field is next to mine, and he has barley there; go and set it on fire." So Ab'salom's servants set the field on fire. 31Then Jo'ab arose and went to Ab'salom at his house, and said to him, "Why have your servants

---

14:11 As the LORD lives: An oath formula, making David's promise to intervene a binding pledge in Yahweh's name. **not one hair:** An (unwitting) allusion to Absalom, famous for his long, thick hair (14:26). The oath is eerily prophetic, for Absalom will die with his head and hair suspended above the ground in a tree branch (18:9–15).

14:17 like the angel of God: Words of flattery, implying that David is gifted with angelic wisdom and a clear perception of all things right and wrong (14:20; 19:27). They are also words of irony, for the king has failed to distinguish between good and evil in the treatment of his exiled son, Absalom. See word study: *Angel of the LORD* at Gen 16:7.

14:18 Do not hide: Excessive flattery makes David suspicious. Also, he probably wonders how a peasant woman could know so much about the internal affairs of the royal family unless she has been coached by someone from inside his administration (Joab, 14:3).

14:23 Geshur: The place of Absalom's exile, east of the Sea of Galilee (13:37).

14:24 dwell apart: Away from the royal palace in isolated quarters. Evidently no genuine reconciliation has taken place between the king and his heir for "two full years" (14:28).

14:25 his beauty: Reminiscent of the initial description of Saul, which likewise focused on outward appearances (1 Sam 9:2). In both cases, it bodes trouble for the days ahead, since God is more interested in the hidden thoughts and motives of the heart (1 Sam 16:7).

14:26 hair of his head: Details about Absalom's hair prepare for the bizarre circumstances of his death. See note on 14:11. **two hundred shekels:** Rhetorical exaggeration, since this would mean that Absalom's hair weighed over five pounds.

14:27 three sons: Apparently died young, since Absalom laments the lack of a male heir in 18:18. **Tamar:** Named after her aunt Tamar, the sister of Absalom (13:1).

14:30 set it on fire: A drastic way of getting Joab's attention.

---

¹ Cn: Heb *and he devises*.

set my field on fire?" ³²Ab′salom answered Jo′ab, "Behold, I sent word to you, 'Come here, that I may send you to the king, to ask, "Why have I come from Ge′shur? It would be better for me to be there still." Now therefore let me go into the presence of the king; and if there is guilt in me, let him kill me.'" ³³Then Jo′ab went to the king, and told him; and he summoned Ab′salom. So he came to the king, and bowed himself on his face to the ground before the king; and the king kissed Absalom.

Absalom Usurps the Throne

15 After this Ab′salom got himself a chariot and horses, and fifty men to run before him. ²And Ab′salom used to rise early and stand beside the way of the gate; and when any man had a suit to come before the king for judgment, Absalom would call to him, and say, "From what city are you?" And when he said, "Your servant is of such and such a tribe in Israel," ³Ab′salom would say to him, "See, your claims are good and right; but there is no man deputed by the king to hear you." ⁴Ab′salom said moreover, "Oh that I were judge in the land! Then every man with a suit or cause might come to me, and I would give him justice." ⁵And whenever a man came near to do obeisance to him, he would put out his hand, and take hold of him, and kiss him. ⁶Thus Ab′salom did to all of Israel who came to the king for judgment; so Absalom stole the hearts of the men of Israel.

7 And at the end of four ʲ years Ab′salom said to the king, "Please let me go and pay my vow, which I have vowed to the LORD, in He′bron. ⁸For your servant vowed a vow while I dwelt at Ge′shur in Ar′am, saying, 'If the LORD will indeed bring me back to Jerusalem, then I will offer worship to the LORD.'" ⁹The king said to him, "Go in peace." So he arose, and went to He′bron. ¹⁰But Ab′salom sent secret messengers throughout all the tribes of Israel, saying, "As soon as you hear the sound of the trumpet, then say, 'Ab′salom is king at He′bron!'" ¹¹With Ab′salom went two hundred men from Jerusalem who were invited guests, and they went in their simplicity, and knew nothing. ¹²And while Ab′salom was offering the sacrifices, he sent for ᵏ Ahith′ophel the Gi′lonite, David's counselor, from his city Gi′loh. And the conspiracy grew strong, and the people with Absalom kept increasing.

David Flees from Jerusalem

13 And a messenger came to David, saying, "The hearts of the men of Israel have gone after Ab′salom." ¹⁴Then David said to all his servants who were with him at Jerusalem, "Arise, and let us flee; or else there will be no escape for us from Ab′salom; go in haste, lest he overtake us quickly, and bring down evil upon us, and strike the city with the edge of the sword." ¹⁵And the king's servants said to the king, "Behold, your servants are ready to do whatever my lord the king decides." ¹⁶So the king went forth, and all his household after him. And the king left ten concubines to keep the house. ¹⁷And the king went forth, and all the people after him; and they halted at the last house. ¹⁸And all his servants passed by him;

14:33 kissed Absalom: Suggests some level of reconciliation (Lk 15:20). Although the gesture is good in itself, Absalom will continue to go unpunished by David, and this will come back to haunt the king when Absalom stages a coup d'état in chaps. 15–18. For a parallel situation where David's failure to discipline his sons ends in tragedy, see note on 13:21.

15:1—18:33 Absalom's revolt. In a carefully plotted conspiracy, David's third son and heir to the throne launches a campaign of self-promotion, gains a significant following in Israel, and executes a takeover of his father's capital city and kingdom. Absalom even wins to his side a high-ranking official from David's court (Ahithophel, 15:12). The ordeal forces David and his supporters to flee Jerusalem (15:14) and to seek refuge east of the Jordan (17:22).

15:1 chariot ... horses: Symbols of royalty, advertising Absalom's ambitions to be king. **fifty men:** Armed soldiers and bodyguards. Adonijah, the fourth son of David (3:4), will take the same initial step when he makes his own bid for the throne (1 Kings 1:5).

15:2 before the king for judgment: Israel's monarch is also akin to a chief justice who settles disputed civil cases (1 Kings 3:16–28).

15:3 no man deputed: Insinuates that David is inattentive to the concerns of the common folk. Notice that Absalom is churning up discontent with the current administration while posturing as a sympathetic "man of the people" (cf. 15:4).

15:6 the men of Israel: The general population and perhaps the national militia of tribal warriors as well.

15:7 let me ... pay my vow: Absalom hides his plans for a coup behind a cloak of piety. In the Bible, vows are conditional promises (If ... then ...) that depend upon God's willingness to answer specific prayers favorably (cf. Gen 28:20–21; Judg 11:30–31). **Hebron:** Absalom's birthplace, nearly 20 miles south of Jerusalem (3:2–3). It was in Hebron that David was first proclaimed king (2:1–4). See note on 2:1.

15:8 Geshur: East of the Sea of Galilee, where Absalom spent three years in exile (13:38).

15:12 Ahithophel: Grandfather of Bathsheba (11:3; 23:34) and possibly the trusted friend whose betrayal of David is lamented in Ps 41:9 and 55:12–14. One suspects that his loyalty to David was shaken when the king had sinful relations with his granddaughter, Bathsheba, and arranged the death of his grandson-in-law, Uriah (11:2–25). • The treachery of Ahithophel prefigures the treachery of Judas Iscariot in the Gospels. Not only do both men betray the Lord's anointed king, despite being close associates, but both consent to a nighttime ambush (17:1–4; Mt 26:47–48), and, regretting their actions, both commit suicide by hanging (17:23; Mt 27:5). By implication, the painful exile of David, crossing the Kidron (15:23) to the Mount of Olives (15:30), foreshadows the beginning of Jesus' Passion, when he, too, crosses the Kidron (Jn 18:1) to the garden of Gethsemane, which lies on the western slope of the Mount of Olives (Mk 14:26). See note on Mt 26:56. **Gilonite:** I.e., from the town of Giloh in the hill country of Judah (Josh 15:51).

15:16 left ten concubines: An indication that David hopes to return to Jerusalem once the political storm blows over. He is unaware that he is setting the stage for Nathan's prophecy in 12:11 to be fulfilled (see 16:21–22).

15:18 Cherethites ... Pelethites: Foreign mercenaries serving as David's bodyguards (8:18; 20:7). **Gittites:** Persons from the Philistine city of "Gath" (1 Sam 6:17).

ʲ Gk Syr: Heb *forty*.
ᵏ Or *sent*.

and all the Cher'ethites, and all the Pel'ethites, and all the six hundred Gittites who had followed him from Gath, passed on before the king.

19 Then the king said to Ittai the Gittite, "Why do you also go with us? Go back, and stay with the king; for you are a foreigner, and also an exile from[1] your home. [20]You came only yesterday, and shall I today make you wander about with us, seeing I go I know not where? Go back, and take your brethren with you; and may the Lord show[m] mercy and faithfulness to you." [21]But Ittai answered the king, "As the Lord lives, and as my lord the king lives, wherever my lord the king shall be, whether for death or for life, there also will your servant be." [22]And David said to Ittai, "Go then, pass on." So Ittai the Gittite passed on, with all his men and all the little ones who were with him. [23]And all the country wept aloud as all the people passed by, and the king crossed the brook Kidron, and all the people passed on toward the wilderness.

24 And Abi'athar came up, and behold, Za'dok came also, with all the Levites, bearing the ark of the covenant of God; and they set down the ark of God, until the people had all passed out of the city. [25]Then the king said to Za'dok, "Carry the ark of God back into the city. If I find favor in the eyes of the Lord, he will bring me back and let me see both it and his habitation; [26]but if he says, 'I have no pleasure in you,' behold, here I am, let him do to me what seems good to him." [27]The king also said to Za'dok the priest, "Look,[n] go back to the city in peace, you and Abi'athar,[o] with your two sons, Ahim'a-az your son, and Jonathan the son of Abiathar. [28]See, I will wait at the fords of the wilderness, until word comes from you to inform me." [29]So Za'dok and Abi'athar carried the ark of God back to Jerusalem; and they remained there.

30 But David went up the ascent of the Mount of Olives, weeping as he went, barefoot and with his head covered; and all the people who were with him covered their heads, and they went up, weeping as they went. [31]And it was told David, "Ahith'ophel

is among the conspirators with Ab'salom." And David said, "O Lord, I pray you, turn the counsel of Ahithophel into foolishness."

Hushai Becomes David's Spy

32 When David came to the summit, where God was worshiped, behold, Hu'shai the Ar'chite came to meet him with his coat torn and earth upon his head. [33]David said to him, "If you go on with me, you will be a burden to me. [34]But if you return to the city, and say to Ab'salom, 'I will be your servant, O king; as I have been your father's servant in time past, so now I will be your servant,' then you will defeat for me the counsel of Ahith'ophel. [35]Are not Za'dok and Abi'athar the priests with you there? So whatever you hear from the king's house, tell it to Zadok and Abiathar the priests. [36]Behold, their two sons are with them there, Ahim'a-az, Za'dok's son, and Jonathan, Abi'athar's son; and by them you shall send to me everything you hear." [37]So Hu'shai, David's friend, came into the city, just as Ab'salom was entering Jerusalem.

David Meets Ziba

16 When David had passed a little beyond the summit, Zi'ba the servant of Mephib'osheth met him, with a couple of donkeys saddled, bearing two hundred loaves of bread, a hundred bunches of raisins, a hundred of summer fruits, and a skin of wine. [2]And the king said to Zi'ba, "Why have you brought these?" Ziba answered, "The donkeys are for the king's household to ride on, the bread and summer fruit for the young men to eat, and the wine for those who faint in the wilderness to drink." [3]And the king said, "And where is your master's son?" Zi'ba said to the king, "Behold, he remains in Jerusalem; for he said, 'Today the house of Israel will give me back the kingdom of my father.'" [4]Then the king said to Zi'ba, "Behold, all that belonged to Mephib'osheth is now yours." And Ziba said, "I do obeisance; let me ever find favor in your sight, my lord the king."

Shime-i Curses David

5 When King David came to Bahu'rim, there came out a man of the family of the house of Saul,

---

15:20 only yesterday: Perhaps the real concern is that the loyalty of Ittai and his Philistine comrades has not been sufficiently tested. They could easily turn against David when he is most vulnerable.

15:21 As the Lord lives: Introduces an oath of loyalty, similar to the one in Ruth 1:16–17.

15:23 the brook Kidron: A seasonal watercourse in the ravine directly east of Jerusalem. It runs between the city and the Mount of Olives.

15:24 Abiathar ... Zadok: The two chief priests in David's time (20:25). They and their sons will continue to serve David in Jerusalem as secret informants (15:27–28).

15:25 If I find favor: David humbles himself in acceptance of the Lord's will. As a result, he shows remarkable serenity in

the face of this upheaval. **his habitation:** The tent that David pitched for the ark on Mt. Zion (6:17).

15:27 Ahimaaz ... Jonathan: Recruited as messengers to bring David news from Jerusalem (15:36).

15:30 barefoot: A sign of mourning (Ezek 24:17).

15:32 Hushai the Archite: One of David's royal court advisors (1 Chron 27:33), officially titled the king's "friend" (15:37). His name suggests he is a Canaanite from west of Bethel (Josh 16:2). David wants him to counteract the influence of Ahithophel on Absalom (15:34).

16:1 the summit: The crest of the Mount of Olives, directly east of Jerusalem (15:30). **Ziba:** Former royal servant put in charge of farming the lands of King Saul's crippled grandson, **Mephibosheth** (9:2, 9–10). See note on 4:4.

16:3 Today ... kingdom of my father: Utterly false and slanderous words, judging from Mephibosheth's account in 19:24–30.

16:5 Bahurim: A town of Benjamin northeast of Jerusalem. **Shimei:** A deeply embittered supporter of Saul and his

---

[1]Gk Syr Vg: Heb *to*.
[m]Gk: Heb lacks *may the Lord show*.
[n]Gk: Heb *Are you a seer* or *Do you see?*
[o]Cn: Heb lacks *and Abiathar*.

whose name was Shim'e-i, the son of Gera; and as he came he cursed continually. [6]And he threw stones at David, and at all the servants of King David; and all the people and all the mighty men were on his right hand and on his left. [7]And Shim'e-i said as he cursed, "Begone, begone, you man of blood, you worthless fellow! [8]The LORD has avenged upon you all the blood of the house of Saul, in whose place you have reigned; and the LORD has given the kingdom into the hand of your son Ab'salom. See, your ruin is on you; for you are a man of blood."

9 Then Abi'shai the son of Zeru'iah said to the king, "Why should this dead dog curse my lord the king? Let me go over and take off his head." [10]But the king said, "What have I to do with you, you sons of Zeru'iah? If he is cursing because the LORD has said to him, 'Curse David,' who then shall say, 'Why have you done so?'" [11]And David said to Abi'shai and to all his servants, "Behold, my own son seeks my life; how much more now may this Benjaminite! Let him alone, and let him curse; for the LORD has bidden him. [12]It may be that the LORD will look upon my affliction,[p] and that the LORD will repay me with good for this cursing of me today." [13]So David and his men went on the road, while Shim'e-i went along on the hillside opposite him and cursed as he went, and threw stones at him and flung dust. [14]And the king, and all the people who were with him, arrived weary at the Jordan;[q] and there he refreshed himself.

The Counsel of Ahithophel

15 Now Ab'salom and all the people, the men of Israel, came to Jerusalem, and Ahith'ophel with him. [16]And when Hu'shai the Ar'chite, David's friend, came to Ab'salom, Hushai said to Absalom, "Long live the king! Long live the king!" [17]And Ab'salom said to Hu'shai, "Is this your loyalty to your friend? Why did you not go with your friend?" [18]And Hu'shai said to Ab'salom, "No; for whom the LORD and this people and all the men of Israel have chosen, his I will be, and with him I will remain. [19]And again, whom should I serve? Should it not be his son? As I have served your father, so I will serve you."

20 Then Ab'salom said to Ahith'ophel, "Give your counsel; what shall we do?" [21]Ahith'ophel said to Ab'salom, "Go in to your father's concubines, whom he has left to keep the house; and all Israel will hear that you have made yourself odious to your father, and the hands of all who are with you will be strengthened." [22]So they pitched a tent for Ab'salom upon the roof; and Absalom went in to his father's concubines in the sight of all Israel.* [23]Now in those days the counsel which Ahith'ophel gave was as if one consulted the oracle[r] of God; so was all the counsel of Ahithophel esteemed, both by David and by Ab'salom.

17 Moreover Ahith'ophel said to Ab'salom, "Let me choose twelve thousand men, and I will set out and pursue David tonight. [2]I will come upon him while he is weary and discouraged, and throw him into a panic; and all the people who are with him will flee. I will strike down the king only, [3]and I will bring all the people back to you as a bride comes home to her husband. You seek the life of only one man,[s] and all the people will be at peace." [4]And the advice pleased Ab'salom and all the elders of Israel.

The Counsel of Hushai

5 Then Ab'salom said, "Call Hu'shai the Ar'chite also, and let us hear what he has to say." [6]And when Hu'shai came to Ab'salom, Absalom said to him, "Thus has Ahith'ophel spoken; shall we do as he advises? If not, you speak." [7]Then Hu'shai said to Ab'salom, "This time the counsel which Ahith'ophel

---

defunct regime. Here he displays a rabid hatred for David, whom he considers a usurper of Saul's throne (16:8); later, after Absalom's rebellion fizzles out, he acknowledges his wrongdoing and submits to David's rule (19:18–23).

16:6 the mighty men: David's most accomplished warriors. See note on 23:8–39.

16:8 blood of the house of Saul: David is declared responsible for the slaying of Abner (3:27) and Ish-bosheth (4:7), and possibly for the execution of seven of Saul's male descendants (21:1–14).

16:9 Abishai: One of David's nephews and military lieutenants. He is quick to recommend violence as the fast solution to David's political problems (19:21; 1 Sam 26:8).

16:11 let him curse: David is learning to accept his trials as divine discipline and to see that resisting the Lord's will is futile.

16:16 Hushai the Archite: Pretends to shift his allegiance from David to Absalom. His fake defection is a clever way to gather intelligence from Absalom's inner council and smuggle it out to David (17:15–16). See note on 15:32.

16:18 whom the LORD ... this people ... have chosen: A strategically ambiguous declaration of loyalty. Absalom assumes the reference is to him, but readers know that David is actually the one chosen by God (6:21) and by all Israel (5:1–3).

16:20–23 Absalom takes control of Jerusalem and makes a public claim on David's throne. His seizure of power is advertised by sleeping with the king's harem in plain sight of the city. Nathan prophesied this very thing would happen as a manifestation of God's judgment on David for his adultery with Bathsheba (12:11–12). Notice that Absalom has sexual relations with his father's concubines on the rooftop of the royal palace—the very same place where David looked with lust on the bathing Bathsheba (11:2).

17:1–14 Absalom receives conflicting counsel on how best to eliminate David. Ahithophel recommends *swift* action to assassinate the king while he is close and still vulnerable, but Hushai advises *delayed* action in the interests of wiping out both David and his defenders. Only pretending to support Absalom and his aims, Hushai is actually trying to buy time for David to escape, regroup, and establish a strong defensive position against attack. For more on Ahithophel and Hushai, see notes on 15:12 and 16:16.

---

[p] Gk Vg: Heb *iniquity*.
[q] Gk: Heb lacks *at the Jordan*.
[r] Heb *word*.
[s] Gk: Heb *like the return of the whole (is) the man whom you seek*.
*16:22: Absalom's action meant that he was supplanting his father in the kingship; cf. 3:7; 12:8.

has given is not good." ⁸Hu′shai said moreover, "You know that your father and his men are mighty men, and that they are enraged, like a bear robbed of her cubs in the field. Besides, your father is expert in war; he will not spend the night with the people. ⁹Behold, even now he has hidden himself in one of the pits, or in some other place. And when some of the people fall[t] at the first attack, whoever hears it will say, 'There has been a slaughter among the people who follow Ab′salom.' ¹⁰Then even the valiant man, whose heart is like the heart of a lion, will utterly melt with fear; for all Israel knows that your father is a mighty man, and that those who are with him are valiant men. ¹¹But my counsel is that all Israel be gathered to you, from Dan to Be′er-she′ba, as the sand by the sea for multitude, and that you go to battle in person. ¹²So we shall come upon him in some place where he is to be found, and we shall light upon him as the dew falls on the ground; and of him and all the men with him not one will be left. ¹³If he withdraws into a city, then all Israel will bring ropes to that city, and we shall drag it into the valley, until not even a pebble is to be found there." ¹⁴And Ab′salom and all the men of Israel said, "The counsel of Hu′shai the Ar′chite is better than the counsel of Ahith′ophel." For the Lord had ordained to defeat the good counsel of Ahithophel, so that the Lord might bring evil upon Ab′salom.

Hushai Warns David to Escape

15 Then Hu′shai said to Za′dok and Abi′athar the priests, "Thus and so did Ahith′ophel counsel Ab′salom and the elders of Israel; and thus and so have I counseled. ¹⁶Now therefore send quickly and tell David, 'Do not lodge tonight at the fords of the wilderness, but by all means pass over; lest the king and all the people who are with him be swallowed up.'" ¹⁷Now Jonathan and Ahim′a-az were waiting at En-ro′gel; a maidservant used to

go and tell them, and they would go and tell King David; for they must not be seen entering the city. ¹⁸But a lad saw them, and told Ab′salom; so both of them went away quickly, and came to the house of a man at Bahu′rim, who had a well in his courtyard; and they went down into it. ¹⁹And the woman took and spread a covering over the well's mouth, and scattered grain upon it; and nothing was known of it. ²⁰When Ab′salom's servants came to the woman at the house, they said, "Where are Ahim′a-az and Jonathan?" And the woman said to them, "They have gone over the brook[u] of water." And when they had sought and could not find them, they returned to Jerusalem.

21 After they had gone, the men came up out of the well, and went and told King David. They said to David, "Arise, and go quickly over the water; for thus and so has Ahith′ophel counseled against you." ²²Then David arose, and all the people who were with him, and they crossed the Jordan; by daybreak not one was left who had not crossed the Jordan.

23 When Ahith′ophel saw that his counsel was not followed, he saddled his donkey, and went off home to his own city. And he set his house in order, and hanged himself; and he died, and was buried in the tomb of his father.

24 Then David came to Ma″hana′im. And Ab′-salom crossed the Jordan with all the men of Israel. ²⁵Now Ab′salom had set Ama′sa over the army instead of Jo′ab. Amasa was the son of a man named Ithra the Ish′maelite,[v] who had married Ab′igail the daughter of Na′hash, sister of Zeru′iah, Jo′ab's mother. ²⁶And Israel and Ab′salom encamped in the land of Gilead.

27 When David came to Ma″hana′im, Shobi the son of Na′hash from Rabbah of the Am′monites, and Ma′chir the son of Am′mi-el from Lo-de′bar, and Barzil′lai the Gileadite from Ro′gelim, ²⁸brought

---

17:8 expert in war: A shrewd rhetorical reminder. Hushai is putting fear into the heart of Absalom in the hopes he will initiate a nationwide muster of warriors from all Israel before engaging David in combat.

17:11 Dan to Beer-sheba: The full extent of Israelite territory from north to south.

17:14 defeat the good counsel: Shows that the Lord has answered David's prayer (15:31).

17:15–22 David's secret communications network. Information passes from Hushai to the two chief priests (17:15), out of Jerusalem by an inconspicuous maidservant (17:17), to the sons of the chief priests, waiting south of the city (17:17), and finally out to David and his exiled supporters at the Jordan (17:21).

17:17 En-rogel: A spring in the valley south of Jerusalem.

17:18 Bahurim: A town of Benjamin northeast of Jerusalem.

17:23 not followed: Ahithophel realizes that failure to eliminate David by surprise, as he advised in 17:1–2, increases the likelihood that David will regain power in Jerusalem and

avenge himself on all traitors. **hanged himself:** The only premeditated suicide in the OT. Other instances of suicide are mentioned, but these are acts of desperation that occur in combat situations (Judg 9:54; 1 Sam 31:4; 1 Kings 16:18; 2 Mac 14:41). For the significance of Ahithophel's hanging, see note on 15:12.

17:24 Mahanaim: East of the Jordan River and formerly the command center of Saul's son and would-be successor, Ish-bosheth (2:8–9). The name in Hebrew means "two armies" or "two camps" (Gen 32:2).

17:25 Amasa: David's nephew (1 Chron 2:13–17). This means that Amasa, Absalom, and Joab are all cousins. The political crisis that rumbles on is thus a family feud at more than one level. **Joab:** David's military commander (8:16). **Ishmaelite:** A descendant of Ishmael, the half-Egyptian son of Abraham (Gen 25:12).

17:26 Gilead: The land east of central Canaan, across the Jordan River.

17:27–29 Food, supplies, and encouragement come to David from wealthy sympathizers in the Transjordan.

17:27 Machir: Formerly the caretaker of Mephibosheth (9:4). **Barzillai:** Remembered for his kindness and rewarded by David in 19:31–40.

---

[t] Or *when he falls upon them.*
[u] The meaning of the Hebrew word is uncertain.
[v] 1 Chron 2:17: Heb *Israelite.*

beds, basins, and earthen vessels, wheat, barley, meal, parched grain, beans and lentils,[w] [29]honey and curds and sheep and cheese from the herd, for David and the people with him to eat; for they said, "The people are hungry and weary and thirsty in the wilderness."

The Defeat and Death of Absalom

18 Then David mustered the men who were with him, and set over them commanders of thousands and commanders of hundreds. [2]And David sent forth the army, one third under the command of Jo'ab, one third under the command of Abi'shai the son of Zeru'iah, Joab's brother, and one third under the command of Ittai the Gittite. And the king said to the men, "I myself will also go out with you." [3]But the men said, "You shall not go out. For if we flee, they will not care about us. If half of us die, they will not care about us. But you are worth ten thousand of us;[x] therefore it is better that you send us help from the city." [4]The king said to them, "Whatever seems best to you I will do." So the king stood at the side of the gate, while all the army marched out by hundreds and by thousands. [5]And the king ordered Jo'ab and Abi'shai and Ittai, "Deal gently for my sake with the young man Ab'salom." And all the people heard when the king gave orders to all the commanders about Absalom.

[6] So the army went out into the field against Israel; and the battle was fought in the forest of E'phraim. [7]And the men of Israel were defeated there by the servants of David, and the slaughter there was great on that day, twenty thousand men. [8]The battle spread over the face of all the country; and the forest devoured more people that day than the sword.

[9] And Ab'salom chanced to meet the servants of David. Absalom was riding upon his mule, and the mule went under the thick branches of a great oak, and his head caught fast in the oak, and he was left hanging[y] between heaven and earth, while the mule that was under him went on. [10]And a certain man saw it, and told Jo'ab, "Behold, I saw Ab'salom hanging in an oak." [11]Jo'ab said to the man who told him, "What, you saw him! Why then did you not strike him there to the ground? I would have been glad to give you ten pieces of silver and a belt." [12]But the man said to Jo'ab, "Even if I felt in my hand the weight of a thousand pieces of silver, I would not put forth my hand against the king's son; for in our hearing the king commanded you and Abi'shai and Ittai, 'For my sake protect the young man Ab'salom.' [13]On the other hand, if I had dealt treacherously against his life[z] (and there is nothing hidden from the king), then you yourself would have stood aloof." [14]Jo'ab said, "I will not waste time like this with you." And he took three darts in his hand, and thrust them into the heart of Ab'salom, while he was still alive in the oak. [15]And ten young men, Jo'ab's armor-bearers, surrounded Ab'salom and struck him, and killed him.

[16] Then Jo'ab blew the trumpet, and the troops came back from pursuing Israel; for Joab restrained them. [17]And they took Ab'salom, and threw him into a great pit in the forest, and raised over him a very great heap of stones; and all Israel fled every one to his own home. [18]Now Ab'salom in his lifetime had taken and set up for himself the pillar which is in the King's Valley, for he said, "I have no son to keep my name in remembrance"; he called the pillar after his own name, and it is called Absalom's monument to this day.

David Hears Tidings

[19] Then said Ahim'a-az the son of Za'dok, "Let me run, and carry tidings to the king that the LORD has delivered him from the power of his enemies." [20]And Jo'ab said to him, "You are not to carry

---

18:1–33 David quickly organizes his men to meet Absalom's forces in battle. Despite being greatly outnumbered, the king's men prevail, putting Absalom to death and putting down the uprising that he spearheaded. Despite victory and the end of his exile, David is utterly heartbroken at the news of his son's death (18:33).

18:2 one third: For the division of military forces into three companies, see 1 Sam 11:11. **Joab ... Abishai:** David's nephews, born to his sister Zeruiah (2:18). **Ittai:** A loyal supporter from Gath. See note on 15:18.

18:6 the forest of Ephraim: Northwest of David's command center, Mahanaim (17:24). It was an unusual setting for a battle, but it was prime terrain for David's guerilla fighters to divide Absalom's soldiers and thus reduce his advantage of numbers.

18:9 his mule: The transportation of choice for the royal family (13:29; 1 Kings 1:33). **his head caught:** Apparently his head wedged between low-hanging branches, and his hair became entangled in the tree limbs (14:26). So it happened that David's oath in 14:11 was fulfilled: not one hair of his son's head touched the ground.

18:11 a belt: A type worn by warriors (20:8).

18:12 in our hearing: Confirms the comment in 18:5 that David's order to spare the life of Absalom was public knowledge among the troops.

18:14 Joab: Involved in several murders in the book (Abner, 3:26–27; Uriah, 11:14–17; Absalom, 18:14; Amasa, 20:10). Like his brother Abishai, he seems to think that violence is the most efficient way to achieve political goals. David disagrees and finds these brothers (his nephews) annoyingly difficult to manage (3:39; 19:22). See note on 16:9. **three darts:** I.e., three javelins.

18:17 heap of stones: A burial marker for traitors and enemies of war (Josh 7:26; 8:29).

18:18 King's Valley: In the vicinity of Jerusalem (Gen 14:17). **I have no son:** Absalom had three sons according to 14:27, so either he speaks these words before they are born, or all of them have died.

18:20 You are not to carry tidings: Joab is probably concerned because David previously killed messengers who delivered distressing news about the death of important individuals (Saul, 1:4–16; Ish-bosheth, 4:8–12).

---

[w] Heb *lentils and parched grain.*
[x] Gk Vg Symmachus: Heb *for now there are ten thousand such as we.*
[y] Gk Syr Tg: Heb *was put.*
[z] Another reading is *at the risk of my life.*

tidings today; you may carry tidings another day, but today you shall carry no tidings, because the king's son is dead." ²¹Then Jo'ab said to the Cushite, "Go, tell the king what you have seen." The Cushite bowed before Jo'ab, and ran. ²²Then Ahim'a-az the son of Za'dok said again to Jo'ab, "Come what may, let me also run after the Cushite." And Jo'ab said, "Why will you run, my son, seeing that you will have no reward for the tidings?" ²³"Come what may," he said, "I will run." So he said to him, "Run." Then Ahim'a-az ran by the way of the plain, and outran the Cushite.

24 Now David was sitting between the two gates; and the watchman went up to the roof of the gate by the wall, and when he lifted up his eyes and looked, he saw a man running alone. ²⁵And the watchman called out and told the king. And the king said, "If he is alone, there are tidings in his mouth." And he came apace, and drew near. ²⁶And the watchman saw another man running; and the watchman called to the gate and said, "See, another man running alone!" The king said, "He also brings tidings." ²⁷And the watchman said, "I think the running of the foremost is like the running of Ahim'a-az the son of Za'dok." And the king said, "He is a good man, and comes with good tidings."

28 Then Ahim'a-az cried out to the king, "All is well." And he bowed before the king with his face to the earth, and said, "Blessed be the LORD your God, who has delivered up the men who raised their hand against my lord the king." ²⁹And the king said, "Is it well with the young man Ab'salom?" Ahim'a-az answered, "When Jo'ab sent your servant,ᵇ I saw a great tumult, but I do not know what it was." ³⁰And the king said, "Turn aside, and stand here." So he turned aside, and stood still.

31 And behold, the Cushite came; and the Cushite said, "Good tidings for my lord the king! For the LORD has delivered you this day from the power of all who rose up against you." ³²The king said to the Cushite, "Is it well with the young man Ab'salom?" And the Cushite answered, "May the enemies of my lord the king, and all who rise up against you for evil, be like that young man." ³³ᶜAnd the king was deeply moved, and went up to the chamber over the gate, and wept; and as he went, he said, "O my son Ab'salom, my son, my son Absalom! Would I had died instead of you, O Absalom, my son, my son!"

David Mourns for Absalom

19 It was told Jo'ab, "Behold, the king is weeping and mourning for Ab'salom." ²So the victory that day was turned into mourning for all the people; for the people heard that day, "The king is grieving for his son." ³And the people stole into the city that day as people steal in who are ashamed when they flee in battle. ⁴The king covered his face, and the king cried with a loud voice, "O my son Ab'salom, O Absalom, my son, my son!" ⁵Then Jo'ab came into the house to the king, and said, "You have today covered with shame the faces of all your servants, who have this day saved your life, and the lives of your sons and your daughters, and the lives of your wives and your concubines, ⁶because you love those who hate you and hate those who love you. For you have made it clear today that commanders and servants are nothing to you; for today I perceive that if Ab'salom were alive and all of us were dead today, then you would be pleased. ⁷Now therefore arise, go out and speak kindly to your servants; for I swear by the LORD, if you do not go, not a man will stay with you this night; and this will be worse for you than all the evil that has come upon you from your youth until now." ⁸Then the king arose, and took his seat in the gate. And the people were all told, "Behold, the king is sitting in the gate"; and all the people came before the king.

Now Israel had fled every man to his own home. ⁹And all the people were at strife throughout all the tribes of Israel, saying, "The king delivered us from the hand of our enemies, and saved us from the hand of the Philis'tines; and now he has fled out of the land from Ab'salom. ¹⁰But Ab'salom, whom we anointed over us, is dead in battle. Now therefore why do you say nothing about bringing the king back?"

18:21 Cushite: A man from Ethiopia, which the Bible calls "Cush" (Gen 10:6).

18:24 the two gates: Of the town of Mahanaim (17:24). **running alone:** A single runner is usually a messenger bringing news of victory from the battlefront; several runners could indicate that soldiers are fleeing in defeat from the enemy.

18:29 I do not know: Ahimaaz sidesteps the king's question and withholds the tragic news about Absalom's demise.

18:33 my son Absalom!: David sobs words of tenderness and gives no thought to his son's treachery. **died instead of you:** In the midst of his paternal anguish, David may be thinking that Absalom's death is ultimately the result of his own sins, which brought a "sword" of divine judgment against the royal family (12:10).

19:1–8 Joab rebukes David for wallowing in grief while neglecting to express gratitude to the fighters who risked life and limb to restore his kingship. Left unaddressed, this would be a damaging blow to the morale of the king's supporters. It is time for the bereaved father to pull himself together and to fulfill his duties as commander and king.

19:7 not a man will stay: The king's behavior has the potential to turn supporters away. Traditionally, triumphant warriors returning from battle were greeted with songs, dancing, and celebration (Judg 11:34; 1 Sam 18:6–7).

19:8 the gate: The fortified entryway into the walled town of Mahanaim (17:24).

ᵇHeb *the king's servant, your servant.*
ᶜCh 19:1 in Heb.

David Is Recalled

11 And King David sent this message to Za′dok and Abi′athar the priests, "Say to the elders of Judah, 'Why should you be the last to bring the king back to his house, when the word of all Israel has come to the king? ᵈ ¹²You are my kinsmen, you are my bone and my flesh; why then should you be the last to bring back the king?' ¹³And say to Ama′sa, 'Are you not my bone and my flesh? God do so to me, and more also, if you are not commander of my army henceforth in place of Jo′ab.'" ¹⁴And he swayed the heart of all the men of Judah as one man; so that they sent word to the king, "Return, both you and all your servants." ¹⁵So the king came back to the Jordan; and Judah came to Gilgal to meet the king and to bring the king over the Jordan.

Shime-i Meets David and Is Forgiven

16 And Shim′e-i the son of Gera, the Benjaminite, from Bahu′rim, made haste to come down with the men of Judah to meet King David; ¹⁷and with him were a thousand men from Benjamin. And Zi′ba the servant of the house of Saul, with his fifteen sons and his twenty servants, rushed down to the Jordan before the king, ¹⁸and they crossed the fordᵉ to bring over the king's household, and to do his pleasure. And Shim′e-i the son of Gera fell down before the king, as he was about to cross the Jordan, ¹⁹and said to the king, "Let not my lord hold me guilty or remember how your servant did wrong on the day my lord the king left Jerusalem; let not the king bear it in mind. ²⁰For your servant knows that I have sinned; therefore, behold, I have come this day, the first of all the house of Joseph to come down to meet my lord the king." ²¹Abi′shai the son of Zeru′iah answered, "Shall not Shim′e-i be put to death for this, because he cursed the LORD's anointed?" ²²But David said, "What have I to do

with you, you sons of Zeru′iah, that you should this day be as an adversary to me? Shall any one be put to death in Israel this day? For do I not know that I am this day king over Israel?" ²³And the king said to Shim′e-i, "You shall not die." And the king gave him his oath.

David and Mephibosheth Meet

24 And Mephib′osheth the son of Saul came down to meet the king; he had neither dressed his feet, nor trimmed his beard, nor washed his clothes, from the day the king departed until the day he came back in safety. ²⁵And when he came fromᶠ Jerusalem to meet the king, the king said to him, "Why did you not go with me, Mephib′osheth?" ²⁶He answered, "My lord, O king, my servant deceived me; for your servant said to him, 'Saddle a donkey for me,ᵍ that I may ride upon it and go with the king.' For your servant is lame. ²⁷He has slandered your servant to my lord the king. But my lord the king is like the angel of God; do therefore what seems good to you. ²⁸For all my father's house were but men doomed to death before my lord the king; but you set your servant among those who eat at your table. What further right have I, then, to cry to the king?" ²⁹And the king said to him, "Why speak any more of your affairs? I have decided: you and Zi′ba shall divide the land." ³⁰And Mephib′osheth said to the king, "Oh, let him take it all, since my lord the king has come safely home."

David Blesses Barzillai

31 Now Barzil′lai the Gileadite had come down from Ro′gelim; and he went on with the king to the Jordan, to escort him over the Jordan. ³²Barzil′lai was a very aged man, eighty years old; and he had provided the king with food while he stayed at Ma″hana′im; for he was a very wealthy man. ³³And the king said to Barzil′lai, "Come over

---

19:11 Zadok and Abiathar: The chief priests of Israel (20:25) left behind in Jerusalem to spy on David's behalf (15:24–29; 17:15–16).

19:12 my kinsmen: David is a fellow member of the tribe of Judah (1 Chron 2:3–15).

19:13 Amasa: David's nephew by his sister Abigail (17:25). Even though Amasa sided with Absalom during the rebellion, David promotes him to the position of army commander, no doubt as a political move to help win back the Judahite supporters of Absalom. Besides that, **Joab** earned a demotion by his insubordination to David, specifically to the king's order to spare the life of Absalom (18:10–15).

19:15 Gilgal: In the western Jordan valley, northeast of Jericho.

19:16–40 Several notable figures greet the king on his return to Jerusalem. Relieved that the crisis has passed and order is being restored, David shows remarkable largeness of heart, pardoning offenses (19:16–23), settling disputes (19:24–30), and rewarding fidelity (19:31–40).

19:16 Shime-i: The Benjaminite who cursed and reviled David on his flight from Jerusalem (16:5–13). On this occasion, the king swears to grant him royal clemency, allowing him to live another day (19:23); however, on his deathbed, David will remind Solomon of Shimei's treachery and recommend his execution (1 Kings 2:8–9).

19:20 the house of Joseph: The northern tribes of Israel, the two largest tribes being Ephraim and Manasseh, which are descended from the patriarch Joseph (Gen 48:1–5).

19:24 Mephibosheth: Grandson of Saul. His haggard appearance, typically associated with periods of mourning, shows that the crippled Mephibosheth is not the cunning opportunist that Ziba claimed he was in 16:3. Evidently he wished to join David in his flight from the city but no donkey was provided for him to make the journey (19:26). For the dispute over Saul's estate, now divided between Mephibosheth and Ziba, see 9:1–13 and 16:1–4.

19:27 like the angel of God: A compliment for a king (14:17, 20).

19:31 Barzillai: One of David's wealthy benefactors (17:27–29). The king wants to reward his generosity by providing for his needs in Jerusalem; however, the pleasures of the royal court no longer hold appeal for a man of his age. **Rogelim:** Approximately 50 miles north of the Jordan crossing near Jericho.

ᵈGk: Heb *to the king, to his house.*
ᵉCn: Heb *the ford crossed.*
ᶠHeb *to.*
ᵍGk Syr Vg: Heb *said, I will saddle a donkey for myself.*

with me, and I will provide for you with me in Jerusalem." ³⁴But Barzil′lai said to the king, "How many years have I still to live, that I should go up with the king to Jerusalem? ³⁵I am this day eighty years old; can I discern what is pleasant and what is not? Can your servant taste what he eats or what he drinks? Can I still listen to the voice of singing men and singing women? Why then should your servant be an added burden to my lord the king? ³⁶Your servant will go a little way over the Jordan with the king. Why should the king recompense me with such a reward? ³⁷Please let your servant return, that I may die in my own city, near the grave of my father and my mother. But here is your servant Chimham; let him go over with my lord the king; and do for him whatever seems good to you." ³⁸And the king answered, "Chimham shall go over with me, and I will do for him whatever seems good to you; and all that you desire of me I will do for you." ³⁹Then all the people went over the Jordan, and the king went over; and the king kissed Barzil′lai and blessed him, and he returned to his own home. ⁴⁰The king went on to Gilgal, and Chimham went on with him; all the people of Judah, and also half the sons of Israel, brought the king on his way.

Dissension between Israel and Judah

41 Then all the men of Israel came to the king, and said to the king, "Why have our brethren the men of Judah stolen you away, and brought the king and his household over the Jordan, and all David's men with him?" ⁴²All the men of Judah answered the men of Israel, "Because the king is near of kin to us. Why then are you angry over this matter? Have we eaten at all at the king's expense? Or has he given us any gift?" ⁴³And the men of Israel answered the men of Judah, "We have ten shares in the king, and in David also we have more than you. Why then did you despise us? Were we not the first to speak of bringing back our king?" But the words of the men of Judah were fiercer than the words of the men of Israel.

The Rebellion of Sheba

20 Now there happened to be there a worthless fellow, whose name was Sheba, the son of Bichri, a Benjaminite; and he blew the trumpet, and said,

"We have no portion in David,
and we have no inheritance in the son of Jesse;
every man to his tents, O Israel!"

²So all the men of Israel withdrew from David, and followed Sheba the son of Bichri; but the men of Judah followed their king steadfastly from the Jordan to Jerusalem.

3 And David came to his house at Jerusalem; and the king took the ten concubines whom he had left to care for the house, and put them in a house under guard, and provided for them, but did not go in to them. So they were shut up until the day of their death, living as if in widowhood.

4 Then the king said to Ama′sa, "Call the men of Judah together to me within three days, and be here yourself." ⁵So Ama′sa went to summon Judah; but he delayed beyond the set time which had been appointed him. ⁶And David said to Abi′shai, "Now Sheba the son of Bichri will do us more harm than Ab′salom; take your lord's servants and pursue him, lest he get himself fortified cities, and cause us trouble." ʰ ⁷And there went out after Abi′shai, Jo′abⁱ and the Cher′ethites and the Pel′ethites, and all the mighty men; they went out from Jerusalem to pursue Sheba the son of Bichri. ⁸When they were at the great stone which is in Gib′eon, Ama′sa came to meet them. Now Jo′ab was wearing a soldier's garment, and over it was a belt with a sword in its sheath fastened upon his loins, and as he went forward it fell out. ⁹And Jo′ab said to Ama′sa, "Is it well with you, my brother?" And Joab took Amasa by the beard with his right hand to kiss him. ¹⁰But Ama′sa did not observe the sword which was in

---

19:37 Chimham: A kinsman of Barzillai, probably his son (1 Kings 2:7).

19:41–43 Longstanding tensions between Judah (the southernmost tribe) and Israel (the northern tribes) explode into a shouting match. The north feels slighted—even insulted—that Judah acted alone in escorting the king back across the Jordan.

19:43 ten shares: Represents the ten northern tribes (excludes Judah and Benjamin).

20:1 Sheba: Instigates a second rebellion against David. The revolt, although short-lived, is fueled by lingering resentment over the transfer of kingship from Benjamin and the house of Saul to Judah and the house of David (3:1). The depth of this tribal animosity is revealed as the northern Israelites detach themselves from David in an act of mass defection (20:2). **worthless fellow:** A troublemaker or rabble rouser. **no portion in David:** Anticipates the war cry that later divides

Solomon's empire into northern and southern kingdoms (1 Kings 12:16).

20:3 the ten concubines: Raped and defiled by Absalom (16:20–22). Innocent victims of a palace coup, they are cared for by the king and yet quarantined at a location outside his royal residence.

20:4 Amasa: Newly appointed as David's military commander (19:13).

20:5 he delayed: The reason for this is uncertain, but it must raise suspicions about his loyalty to David. One suspects that Amasa is finding it difficult to rally support, given his leadership role in Absalom's rebellion (17:25).

20:7 Cherethites … Pelethites: David's royal bodyguards (8:18; 15:18).

20:8 the great stone: Its precise location and significance are unknown. **Gibeon:** Roughly six miles northwest of Jerusalem.

20:9 with his right hand: Normally the hand for wielding a weapon.

20:10 Joab struck him: One of several murders in which Joab is involved. See note on 18:14.

ʰTg: Heb *snatch away our eyes.*
ⁱCn Compare Gk: Heb *after him Joab's men.*

Jo'ab's hand; so Joab struck him with it in the body, and shed his bowels to the ground, without striking a second blow; and he died.*

Then Joab and Abi'shai his brother pursued Sheba the son of Bichri. [11]And one of Jo'ab's men took his stand by Ama'sa, and said, "Whoever favors Joab, and whoever is for David, let him follow Joab." [12]And Ama'sa lay wallowing in his blood in the highway. And any one who came by, seeing him, stopped;[j] and when the man saw that all the people stopped, he carried Amasa out of the highway into the field, and threw a garment over him. [13]When he was taken out of the highway, all the people went on after Jo'ab to pursue Sheba the son of Bichri.

14 And Sheba passed through all the tribes of Israel to Abel of Beth-ma'acah;[k] and all the Bichrites[l] assembled, and followed him in. [15]And all the men who were with Jo'ab came and besieged him in Abel of Beth-ma'acah; they cast up a mound against the city, and it stood against the rampart; and they were battering the wall, to throw it down. [16]Then a wise woman called from the city, "Hear! Hear! Tell Jo'ab, 'Come here, that I may speak to you.'" [17]And he came near her; and the woman said, "Are you Jo'ab?" He answered, "I am." Then she said to him, "Listen to the words of your maidservant." And he answered, "I am listening." [18]Then she said, "They were wont to say in old time, 'Let them but ask counsel at Abel'; and so they settled a matter. [19]I am one of those who are peaceable and faithful in Israel; you seek to destroy a city which is a mother in Israel; why will you swallow up the heritage of the LORD?" [20]Jo'ab answered, "Far be it from me, far

be it, that I should swallow up or destroy! [21]That is not true. But a man of the hill country of E'phraim, called Sheba the son of Bichri, has lifted up his hand against King David; give up him alone, and I will withdraw from the city." And the woman said to Jo'ab, "Behold, his head shall be thrown to you over the wall." [22]Then the woman went to all the people in her wisdom. And they cut off the head of Sheba the son of Bichri, and threw it out to Jo'ab. So he blew the trumpet, and they dispersed from the city, every man to his home. And Joab returned to Jerusalem to the king.

23 Now Jo'ab was in command of all the army of Israel; and Bena'iah the son of Jehoi'ada was in command of the Cher'ethites and the Pel'ethites; [24]and Ador'am was in charge of the forced labor; and Jehosh'aphat the son of Ahi'lud was the recorder; [25]and Sheva was secretary; and Za'dok and Abi'athar were priests; [26]and Ira the Ja'irite was also David's priest.

David Avenges the Gibeonites

21 Now there was a famine in the days of David for three years, year after year; and David sought the face of the LORD. And the LORD said, "There is bloodguilt on Saul and on his house, because he put the Gib'eonites to death." [2]So the king called the Gib'eonites.[m] Now the Gibeonites were not of the sons of Israel, but of the remnant of the Am'orites; although the sons of Israel had sworn to spare them, Saul had sought to slay them in his zeal for the sons of Israel and Judah. [3]And David said to the Gib'eonites, "What shall I do for you? And how shall I make expiation, that you may bless

---

20:23–26: 8:15–18; 1 Chron 18:14–17.

20:14 Abel of Beth-maacah: Nearly 30 miles north of the Sea of Galilee in the far north of Israel. The site has been identified as modern Tell Abil.

20:16 a wise woman: Negotiates an end to the siege. Recall that a wise woman earlier worked with Joab to end the exile of Absalom (14:1–24).

20:18 Let them but ask: A proverb indicating the town of Abel had a reputation for wise decision making.

20:19 heritage of the LORD?: The question is rhetorical, implying there is no need to inflict suffering and death on the peaceful town of Abel when Sheba, the leader of the revolt, could be quickly eliminated.

20:23–26 A list of court officials who serve David in the latter years of his reign. The roster is similar to that in 8:15–18, except that **(1)** David's sons are no longer mentioned as holding leadership positions, as in 8:18, and **(2)** a new position has been created to oversee labor gangs conscripted to work on state construction projects (20:24).

20:23 Joab: Reclaims his former position as chief military commander (8:16) after being temporarily replaced by Amasa (19:13; 20:10).

20:25 Sheva: Successor to Seraiah as the scribe in charge of royal correspondence (8:17). **Zadok and Abiathar:** The two chief priests. See note on 8:17.

20:26 Ira the Jairite: Otherwise unknown. He may be from the Levitical city of Jattir, as this would help to explain his position as priest (Josh 21:14).

21:1—24:25 Chapters 21–24 form an appendix to the Books of Samuel. They consist of six accounts arranged according to a literary chiasm (the pattern a-b-c-c'-b'-a'). Accounts one and six concern *plagues* that troubled David's reign (21:1–14; 24:1–25); accounts two and five inform us about *warriors* in David's army (21:15–22; 23:8–39); and accounts three and four preserve *poems* from the hand of David himself (22:1–51; 23:1–7). This final section of the book, which records events that took place at various times during the life and reign of David, serves as a tribute to his legacy as a king, priest, prophet, and military commander.

21:1 bloodguilt: Saul ordered a massacre of Gibeonites at some point before his death in 1 Sam 31. His attempt at genocide was a violation of the Gibeonite covenant, an ancient peace treaty in which Joshua and the Israelites swore an oath to spare the lives of the Gibeonites (Josh 9:3–15). Saul's disregard for this oath brought the curse of a severe famine upon the land. **Gibeonites:** Residents of Gibeon, a town roughly six miles northwest of Jerusalem.

21:2 Amorites: Inhabitants of Canaan before Israel's invasion and conquest of the land. All but the Gibeonites were to be eliminated by war (Deut 7:1–2).

---

[j] This clause is transposed from the end of the verse.
[k] With 20:15: Heb *and Beth-maacah.*
[l] Heb *Berites.*
[m] Heb *the Gibeonites and said to them.*
*20:10: Thus did Joab remove his last rival and remain in power till David's death, in spite of the king's dislike of him.

the heritage of the LORD?" [4]The Gib'eonites said to him, "It is not a matter of silver or gold between us and Saul or his house; neither is it for us to put any man to death in Israel." And he said, "What do you say that I shall do for you?" [5]They said to the king, "The man who consumed us and planned to destroy us, so that we should have no place in all the territory of Israel, [6]let seven of his sons be given to us, so that we may hang them up before the LORD at Gib'eon on the mountain of the LORD."[n] And the king said, "I will give them."

7 But the king spared Mephib'osheth, the son of Saul's son Jonathan, because of the oath of the LORD which was between them, between David and Jonathan the son of Saul. [8]The king took the two sons of Rizpah the daughter of Ai'ah, whom she bore to Saul, Armo'ni and Mephib'osheth; and the five sons of Merab[o] the daughter of Saul, whom she bore to A'dri-el the son of Barzil'lai the Meho'-lathite; [9]and he gave them into the hands of the Gib'eonites, and they hanged them on the mountain before the LORD, and the seven of them perished together. They were put to death in the first days of harvest, at the beginning of barley harvest.

10 Then Rizpah the daughter of Ai'ah took sackcloth, and spread it for herself on the rock, from the beginning of harvest until rain fell upon them from the heavens; and she did not allow the birds of the air to come upon them by day, or the beasts of the field by night. [11]When David was told what Rizpah the daughter of Ai'ah, the concubine of Saul, had done, [12]David went and took the bones of Saul and the bones of his son Jonathan from the men of Ja'besh-gil'ead, who had stolen them from the public square of Beth-shan, where the Philis'tines had hanged them, on the day the Philistines killed Saul on Gilbo'a; [13]and he brought up from there the bones of Saul and the bones of his son Jonathan; and they gathered the bones of those who were hanged. [14]And they buried the bones of Saul and his son Jonathan in the land of Benjamin in Ze'la, in the tomb of Kish his father; and they did all that the king commanded. And after that God heeded supplications for the land.

Wars with the Philistines

15 The Philis'tines had war again with Israel, and David went down together with his servants, and they fought against the Philistines; and David grew weary. [16]And Ish'bi-be'nob, one of the descendants of the giants, whose spear weighed three hundred shekels of bronze, and who was armed with a new sword, thought to kill David. [17]But Abi'-shai the son of Zeru'iah came to his aid, and attacked the Philis'tine and killed him. Then David's men adjured him, "You shall no more go out with us to battle, lest you quench the lamp of Israel."

18 After this there was again war with the Philis'tines at Gob; then Sib'becai the Hu'shathite

---

21:18–22: 1 Chron 20:4–8.

WORD STUDY

Make Expiation (21:3)

Kaphar (Heb.): the verb has a basic meaning "to cover" and a theological meaning "to make atonement". Its basic meaning appears in Genesis, where Noah is told to water seal the ark by coating its hull with pitch (Gen 6:14). Its theological meaning is more prominent in the Bible, especially in Leviticus, where atonement for sin is made by the sacrifice of burnt offerings (Lev 1:4), sin offerings (Lev 4:20), and guilt offerings (Lev 5:16), most notably on the yearly Day of Atonement (Lev 16:11, 16–17). In OT theology, atonement is more or less equivalent to reconciliation, the mending of man's relationship with God made possible by his mercy and forgiveness (Ps 65:3; 78:38). On the one hand, it involves "expiation", the taking away of sin (Is 6:7; 27:9; Jer 18:23). On the other, it also involves "propitiation", the turning away of God's wrath from sinners (Num 25:10–13; cf. Prov 16:14). Both ideas are present in 2 Sam 21:1–14, where seven descendants of Saul are sacrificed in order to make atonement for Saul's bloodguilt (his murder of the Gibeonites) and to lift the famine from the land (a manifestation of Yahweh's anger).

21:6 seven of his sons: Saul did not have seven living sons, so David hands over two of Saul's sons and five of his grandsons (21:8). **hang them up:** I.e., make a public display of their corpses. Bodies disgraced and exposed in this way were fastened to such things as trees (Deut 21:22; Josh 10:26) and city walls (1 Sam 31:10–12). The manner of their execution is uncertain; possibilities include crucifixion, stoning, and dismemberment. **before the LORD at Gibeon:** The Mosaic Tabernacle is stationed there at this time (1 Chron 16:39).

21:7 the oath: Sworn when David made a pledge to remain loyal to the house of Jonathan (1 Sam 20:14–17).

21:8 Rizpah: Saul's concubine (3:7; 21:11). **Mephibosheth:** Saul's son, not to be confused with Saul's grandson of the same name (21:7). **Merab:** Saul's eldest daughter (1 Sam 18:17–19).

21:9 barley harvest: In the spring month of Nisan (corresponds to March–April).

21:10 sackcloth: Associated with mourning (3:31). **she did not allow:** Rizpah keeps vigil to guard the remains of her deceased sons from scavengers. Her maternal devotion moves David to provide them with an honorable burial (21:11–14).

21:12 men of Jabesh-gilead: The valiant heroes of 1 Sam 31:11–13.

21:14 Zela: A few miles north of Jerusalem (Josh 18:28). **heeded supplications:** I.e., lifted the famine from the land in answer to prayer (21:1).

21:15–22 A sampling of clashes between David and the Philistines (see 5:17–25; 8:1). The focus is on four Israelite warriors who fell four Philistine giants.

21:16 three hundred shekels: Over seven pounds.

21:17 the lamp of Israel: David, whose death would leave Israel in darkness.

21:18 Gob: Location undetermined.

---

[n] Cn Compare Gk and 21:9: Heb *at Gibeah of Saul, the chosen of the* LORD.
[o] Two Hebrew Mss Gk: Heb *Michal*.

slew Saph, who was one of the descendants of the giants. ¹⁹And there was again war with the Philis'tines at Gob; and Elha'nan the son of Ja'are-or'egim, the Bethlehemite, slew Goliath the Gittite, the shaft of whose spear was like a weaver's beam. ²⁰And there was again war at Gath, where there was a man of great stature, who had six fingers on each hand, and six toes on each foot, twenty-four in number; and he also was descended from the giants. ²¹And when he taunted Israel, Jonathan the son of Shim'e-i, David's brother, slew him. ²²These four were descended from the giants in Gath; and they fell by the hand of David and by the hand of his servants.

David's Song of Thanksgiving

22 And David spoke to the LORD the words of this song on the day when the LORD delivered him from the hand of all his enemies, and from the hand of Saul. ²He said,*

"The LORD is my rock, and my fortress, and my
    deliverer,
³   myᴾ God, my rock, in whom I take refuge,
my shield and the horn of my salvation,
    my stronghold and my refuge,
    my savior; you save me from violence.
⁴I call upon the LORD, who is worthy to be praised,
    and I am saved from my enemies.

⁵"For the waves of death encompassed me,
    the torrents of perdition assailed me;
⁶the cords of Sheol entangled me,
    the snares of death confronted me.

⁷"In my distress I called upon the LORD;
    to my God I called.

From his temple he heard my voice,
    and my cry came to his ears.

⁸"Then the earth reeled and rocked;
    the foundations of the heavens trembled
    and quaked, because he was angry.
⁹Smoke went up from his nostrils,
    and devouring fire from his mouth;
    glowing coals flamed forth from him.
¹⁰He bowed the heavens, and came down;
    thick darkness was under his feet.
¹¹He rode on a cherub, and flew;
    he was seen upon the wings of the wind.
¹²He made darkness around him
    his canopy, thick clouds, a gathering of water.
¹³Out of the brightness before him
    coals of fire flamed forth.
¹⁴The LORD thundered from heaven,
    and the Most High uttered his voice.
¹⁵And he sent out arrows, and scattered them;
    lightning, and routed them.
¹⁶Then the channels of the sea were seen,
    the foundations of the world were laid bare,
  at the rebuke of the LORD,
    at the blast of the breath of his nostrils.

¹⁷"He reached from on high, he took me,
    he drew me out of many waters.
¹⁸He delivered me from my strong enemy,
    from those who hated me;
    for they were too mighty for me.
¹⁹They came upon me in the day of my calamity;
    but the LORD was my stay.
²⁰He brought me forth into a broad place;
    he delivered me, because he delighted in me.

22:2–51: Ps 18:2–50.

21:19 Elhanan ... slew Goliath: The statement as worded clashes with 1 Sam 17:1–51, the story of David taking down the mighty Goliath. The most likely reason for this incongruity is a transcriptional error, meaning the verse was accidentally miscopied by a scribe in the process of transmitting the text. The parallel passage in 1 Chron 20:5 seems to preserve the original wording: it says that Elhanan slew "Lahmi the brother of Goliath".
21:20 six fingers: An abnormality known as hexadigitation.
22:1–51 David's Song. It is a prayer of praise closely resembling Ps 18. Its theme is that "salvation" and "strength" belong to Yahweh, the God of Israel. David experienced these in his own life every time the Lord rescued him from danger and rewarded his faithfulness by prospering his endeavors. Chronologically, the song is best situated *after* David's subjugation of several nations (compare 22:44–46 with 8:1–12) but *before* his adulterous affair with Bathsheba (his confession of innocence in 22:21–25 does not account for his sins in 11:2–15). Compositionally, the Books of Samuel are framed by lyrical poetry: Hannah's Song rings out in the beginning (1 Sam 2:1–10), just as David's Song brings melody to the end (2 Sam 22:1–51) (CCC 2579).

22:1–4 Dominated by metaphors portraying Yahweh as the Defender and Protector of the king (**my rock ... fortress ... deliverer ... shield ... salvation ... stronghold ... refuge**). These and similar expressions in the song depict David's relationship with the Lord in deeply personal terms.
22:3 the horn: A symbol of strength (Mic 4:13; Lk 1:69).
22:6 Sheol: The realm of the dead. See word study: *Sheol* at Num 16:30.
22:7 his temple: The Lord's sanctuary in heaven (Ps 11:4). It is from this celestial height that Yahweh bends down to work powerfully in David's life (22:10).
22:8–16 Yahweh faces his enemy with a dreadful display of cosmic power. Earthquakes, fire, and thunderstorms are themes often associated with extraordinary manifestations of God's presence and power in the world (called "theophanies"). Reference is made to them in both historical (Ex 19:16–18) and poetical contexts (Judg 5:4–5; Ps 97:2–5).
22:11 a cherub: A winged angelic figure. In biblical poetry, powerful winds are linked with the movement of angels (Ps 104:4; Heb 1:7).
22:14–15 In Ugaritic mythology, the god Baal speaks in thunder and wields lightning as his weapon. David adapts these traditional concepts, so that thunder is Yahweh's **voice** and the shaft of lightning his **arrow**.

ᴾGk Ps 18:2: Heb lacks *my*.
*22:2–51: This song, probably inserted later, is very similar to Psalm 18.

21 "The Lord rewarded me according to my
    righteousness;
    according to the cleanness of my hands he
    recompensed me.
22 For I have kept the ways of the Lord,
    and have not wickedly departed from my God.
23 For all his ordinances were before me,
    and from his statutes I did not turn aside.
24 I was blameless before him,
    and I kept myself from guilt.
25 Therefore the Lord has recompensed me
    according to my righteousness,
    according to my cleanness in his sight.

26 "With the loyal you show yourself loyal;
    with the blameless man you show yourself
    blameless;
27 with the pure you show yourself pure,
    and with the crooked you show yourself
    perverse.
28 You deliver a humble people,
    but your eyes are upon the haughty to bring
    them down.
29 Yes, you are my lamp, O Lord,
    and my God lightens my darkness.
30 Yes, by you I can crush a troop,
    and by my God I can leap over a wall.
31 This God—his way is perfect;
    the promise of the Lord proves true;
    he is a shield for all those who take refuge in
    him.

32 "For who is God, but the Lord?
    And who is a rock, except our God?
33 This God is my strong refuge,
    and has made ͬ my ˢ way safe.
34 He made my ˢ feet like deer's feet,
    and set me secure on the heights.
35 He trains my hands for war,
    so that my arms can bend a bow of bronze.
36 You have given me the shield of your salvation,
    and your help ͭ made me great.

37 You gave a wide place for my steps under me,
    and my feet ͧ did not slip;
38 I pursued my enemies and destroyed them,
    and did not turn back until they were
    consumed.
39 I consumed them; I thrust them through, so that
    they did not rise;
    they fell under my feet.
40 For you girded me with strength for the battle;
    you made my assailants sink under me.
41 You made my enemies turn their backs to me,
    those who hated me, and I destroyed them.
42 They looked, but there was none to save;
    they cried to the Lord, but he did not answer
    them.
43 I beat them fine as the dust of the earth,
    I crushed them and stamped them down like
    the mire of the streets.

44 "You delivered me from strife with the peoples; ͮ
    you kept me as the head of the nations;
    people whom I had not known served me.
45 Foreigners came cringing to me;
    as soon as they heard of me, they obeyed me.
46 Foreigners lost heart,
    and came trembling ͷ out of their fastnesses.

47 "The Lord lives; and blessed be my rock,
    and exalted be my God, the rock of my
    salvation,
48 the God who gave me vengeance
    and brought down peoples under me,
49 who brought me out from my enemies;
    you exalted me above my adversaries,
    you delivered me from men of violence.

50 "For this I will extol you, O Lord, among the
    nations,
    and sing praises to your name.
51 Great triumphs he gives ˣ to his king,
    and shows mercy to his anointed,
    to David, and his descendants for ever."

22:50: Rom 15:9.

22:24 blameless: Not absolutely sinless, but heroically faithful to the commandments of the Torah (Lk 1:6; Phil 3:6). Contrast these words with David's penitential words in Ps 51, composed after the Bathsheba incident. See note on 22:1–51.

22:32 who is a rock: A depiction of Yahweh that is also found in the Song of Moses (Deut 32:4).

22:34 my feet like deer's feet: Thanks to the influence of grace, David is made swift and sure-footed in doing God's will (Hab 3:19).

22:42 they cried: The pleas of the wicked go unheeded by the Lord (Ps 66:18), but the prayers of righteous David have the opposite effect (22:4, 7; Jas 5:16).

22:44 head of the nations: Israel becomes an international power under David, ruling over several neighboring peoples in the region (8:1–12). The subjugation of these vassal states, which transforms the nation of Israel into a kingdom, is really the work of Yahweh (8:6, 14). According to Deuteronomy, the rise to political prominence in the world is a blessing bestowed for obedience to the covenant (Deut 26:18–19; 28:1, 13).

22:51 his king . . . his anointed: Mirrors the climax of Hannah's Song in 1 Sam 2:10.

ͬ Ps 18:32: Heb *set free.*
ˢ Another reading is *his.*
ͭ Or *gentleness.*
ͧ Heb *ankles.*
ͮ Gk: Heb *from strife with my people.*
ͷ Ps 18:45: Heb *armed themselves.*
ˣ Another reading is *He is a tower of salvation.*

Last Words of David

23 Now these are the last words of David:
The oracle of David, the son of Jesse,
the oracle of the man who was raised on high,
the anointed of the God of Jacob,
the sweet psalmist of Israel:ʸ

²"The Spirit of the LORD speaks by me,
his word is upon my tongue.
³The God of Israel has spoken,
the Rock of Israel has said to me:
When one rules justly over men,
ruling in the fear of God,
⁴he dawns on them like the morning light,
like the sun shining forth upon a cloudless
morning,
like rainᶻ that makes grass to sprout from the
earth.
⁵Yes, does not my house stand so with God?
For he has made with me an everlasting
covenant,
ordered in all things and secure.
For will he not cause to prosper
all my help and my desire?
⁶But godless menᵃ are all like thorns that are
thrown away;
for they cannot be taken with the hand;
⁷but the man who touches them
arms himself with iron and the shaft of a
spear,
and they are utterly consumed with
fire."ᵇ

David's Mighty Men

8 These are the names of the mighty men whom David had: Jo'sheb-basshe'beth a Tah-che'monite;

he was chief of the three;ᶜ he wielded his spearᵈ against eight hundred whom he slew at one time.

9 And next to him among the three mighty men was Elea'zar the son of Dodo, son of Aho'hi. He was with David when they defied the Philis'tines who were gathered there for battle, and the men of Israel withdrew. ¹⁰He rose and struck down the Philis'tines until his hand was weary, and his hand clung to the sword; and the LORD wrought a great victory that day; and the men returned after him only to strip the slain.

11 And next to him was Shammah, the son of Agee the Har'arite. The Philis'tines gathered together at Lehi, where there was a plot of ground full of lentils; and the men fled from the Philistines. ¹²But he took his stand in the midst of the plot, and defended it, and slew the Philis'tines; and the LORD wrought a great victory.

13 And three of the thirty chief men went down, and came about harvest time to David at the cave of Adul'lam, when a band of Philis'tines was encamped in the valley of Reph'aim. ¹⁴David was then in the stronghold; and the garrison of the Philis'tines was then at Bethlehem. ¹⁵And David said longingly, "O that some one would give me water to drink from the well of Bethlehem which is by the gate!" ¹⁶Then the three mighty men broke through the camp of the Philis'tines, and drew water out of the well of Bethlehem which was by the gate, and took and brought it to David. But he would not drink of it; he poured it out to the LORD, ¹⁷and said, "Far be it from me, O LORD, that I should do this. Shall I drink the blood of the men who went at the risk of their lives?" Therefore he would not drink it. These things did the three mighty men.

23:8-39: 1 Chron 11:10–41.

23:1-7 David's final written testament. The king looks back on his life and its lessons. More than anything, he has learned that an upright king is blessed by the Lord and, in turn, becomes a blessing to his subjects. Compare this to the testaments of Jacob (Gen 49:1–27) and Moses (Deut 33:1–29).

23:1 the last words: Not the final words of David uttered before death, as these are found in 1 Kings 2:1–9, but his final composition as a poet and songwriter. **sweet psalmist of Israel:** Among other possible translations, the expression could also be rendered "singer of the songs of Israel" or "beloved of the songs of Israel".

23:2 the LORD speaks by me: David is a divinely inspired prophet; his tongue and pen are instruments used by Yahweh for speaking to his people (2 Pet 1:21). David's status as a prophet is later acknowledged by Jesus (Mk 12:36) and Peter (Acts 2:30).

23:5 everlasting covenant: Delineated in the oracle of Nathan in 7:8–16. See essay: *The Davidic Covenant* at 2 Sam 7.

23:8-39 David's most valiant warriors, known in Hebrew as the *gibborim*. These form an elite corps of men who distinguished themselves from the general army by remarkable feats of bravery and strength. Two distinct ranks are discernible—the three (23:8–12) and the thirty (23:24–39)—with mention made of two commanding officers (23:18–23). The majority of these individuals are Israelites, mainly from the tribes of Judah and Benjamin, while some are non-Israelites.

23:8 eight hundred: Or possibly "three hundred" (see 1 Chron 11:11).

23:13-17 The bond of loyalty between David and his men is underscored in this incident.

23:13 three: Seemingly three warriors from the list in 23:24–39, although some think the three listed in 23:8–12 are meant. **cave of Adullam:** David's hideout southwest of Jerusalem. See note on 1 Sam 22:1. **valley of Rephaim:** Begins a few miles southwest of Jerusalem and slopes downward toward Philistine territory (5:18).

23:16 poured it out: The water from Bethlehem, retrieved at the risk of human life, is treated like blood. David therefore refuses to drink it and instead pours it on the ground in symbolic adherence to the law of blood disposal (Deut 12:23–24).

ʸOr *the favorite of the songs of Israel.*
ᶻHeb *from rain.*
ᵃHeb *worthlessness.*
ᵇHeb *fire in the sitting.*
ᶜOr *captains.*
ᵈ1 Chron 11:11: Heb obscure.

18 Now Abi'shai, the brother of Jo'ab, the son of Zeru'iah, was chief of the thirty.ᵉ And he wielded his spear against three hundred men and slew them, and won a name beside the three. ¹⁹He was the most renowned of the thirty,ᶠ and became their commander; but he did not attain to the three.

20 And Bena'iah the son of Jehoi'ada was a valiant manᵍ of Kab'zeel, a doer of great deeds; he struck two Arielsʰ of Moab. He also went down and slew a lion in a pit on a day when snow had fallen. ²¹And he slew an Egyptian, a handsome man. The Egyptian had a spear in his hand; but Bena'iah went down to him with a staff, and snatched the spear out of the Egyptian's hand, and slew him with his own spear. ²²These things did Bena'iah the son of Jehoi'ada, and won a name beside the three mighty men. ²³He was renowned among the thirty, but he did not attain to the three. And David set him over his bodyguard.

24 As'ahel the brother of Jo'ab was one of the thirty; Elha'nan the son of Dodo of Bethlehem, ²⁵Shammah of Harod, Eli'ka of Harod, ²⁶He'lez the Paltite, Ira the son of Ikkesh of Teko'a, ²⁷Abie'zer, of An'athoth, Mebun'nai the Hu'shathite, ²⁸Zalmon the Aho'hite, Ma'harai of Netoph'ah, ²⁹He'leb the son of Ba'anah of Netoph'ah, Ittai the son of Ribai of Gib'e-ah of the Benjaminites, ³⁰Bena'iah of Pir'athon, Hiddai of the brooks of Ga'ash, ³¹A'bi-al'bon the Ar'bathite, Az'maveth of Bahu'rim, ³²Eli'ahba of Sha-al'bon, the sons of Jashen, Jonathan, ³³Shammah the Har'arite, Ahi'am the son of Sharar the Hararite, ³⁴Eliph'elet the son of Ahas'bai of Ma'acah, Eli'am

the son of Ahith'ophel of Gilo, ³⁵Hezroⁱ of Carmel, Pa'arai the Arbite, ³⁶I'gal the son of Nathan of Zobah, Ba'ni the Gadite, ³⁷Zelek the Am'monite, Na'harai of Be-er'oth, the armor-bearer of Jo'ab the son of Zeru'iah, ³⁸Ira the Ithrite, Ga'reb the Ithrite, ³⁹Uri'ah the Hittite: thirty-seven in all.

David Takes a Census

24 Again the anger of the Lᴏʀᴅ was kindled against Israel, and he incited David against them, saying, "Go, number Israel and Judah."* ²So the king said to Jo'ab and the commanders of the army,ʲ who were with him, "Go through all the tribes of Israel, from Dan to Be'er-she'ba, and number the people, that I may know the number of the people." ³But Jo'ab said to the king, "May the Lᴏʀᴅ your God add to the people a hundred times as many as they are, while the eyes of my lord the king still see it; but why does my lord the king delight in this thing?" ⁴But the king's word prevailed against Jo'ab and the commanders of the army. So Joab and the commanders of the army went out from the presence of the king to number the people of Israel. ⁵They crossed the Jordan, and began from Aro'er,ᵏ and from the city that is in the middle of the valley, toward Gad and on to Ja'zer. ⁶Then they came to Gilead, and to Ka'desh in the land of the Hittites;ˡ and they came to Dan, and from Danᵐ they went around to Si'don, ⁷and came to the fortress of Tyre and to all the cities of the Hi'vites and Canaanites; and they went out to the Neg'eb of Judah at Be'er-she'ba. ⁸So when they had gone through all the land, they came to Jerusalem at the end of nine months and twenty days. ⁹And Jo'ab

---

24:1–25: 1 Chron 21:1–27.

23:18 Abishai: David's nephew, appointed commander of the thirty (23:19). **Joab:** David's nephew, commander of the general army (8:16; 20:23).

23:20 Benaiah: Put in charge of David's bodyguards, the Cherethites and Pelethites (8:18).

23:34 Eliam: The father of Bathsheba (11:3) and the son of David's betrayer, Ahithophel (15:12, 31).

23:39 Uriah: The husband of Bathsheba (11:3). **thirty-seven:** The method of calculation is unclear. Perhaps the narrator is counting the three peerless warriors (Josheb-basshebeth, Eleazar, Shammah, 23:8–9, 11) and the three leaders (Abishai, Joab, Benaiah, 20:23; 23:18–20) along with Asahel (23:24) and the corps of the thirty (Elhanan ... Uriah, 23:24–39). Among other factors, it remains uncertain how many "sons of Jashen" should be counted (23:32).

24:1–25 David sins by conducting a military census (24:10). The fallout is a plague from the Lord let loose upon the people (24:15). The incident shows, among other things, that the fate of Israel rides on the shoulders of the king. When the king is prayerful and pious, the kingdom prospers; but when the king is sinful and selfish, the kingdom suffers. David is eventually able to limit the devastation by acknowledging his guilt and showing repentance through sacrifice (24:10, 17).

24:1 Again the anger: Following the episode in 21:1–14. **he incited David:** The parallel account in 1 Chron 21:1 identifies "Satan" as the instigator of David's wrongdoing. Though worded differently, the two statements are not incompatible. The author of Samuel stresses that all things, good as well as evil, necessarily take place within the parameters set by the will of God. Not even the spiritual forces of darkness operate outside or independently of divine Providence. Whatever creatures, seen or unseen, may be permitted to act as agents of temptation, none discharges this role without the Lord allowing it to happen. See note on 1 Sam 16:14.

24:2 Dan to Beer-sheba: The full extent of Israelite territory from north to south.

24:5 Aroer: Located near the Arnon, a watercourse that flows into the eastern side of the Dead Sea (Josh 13:16). This marks the southern border of Israelite territory east of the Jordan. From here the team travels in a counterclockwise direction, proceeding north, then west, then south.

24:9 the sum: The census return counts 1,300,000 soldiers qualified for active duty.

ᵉTwo Hebrew Mss Syr: MT *three.*
ᶠ1 Chron 11:25: Heb *Was he the most renowned of the three?*
ᵍAnother reading is *the son of Ish-hai.*
ʰGk: *sons of Ariel.* Heb lacks *sons of.*
ⁱ Another reading is *Hezrai.*
ʲ1 Chron 21:2 Gk: Heb *to Joab the commander of the army.*
ᵏGk: Heb *encamped in Aroer.*
ˡGk: Heb *to the land of Tahtim-hodshi.*
ᵐCn Compare Gk: Heb *they came to Dan-jaan and.*
*24:1: God is here said to command the census, presumably on the general grounds of ascribing the king's policies to him, but in verse 10 David says he has sinned thereby, and in 1 Chron 21:1 the census is ascribed to Satan as an infringement of God's prerogatives.

gave the sum of the numbering of the people to the king: in Israel there were eight hundred thousand valiant men who drew the sword, and the men of Judah were five hundred thousand.

Judgment on David's Sin

10 But David's heart struck him after he had numbered the people. And David said to the LORD, "I have sinned greatly in what I have done. But now, O LORD, I pray you, take away the iniquity of your servant; for I have done very foolishly." [11]And when David arose in the morning, the word of the LORD came to the prophet Gad, David's seer, saying, [12]"Go and say to David, 'Thus says the LORD, Three things I offer[n] you; choose one of them, that I may do it to you.'" [13]So Gad came to David and told him, and said to him, "Shall three[o] years of famine come to you in your land? Or will you flee three months before your foes while they pursue you? Or shall there be three days' pestilence in your land? Now consider, and decide what answer I shall return to him who sent me." [14]Then David said to Gad, "I am in great distress; let us fall into the hand of the LORD, for his mercy is great; but let me not fall into the hand of man."

15 So the LORD sent a pestilence upon Israel from the morning until the appointed time; and there died of the people from Dan to Be'er-she'ba seventy thousand men. [16]And when the angel stretched forth his hand toward Jerusalem to destroy it, the LORD repented of the evil, and said to the angel who was working destruction among the people, "It is enough; now stay your hand." And the angel of the LORD was by the threshing floor of Arau'nah

the Jeb'usite. [17]Then David spoke to the LORD when he saw the angel who was striking down the people, and said, "Behold, I have sinned, and I have done wickedly; but these sheep, what have they done? Let your hand, I pray you, be against me and against my father's house."

David's Altar on the Threshing Floor

18 And Gad came that day to David, and said to him, "Go up, rear an altar to the LORD on the threshing floor of Arau'nah the Jeb'usite." [19]So David went up at Gad's word, as the LORD commanded. [20]And when Arau'nah looked down, he saw the king and his servants coming on toward him; and Araunah went forth, and did obeisance to the king with his face to the ground. [21]And Arau'nah said, "Why has my lord the king come to his servant?" David said, "To buy the threshing floor of you, in order to build an altar to the LORD, that the plague may be averted from the people." [22]Then Arau'nah said to David, "Let my lord the king take and offer up what seems good to him; here are the oxen for the burnt offering, and the threshing sledges and the yokes of the oxen for the wood. [23]All this, O king, Arau'nah gives to the king." And Araunah said to the king, "The LORD your God accept you." [24]But the king said to Arau'nah, "No, but I will buy it of you for a price; I will not offer burnt offerings to the LORD my God which cost me nothing." So David bought the threshing floor and the oxen for fifty shekels of silver. [25]And David built there an altar to the LORD, and offered burnt offerings and peace offerings. So the LORD heeded supplications for the land, and the plague was averted from Israel.

24:10 I have sinned: The narrator never explains why the census is sinful. Perhaps it implies that David is priding himself on Israel's military might and thus putting his trust in the resources at his command. If so, he is guilty, not only of boasting in human strength, but of betraying the Lord, who is ultimately responsible for his many victories on the battlefield (5:24; 8:6, 14; 22:32–43).

24:11 Gad: A court prophet and longtime advisor to David (1 Sam 22:5).

24:12–25 David halts the advance of the plague by sacrifice. • The incident displays subtle parallels with Abraham's sacrifice of Isaac. **(1)** Both take place at the climax of a three-day trial (24:13; Gen 22:4); **(2)** on both occasions, the Lord intervenes to stay the hand of the slaughterer (24:16; Gen 22:11–12); **(3)** both David and Abraham act as priests, building altars and sacrificing animals, with the result that Yahweh's chosen ones, Isaac and Israel, are spared death (24:25; Gen 22:13); **(4)** both sacrifices take place on the mountaintop where Solomon will build the future Temple (compare Gen 22:2 and 1 Chron 22:1 with 2 Chron 3:1).

24:13 three . . . three . . . three: Famines, wars, and plagues are divine curses triggered by transgression of the Mosaic covenant (Lev 26:17, 21, 25; Deut 28:21, 48–52). The prophets sometimes link them together as God's threefold judgment on wayward Israel (Jer 14:12; Ezek 6:11).

24:16 the angel: The executor of Yahweh's judgment on Israel. See word study: *Angel of the LORD* at Gen 16:7. **threshing floor:** A hilltop platform, exposed to the wind, where wheat is sifted and separated from the husk. Here, the hill is Mount Moriah, which rises adjacent to Mount Zion on its north side. This location, sanctified by the Lord's presence, will become the site of the Solomonic Temple (2 Chron 3:1). **Araunah:** Also called "Ornan" (1 Chron 21:15). **Jebusite:** A Canaanite inhabitant of ancient Jerusalem (Josh 15:63).

24:21 may be averted: It is hoped that sacrifice will propitiate the Lord, i.e., turn away his wrath (24:1) before it devours Jerusalem (24:16). • Stopping a plague by priestly action recalls the story of Aaron, the high priest, averting a plague against Israel by offering incense at the command of Moses (Num 16:46–48).

24:25 burnt . . . peace: For these types of offerings, see chart: *The Levitical Sacrifices* at Lev 3. **heeded supplications:** Compare with the similar statement in 21:14.

[n]Or *hold over.*
[o]1 Chron 21:12 Gk: Heb *seven.*

2 Samuel

Chapter 1

For understanding

1. **1:1–16.** How does David receive confirmation of Saul's death? What about the story of his demise is suspicious and ultimately incriminating? With what expectation does the messenger come to David, and what does he receive?
2. **1:14.** For what is the expression "the Lord's anointed" a title? What is David's attitude toward the office of the king? What is the Amalekite's attitude?
3. **1:18.** What is the Book of Jashar? What else is known about this ancient work?
4. **1:26.** Why does David call Jonathan his brother? What sort of kinship underlies this language? What does David mean by saying that his love for Jonathan is "passing the love of women"? What should we *not* take this statement to mean?

For application

1. **1:11–12.** What are some expressions of national mourning that might follow a great national disaster, such as a political assassination or a terrorist act? Why are such expressions important for the life of the nation as a whole? How might people in your own community join in mourning?
2. **1:19.** David's exclamation, "How are the mighty fallen!" has become proverbial. In what contexts do you usually hear it quoted? How do these contexts differ from the meaning David gives his words?
3. **1:26.** In your experience, what are some of the characteristics of real friendship? Why is friendship (as opposed to other forms of social companionship) so necessary to a person? What makes a true friendship spiritually beneficial, and how would you recognize when it is becoming spiritually harmful?

Chapter 2

For understanding

1. **2:1.** What is the importance of Hebron at this time, and where is it located? How long does it serve as David's royal capital? Who settled there at the time of the conquest?
2. **2:4.** Since David has previously been anointed by Samuel, what is the purpose of this anointing? What is the "house of Judah"? Why does David praise the city of Jabesh-gilead, and what does he invite the people to do? Who apparently causes him to fail to win their support?
3. **2:8.** Who is Abner? Who is Ish-bosheth? What does the latter's name mean? Why is Abner's attempt to make Ish-bosheth the successor to Saul doomed from the start? Where is Mahanaim, and what brief role does it have for northern Israel? What does its name in Hebrew mean?
4. **2:13.** Who is Joab? What is the pool of Gibeon, and how large is it? What is it known as?

For application

1. **2:8–9.** When a strong man sets up a weaker person as his superior, who usually exercises the real power? When the devil grants the wishes of a suppliant for control or influence, who exercises the real power in the long run? How can his power be broken?
2. **2:12–17.** Read the note for v. 14. Why do you think this "entertainment" takes place to begin with? In some of our country's larger cities, what is behind the violence between gangs that happens there? What often happens to ordinary citizens when the violence explodes beyond a mere street fight?
3. **2:19–23.** Suppose you are involved in a heated controversy where you are trying to stop the quarrel, and your opponent insists on pursuing it. What does your goal become—getting out of the situation, reaching agreement, or winning the argument? Do you follow Jesus' admonition in Mt 5:38–42, or do you try to end things forcibly by humiliating your opponent?

Chapter 3

For understanding

1. **3:2–5.** How many sons by how many wives does David father during his time in Hebron? Why is this not surprising? Why is it not commendable? What are we to notice about how the author of 2 Samuel describes the situation?
2. **3:7.** What kind of move is Abner's taking one of Saul's concubines? What is Abner trying to do? What will Absalom, in his turn, later use sexual aggression to accomplish?
3. **3:12–16.** To whom does Abner shift allegiance? Why is this surprising? What must have dawned upon him about Ish-bosheth?
4. **3:27.** How does Joab regard himself in relation to Abner? How was retribution for murder customary among ancient tribal societies?

For application

1. **3:6–11.** If you were in the position of Ish-bosheth, what kind of danger would Abner pose to you? What would you want to do about it—or, alternatively, what might you think Abner would do if you attempted anything? In your own career or social position, have you ever had relationships that resemble this one?
2. **3:13–15.** Do you think that David's desire to retrieve his wife Michal is for personal or political reasons? If either, what makes you think so? What might have been Michal's frame of mind in this situation?
3. **3:16.** How would you assess Paltiel's behavior in this verse? Why would he be so demonstrative in following Michal's retinue, then raise no objection on being told to go back?

4. **3:27–30.** Because Abner killed Joab's brother Asahel in a combat situation rather than in cold blood, is Joab's act of revenge as an "avenger of blood" justified according to Israelite law (see Gen 9:6, Num 35:10–28)? What does David think? What are some of the consequences of allowing family members to take blood vengeance in this way?

Chapter 4

For understanding
1. **4:1–12.** What do Ish-bosheth's captains do? How does David consider this action? What does the tribal descent of these men show about Saul's tribe? Why is the way now clear for David to rule over all Israel?
2. **4:4.** Who is Mephibosheth? What does his name probably mean? What did a boyhood accident do to him, and for what does this brief introduction here prepare?
3. **4:9.** What does David often experience from God? With the Lord at his side, of what does David have no need? What do Rechab and Baanah wrongly assume?

For application
1. **4:1.** Since Ish-bosheth is afraid of Abner, whose allegiance is in doubt, why would his courage fail him when Abner is killed? Why would "all Israel" be dismayed as well? What often happens in a country when a power vacuum is created?
2. **4:4.** In our society, what do most people do when a caregiver causes permanent damage to the person being cared for? What difference would it make if the caregiver were a fellow Christian? What do you think of St. Paul's recommendation about lawsuits in 1 Cor 6:1–7?
3. **4:8.** What makes a deliberate act good or evil? Why may one not do evil so that good may come of it, especially if national interest is at stake? (Refer to CCC 1755–56, 1761.)

Chapter 5

For understanding
1. **5:1–5.** What summit has David reached by now? Of what is it the true beginning? How long will it last, and what will happen then?
2. **5:3.** What oath do the northern tribes swear? How do the obligations entailed by this covenant relate to the larger Deuteronomic covenant? Which anointing of David is this?
3. **5:6.** What were other names for Jerusalem? How does David go about making Jerusalem his capital? What strategic motivation prompts the selection of this site for the seat of Israel's government? When is Jerusalem conquered by David? Who are the Jebusites? To what do the taunting words of the Jebusites about the blind and the lame refer?
4. **5:7.** To what geographical location does the name Zion refer? What makes the site naturally defensible? What is the name Zion extended to include? According to the New Testament, of what is Zion a prophetic sign? What is the "city of David"?
5. **5:8.** What are the alternative meanings of the Hebrew word translated as "water shaft"? What is David urging his men to do in either the first or the second case?

For application
1. **5:1–3.** Would you describe the constitution of your country as a *covenant* (which establishes a family bond) or as a *contract* (which provides for the exchange of goods and services)? What allegiance do you as a citizen owe the country? What are the limits of that allegiance?
2. **5:7.** According to the note for this verse, the name "Zion" is sometimes extended to refer to the whole of Jerusalem. How do the psalms envision Zion (e.g., Ps 9:11; 14:7; 50:2; 84:5)? What images come to your mind when you read scriptural references to Zion?
3. **5:8.** Read the note for this verse. What is your attitude toward people who attend church but who are "different" (e.g., physically impaired, poor, tattooed, dressed oddly)? What does the Letter of James (2:1–13) have to say about making distinctions regarding such people?

Chapter 6

For understanding
1. **6:1–23.** What does David do with the Ark of the Covenant? What does that thereby make his capital Jerusalem? What story does this episode resume?
2. **6:3–8.** How is transport of the ark irregular to the point of being irreverent? What sparks a lethal blast of divine wrath against Uzzah?
3. **6:17.** Where has David pitched the tent that will house the ark? At this time, where is the Mosaic sanctuary stationed, and what goes on there? What is the Davidic tent like, and what kind of liturgy do the Levites conduct there?
4. **6:19.** In what ways are the etymology and meaning of the Hebrew term "a portion of meat" uncertain? What does the parallel account in Chronicles indicate? Whose gestures do David's actions recall?

For application
1. **6:6–7.** What does the account of Uzzah's death indicate about respect we should have for holy things? Why is disrespect for them spiritually dangerous?
2. **6:9.** Read Sirach, chap. 1, on fear of the Lord. How is Sirach's description different from the fear that David feels? How might it be similar? What is your own understanding of this virtue? How does it apply to your life?
3. **6:14.** Have you ever experienced feelings of joy and delight in the presence of the Lord, especially during a liturgical celebration? How did you express it? What expressions of joy and delight are appropriate in private prayer? in public (liturgical) prayer?

4. **6:16, 20–23.** Why do you think the love Michal formerly had for David has now turned to contempt? Do her stated reasons in v. 20 explain the shift? When the love between married couples turns sour like this, how can it be renewed? What attitudes in both spouses are necessary for that to happen?

Chapter 7

For understanding
1. **7:1.** What is David's "house"? How is rest from all his enemies achieved? Of what technique is the placing of the discourses of chap. 7 before the events of chap. 8 an example, and what does it mean? In this instance, what does the author's rearrangement of the story show about David? Theologically, what does the attainment of "rest" signal?
2. **7:9.** To what does God's promise of a great name refer? How was historical testimony to this from outside the Bible uncovered? How does the promise made to David link back to the promises made to Abraham?
3. **Word Study: House (7:11).** What does the Hebrew noun *bayit* mean, and how often is it used in the Hebrew Bible? Broadly speaking, to what can it refer? As a place, what is a house—especially if a king or a god lives there? Referring to a people, what is a house? What are some plays on the various meanings of this word in Nathan's oracle?
4. **7:12.** Who is "your offspring" mentioned here? How did the early Christians read this prophecy? According to St. Augustine, what partial reflection of the future do we see in Solomon?
5. **Essay: The Davidic Covenant.** How does the Davidic covenant fit into the rest of the Old Testament covenants? How is Nathan's oracle the foundation of the Davidic covenant? How is the divine plan summarized under the headings of Dynasty, Temple, Adoption, and Law for Mankind? Though worded as a divine promise, how are its terms guaranteed, and who assumed responsibility for its fulfillment? How are the pledges made to David fulfilled definitively in the coming of Jesus Christ?

For application
1. **7:1.** "Rest" is a major theme throughout Scripture (see Heb 3:7—4:11). What kinds of "rest" does Scripture have in mind? How do you observe the Sabbath rest? How *should* you observe it (see CCC 2184–88)?
2. **7:11.** Given the understanding of "house" in the word study for this verse, what kind of house has the Lord made for you? What does Ps 127 suggest about your plans for your home and family?
3. **7:18–29.** David, in awe over the promises of God, expresses his gratitude by an extended prayer before the Ark of the Covenant. What part does gratitude play in your prayer life? How do you express it? Where do you go when you want to spend time in in-depth prayer?

Chapter 8

For understanding
1. **8:1–14.** How does David expand his kingdom by military conquest? What happens to survivors of the wars, with what result?
2. **8:15–18.** How does David take advantage of peacetime? Of what needs is his small administration given charge, and by whom?
3. **8:15.** How is the expression "justice and equity" defined in Genesis? With what are equivalent expressions in the ancient Near East connected?
4. **8:17.** Who has the responsibility for religious leadership? Who are Zadok and Ahimelech? Why is there reason to suspect that the names Abiathar and Ahimelech were switched around during the copying of the book?
5. **8:18.** Who are the Cherethites and Pelethites? How many of David's sons are named in this book? Although the Hebrew calls David's sons priests, how does the Greek LXX translate the Hebrew? What does the parallel passage in 1 Chronicles call them? To what might the priestly ministry of David's sons perhaps be linked?

For application
1. **8:6.** Read the note for this verse. What victories in your life would you ascribe to the Lord's assistance? What has failure taught you about your need for his help?
2. **8:13.** Why is one's good name—or reputation—important, both to the person himself and to others? What care do we owe others for the preservation of their good name? Given the popularity of social media, how easy is it to malign the good name of anyone—and how hard is it to repair any damage? (Refer to CCC 2493–98 for a discussion of communications media in this regard.)
3. **8:18.** According to CCC 1546–47, what characterizes the priesthood of the lay faithful, and how is it expressed? At what is the ministerial priesthood of the ordained hierarchy directed?

Chapter 9

For understanding
1. **9:1—20:26.** What do these chapters comprise, according to scholars? Of what are they the story? How does the story thematically mirror the preceding chapters? How do many consider the quality of these chapters? When did the author probably live?
2. **9:1.** What is David doing beyond simply honoring the memory of Jonathan, his fallen companion? How does David make good on this?
3. **9:7.** How are the circumstances of David's effort to restore to Mephibosheth all of Saul's property unclear?

For application
1. **9:1.** How is a promise made to others in God's name related to the second commandment of the Decalogue (CCC 2147)? Even if not made in God's name, why must promises be kept as long as the commitments are morally just (CCC 2410, 2101–2)?

2. **9:8.** In what position does accepting a gift from someone place the receiver? Why do some feel the urge to refuse gifts or to reciprocate in some way? What is the proper response to receiving gifts from God, for whom adequate repayment is not possible?

Chapter 10

For understanding
1. **10:2.** What does the Hebrew suggest that Israel has established with the kingdom of Ammon?
2. **10:4.** To what does shaving off the beards of David's emissaries amount? Of what is shaving a sign? What does cutting off their garments mean they are being treated like?
3. **10:9–14.** What does the Ammonite coalition do? If they had chosen to engage battle, what would have happened?

For application
1. **10:2.** When a country's leader dies, what do other friendly nations tend to do? How do their ambassadors expect to be treated by the host country?
2. **10:3.** Given David's defeat of the Philistines and Moabites described in chap. 8, on the one hand, as opposed to the likelihood of a treaty covenant between Israel and Ammon, on the other (see the note for v. 2), what cause for concern do the princes of the Ammonites have regarding David's emissaries? How does their suspicion compare with that of modern states?
3. **10:11–12.** When you find yourself beset on all sides with problems, what is your first recourse—to figure out a strategy on your own or to submit the situation to the Lord in prayer? When should you resort to prayer?

Chapter 11

For understanding
1. **11:1–27.** What happens in these verses? In the course of three days, how many commandments does he violate? How does he also abuse his royal authority? Predictably, what is the Lord's reaction?
2. **11:1.** What season is the spring of the year like? For what are farmers available within this window of opportunity? How does the expression "when kings go forth" appear to be a criticism of David? What relation to David is Joab? Where is Rabbah?
3. **11:3.** What is different about David's inquiry from previous occasions? How is Bathsheba designated several times in the text? Who is Uriah the Hittite? What does the meaning of his name suggest about him?
4. **11:11.** Where is the ark kept at this time? How is sexual abstinence in wartime used as a discipline? What is Uriah refusing to do?

For application
1. **11:2.** The note for this verse alludes to a discipline called "custody of the eyes", controlling what you choose to look at. Which virtues is it intended to protect? How often do you need to practice it, and on what occasion? How, for example, might you practice it while using an electronic device such as a computer or Internet-connected phone?
2. **11:6–13.** According to CCC 1778, when should one's conscience be operative? What often happens when a person decides to act despite what his conscience says? What spiritual damage occurs when he covers up a serious wrong that he has done?
3. **11:11.** Why does Uriah refuse to go to his house as the king has asked? What do you think of his reasons? How does his devotion to duty set an example for you?

Chapter 12

For understanding
1. **12:7–14.** How will the sword of violence turn back on the house of David? How will evil rear its head in David's own house? What will David learn from these hardships?
2. **12:14.** What is the child born of David's union with Bathsheba destined to bear? What distinction does Nathan's oracle illustrate? While the Lord remits David's guilt, what debt does he require him to pay?
3. **12:20.** What, presumably, is the house of the Lord that David goes into for worship? What is David's attitude at this time of grief?
4. **12:24.** Which of David's sons is Solomon? What Hebrew word does his name resemble, and where is that connection noted? What is significant from a theological perspective about the Lord's love for Solomon?

For application
1. **12:5–7.** How deserving of death are we when we choose to do what we know is evil? Some people question the possibility of committing a sin that is truly mortal; given David's example and his judgment on himself in v. 5, what do you say? What are the three conditions for a sin to be considered mortal (CCC 1857–59)?
2. **12:10–12.** All sin has consequences that even forgiveness of the sin does not remove. What consequences for David does Nathan outline in these verses? Some consequences affect other people, such as one's family. Are you aware of consequences for your family that have arisen from sins that you have committed? What are some of the consequences that have affected you or your relation with the Lord?
3. **12:16–18.** Even though David prays for the child he has with Bathsheba, for what other person might he be praying? Why might God sometimes refuse to "let us off easy" when he disciplines us? What do we learn from his "tough love"?

Chapter 13

For understanding

1. **13:1.** Which son of David is Absalom, and what does he turn out to be? Who is Tamar? Which son of David is Amnon, and what is his rank? For what will his death open the way?
2. **13:13.** What is Tamar trying to do by saying that David would not withhold her from Amnon? What conjecture do others offer on the basis of ancient precedent?
3. **13:21.** Though David is outraged by the rape of Tamar, what does he fail to do? As a result, what will Absalom do?
4. **13:37.** Why does Absalom flee? Who is Talmai, and why is it no surprise that Absalom should seek asylum with him?

For application

1. **13:14.** The English word *rape* comes from a Latin verb meaning *to steal*. What theft is involved in sexual rape?
2. **13:15.** How unusual is a rapist's hatred for his victim? What causes such hatred, especially when the assault is motivated by lust?
3. **13:19.** For the victim, what are some of the psychological aftereffects of rape? What might be some of the spiritual aftereffects? How might a healing process be pursued?
4. **13:21.** What do you think explains David's failure to discipline his son, since he has shown himself merciless in punishing the crimes of others? How do parents' failures to discipline their children harm them?

Chapter 14

For understanding

1. **14:2.** Where is Tekoa, and whose hometown is it? How, in staging this ruse, does Joab appear to be acting in the interest of the kingdom?
2. **14:4–20.** What is the Tekoa woman's tale designed to elicit from David? In this case, what is it meant to secure? By indicating that the surviving son is his father's "heir", what does the tale assume about Absalom, David's third son? What happened to Chileab, David's second son? What are the parallels between this story and that of Cain and Abel?
3. **14:17.** How are the woman's words both words of flattery and words of irony?
4. **14:33.** What does David's kissing of Absalom suggest about their relationship? Although the gesture is good in itself, what problem arises because Absalom is not punished by David?

For application

1. **14:17.** What is the difference between sincere praise and flattery? According to CCC 2480, when is flattery sinful?
2. **14:18.** Read the note for this verse. What do you think causes David to suspect that his nephew Joab in particular is the person who coached the woman? What have we learned so far about Joab's character?
3. **14:26.** How does our culture evaluate a person's beauty? What does the condition of one's hair have to do with it? Why do we associate physical beauty with good moral character and physical ugliness with bad character? What do we know about Absalom's character so far?

Chapter 15

For understanding

1. **15:1—18:33.** In a carefully plotted conspiracy, what does David's third son and heir to the throne do? What high-ranking official does he win to his side? What does the ordeal force David and his supporters to do?
2. **15:7.** How does Absalom hide his plans for a coup? In the Bible, what are vows? Where is Hebron, and what is its connection with Absalom and David?
3. **15:12.** Who is Ahithophel, and what may be his connection with Ps 41 and 55? How might his loyalty to David have been shaken? Whose treachery does that of Ahithophel prefigure, and how? By implication, what does David's painful crossing of the Kidron to the Mount of Olives foreshadow?
4. **15:16.** What does David's decision to leave ten concubines behind indicate? Of what is he unaware?

For application

1. **15:2–7.** Notice Absalom's patience as he gradually devises his plot. What are David and his officials apparently not doing during this period? What happens in our spiritual lives when we are inattentive to subtle worldly or demonic influences over time?
2. **15:12.** Read the note for this verse. Scripture commands us to forgive those who let us down or even betray us (e.g., Mt 6:12–15). What does forgiveness involve? What does it accomplish, both in ourselves and in our relationships? What happens to us when we refuse to forgive?
3. **15:25–26.** Read the note for v. 25. On what does David base his serenity in the face of suffering? What is the difference between a stoical acceptance of suffering and serene trust in God?

Chapter 16

For understanding

1. **16:5.** Where is Bahurim? Who is Shimei? What does he display here, and how does he change later?
2. **16:18.** How is Hushai's declaration of loyalty to Absalom strategically ambiguous? What does Absalom assume, and what does the reader know?
3. **16:20–23.** Having taken control of Jerusalem and made a public claim to David's throne, how does Absalom advertise his seizure of power? Where does Absalom have sexual relations with his father's concubines, and why is the site significant?

Study Questions

For application

1. **16:4.** David accepts Ziba's accusation of Mephibosheth at face value. How are Christians supposed to speak about one another (see Eph 4:25)? When one hears an accusation of a neighbor, how should he deal with it?
2. **16:7.** What is the difference between venting anger with an expletive and actively cursing someone? Though not specifically mentioned in the *Catechism*, how might cursing be an offense against the fifth commandment (compare CCC 2302–3)?
3. **16:18.** By engaging in strategically ambiguous language, is Hushai being truthful or is he lying? Is the use of "discreet language" (CCC 2489) in effect lying? What is our obligation to tell the truth to one who may use it to endanger others?

Chapter 17

For understanding

1. **17:1–14.** What kind of counsel does Absalom receive concerning David? What does Ahithophel recommend, and what does Hushai advise? What is Hushai actually trying to do?
2. **17:8.** What is Hushai trying to accomplish by his shrewd political reminder to Absalom?
3. **17:15–22.** What are these verses describing? How does information pass from Hushai to David?
4. **17:23.** What does Ahithophel realize about the failure of his advice? How many premeditated suicides occur in the Old Testament, and how is Ahithophel's different from other instances?

For application

1. **17:1–14.** Have you ever received conflicting advice on an important matter from people you trusted? How did you arrive at a decision? How do you see the Lord's hand in what ultimately happened?
2. **17:23.** How, as the *Catechism* mentions (2091), does despair offend against the first commandment? How, as it explains elsewhere (2281), does suicide offend the love of neighbor? If you have ever considered suicide, what made you choose to live?
3. **17:25.** The note for this verse points out that the political situation David faces is a family feud at several levels. Why are disagreements within families often more serious than disagreements between neighbors? Do disagreements exist within your extended family, and, if so, have they disrupted relationships? How can personal holiness help eliminate the "root of bitterness" against which Heb 12:14–15 warns?

Chapter 18

For understanding

1. **18:6.** Where is the forest of Ephraim? Though it is an unusual site for a battle, what advantage does it offer David's guerilla fighters?
2. **18:14.** With which murders is Joab involved in the book? How is he like his brother Abishai? What is David's position?
3. **18:20.** What may be the reason Joab keeps Ahimaaz from carrying tidings of Absalom's death to David?
4. **18:33.** How does David mourn Absalom? In the midst of his paternal anguish, what may David be thinking?

For application

1. **18:9.** Absalom is snared by his most beautiful physical feature, his hair. Why do some people regard their physical beauty as a curse? How can they protect themselves from its dangers?
2. **18:14.** The note for this verse suggests that Joab murders Absalom for political ends. When do ends justify the means, and when do they not? What does the *Catechism* (1887–89) say about the "inversion of means and ends"?
3. **18:33.** What is the worst personal grief you have experienced? How did you express it? What, if anything, provided comfort during this time?

Chapter 19

For understanding

1. **19:1–8.** For what does Joab rebuke David? What might result from David's failure to express gratitude to his soldiers? What is it time for the bereaved father to do?
2. **19:13.** Who is Amasa? Even though Amasa sides with Absalom during the rebellion, how does David treat him, with what end no doubt in view? Besides that, what does Joab earn, and for what act?
3. **19:16.** Who is Shime-i? On this occasion, what does David swear to grant him; however, on his deathbed, what will David do?
4. **19:24.** What does the haggard appearance of Mephibosheth, grandson of Saul, show about him? Why did he not join David in his flight over the Jordan?

For application

1. **19:5–7.** What is the sternest rebuke you have ever received? How deserved was it? What did you do in response? What was your attitude to the person who delivered it, both at the time and after the situation had passed?
2. **19:18–20.** What is the difference between an apology that expresses sorrow for an offense (as in "I'm sorry") and one that asks for forgiveness (as in "Please forgive me")? Which calls for a response from the person offended? How adequate do you think Shime-i's apology is for what he did (16:5–8)?
3. **19:26–30.** The *Catechism* (2477) describes the sins of rash judgment, detraction, and calumny. Of these three, which ones apply to or affect Mephibosheth, David, and Ziba? How equitable is the decision David makes in v. 29? Why do you think he would be so favorable to Ziba?

Chapter 20

For understanding
1. **20:1.** What fuels the short-lived second rebellion against David? How is the depth of this tribal animosity revealed? What does the war cry "no portion in David" anticipate?
2. **20:5.** What suspicions must Amasa's delay raise? What does one suspect Amasa is having difficulty doing, and why?
3. **20:23-26.** What is different about this list of court officials who serve David in the latter years of his reign as compared with the roster in 8:15-18?

For application
1. **20:3.** Read the note for this verse. How are victims of rape often treated in our culture? How do you think they *should* be treated? Since Absalom abused these women to stake his claim to the throne, how justified is David in his treatment of them?
2. **20:9-10.** Since Amasa is Joab's cousin and Joab has no reason to kill him to avenge blood, what is his motive for this murder? Why do you think David does not call Joab to account immediately (refer to 1 Kings 2:5-6) but reinstates him instead?
3. **20:22.** How many definitions can you think of for the word *wisdom*? What seems to be the meaning here? As mentioned in other parts of Scripture (e.g., Prov 1:2; Ps 111:10; Is 11:2), what does it mean?

Chapter 21

For understanding
1. **21:1—24:25.** Of what do these chapters, as an appendix to the books of Samuel, consist, and according to what literary device? What does each of the accounts concern? What function does this final section serve?
2. **21:1.** What was the bloodguilt that Saul incurred before his death? What covenant did his attempt at genocide violate? What did his disregard for this oath bring upon the land?
3. **Word Study: Make Expiation (21:3).** What basic and theological meanings does the Hebrew verb *kaphar* have? In which book does its basic meaning appear? Where is its theological meaning made more prominent, and how? In Old Testament theology, to what is atonement equivalent? What two elements does it involve? How are both ideas present in 2 Sam 21:1-14?
4. **21:6.** Since Saul did not have seven living sons, whom does David hand over to the Gibeonites? What does "hang them up" mean? How is it accomplished? Where is the Mosaic Tabernacle at the time?
5. **21:19.** What is the most likely reason for the statement that Elhanan slew Goliath, which clashes with 1 Sam 17:1-51, which says that David killed him? According to the parallel passage in 1 Chron 20:5, whom did Elhanan slay?

For application
1. **21:3.** According to the word study for this verse ("Make Expiation"), *expiation* in the Old Testament has a theological meaning of making atonement. What do you think the New Testament understanding of expiation is, especially in terms of Jesus' death on the Cross? What is our part in making expiation for our sins (beyond the types of penances usually given in the confessional)?
2. **21:8-9.** According to the *Catechism* (2266-67), what should be the purpose of legitimate public authority in inflicting punishment on a criminal? What is current Church teaching on the use of the death penalty? What expiatory value does it have?
3. **21:11-14.** Given the dignity of the human person, what kind of burial do criminals executed by the State deserve? How should the State proceed if human remains cannot be identified and no one claims them?

Chapter 22

For understanding
1. **22:1-51.** What is the theme of David's prayer of praise? How does David experience Yahweh's strength and salvation? Chronologically, where is the song best situated? Compositionally, how are the Books of Samuel framed?
2. **22:8-16.** How does Yahweh often face his enemies? What are these extraordinary manifestations called?
3. **22:11.** What is a cherub? In biblical poetry, with what are powerful winds linked?
4. **22:44.** What kind of power does Israel become under David? Who is really responsible for the subjugation of these vassal states? According to Deuteronomy, what is one blessing bestowed for obedience to the covenant?

For application
1. **22:4.** When you experience trouble and "call upon the Lord" for help, what is your prayer typically like? How often do you worry even as you pray? How would praise of God, "who is worthy to be praised", change the tenor of your petition?
2. **22:20.** How do you think God looks upon you—for example, do you think his view of you is positive or negative, benevolent or judgmental? How do you believe he regards your failures? What would make him delight in you?
3. **22:26-28.** What does it mean that God shows himself "perverse" to the crooked? Does loyalty to God earn his favor? What does *humility* mean, and why does God respond so favorably to it?
4. **22:35, 40.** How are Christians to be prepared for war? In what kinds of battles are they engaged? According to Eph 6:10-17, what weapons should we be prepared to use, and against what enemy?

Chapter 23

For understanding
1. **23:1.** What does it mean to say that these are the last words of David? What are other possible translations for "sweet psalmist of Israel"?

111

2. **23:2.** How does the Lord speak through David? Who later acknowledges David's status as a prophet?
3. **23:8–39.** With what do these verses deal? What are they known as in Hebrew, and what makes them into an elite corps of men? What two distinct ranks are discernible? Who comprise these ranks?
4. **23:16.** What is the water from Bethlehem, retrieved at the risk of human life, treated like? What does David therefore do with it, in symbolic adherence with what law?

For application
1. **23:2.** How has the Spirit of the Lord spoken to you through others? In what ways might the Spirit of the Lord speak through you? In what ways might your life be an encouraging testimony to others?
2. **23:5.** What do you think of the "prosperity gospel" advocated by some preachers? When you are faithful to the Lord and his covenant, what kind of prosperity do you expect? What happens to your fidelity if material or personal suffering happens instead?
3. **23:13–17.** Read the note for these verses. What is the most striking example of loyalty you can recall in a friend? How does Sir 6:1–16 understand the loyalty involved in friendship?

Chapter 24

For understanding
1. **24:1.** Whom does the parallel account in 1 Chron 21:1 identify as the instigator of David's wrongdoing? Since the two statements are not incompatible, what does the author of 2 Samuel stress? Within what context must even the spiritual forces of darkness operate?
2. **24:10.** Since the narrator never explains why the census is sinful, what might it imply that David is doing? If so, of what is he guilty?
3. **24:12–25.** How does David halt the plague? In what four ways does the incident display subtle parallels with Abraham's sacrifice of Isaac?

For application
1. **24:1–3.** The note for v. 1 discusses the spiritual instigator behind this census. What do you think David's own motivation may have been? Which organizations do you know that count their membership? What probably distinguishes their motives from those of David?
2. **24:10–14.** David is confronted with a choice of three immediate consequences of his sin. Which would you have chosen? What do you think of David's answer? When confronted with the consequences of your sin, how do you choose to respond to the Lord?
3. **24:16–18.** The note for v. 16 suggests that the Lord can turn the evil of sin into great spiritual benefits—in this case, the location of the Temple (see Rom 8:28). How has the Lord turned evil into good in your life or the lives of people you know? How might some of the setbacks of the Church in recent history (e.g., the modern decline in church attendance) be turned to good for those who love the Lord?
4. **24:24.** David's reply to Araunah the Jebusite amounts to a principle of the spiritual life—namely, do not offer God what costs you nothing. What, by definition, is a sacrifice? What did Dietrich Bonhoeffer mean by the expression "cheap grace"? Why should a sacrifice to the Lord your God cost you something?

BOOKS OF THE BIBLE

THE OLD TESTAMENT (OT)

Gen	Genesis
Ex	Exodus
Lev	Leviticus
Num	Numbers
Deut	Deuteronomy
Josh	Joshua
Judg	Judges
Ruth	Ruth
1 Sam	1 Samuel
2 Sam	2 Samuel
1 Kings	1 Kings
2 Kings	2 Kings
1 Chron	1 Chronicles
2 Chron	2 Chronicles
Ezra	Ezra
Neh	Nehemiah
Tob	Tobit
Jud	Judith
Esther	Esther
Job	Job
Ps	Psalms
Prov	Proverbs
Eccles	Ecclesiastes
Song	Song of Solomon
Wis	Wisdom
Sir	Sirach (Ecclesiasticus)
Is	Isaiah
Jer	Jeremiah
Lam	Lamentations
Bar	Baruch
Ezek	Ezekiel
Dan	Daniel
Hos	Hosea
Joel	Joel
Amos	Amos
Obad	Obadiah
Jon	Jonah
Mic	Micah
Nahum	Nahum
Hab	Habakkuk
Zeph	Zephaniah
Hag	Haggai
Zech	Zechariah
Mal	Malachi
1 Mac	1 Maccabees
2 Mac	2 Maccabees

THE NEW TESTAMENT (NT)

Mt	Matthew
Mk	Mark
Lk	Luke
Jn	John
Acts	Acts of the Apostles
Rom	Romans
1 Cor	1 Corinthians
2 Cor	2 Corinthians
Gal	Galatians
Eph	Ephesians
Phil	Philippians
Col	Colossians
1 Thess	1 Thessalonians
2 Thess	2 Thessalonians
1 Tim	1 Timothy
2 Tim	2 Timothy
Tit	Titus
Philem	Philemon
Heb	Hebrews
Jas	James
1 Pet	1 Peter
2 Pet	2 Peter
1 Jn	1 John
2 Jn	2 John
3 Jn	3 John
Jude	Jude
Rev	Revelation (Apocalypse)